Reading
the
Silver
Screen

Also by Thomas C. Foster

Twenty-five Books That Shaped America

How to Read Novels Like a Professor

How to Read Literature Like a Professor

Reading the Silver Screen

A Film Lover's Guide to Decoding
the Art Form That Moves

THOMAS C. FOSTER

HARPER PERENNIAL

NEW YORK • LONDON • TORONTO • SYDNEY • NEW DELHI • AUCKLAND

HARPER ⬤ PERENNIAL

HarperCollins books may be purchased for educational, business, or sales promotional use. For information please email the Special Markets Department at SPsales@harpercollins.com.

First Harper Perennial paperback published 2016.

FIRST EDITION

Library of Congress Cataloging-in-Publication Data has been applied for.

ISBN 978-0-06-211339-9

16 17 18 19 20   DIX/RRD   10 9 8 7 6 5 4 3 2 1

For Brenda: Forever.

Acknowledgments

✦

NO BOOK HAPPENS without a great deal of assistance, and this one is no exception. To begin with, I must remember the late Jim Cash for his help and mentoring in the matter of screenplays and therefore of movies many years ago now. I never see a movie without thinking about him. Among my more recent influences is my colleague Fred Svoboda; it would be impossible to compute all the movies we discussed in our carpool over the years, between talking books, students, and food. My students over the decades have been invaluable resources from the film-and-freshman-writing track at Michigan State University to the literature students at the University of Michigan–Flint. They gave me both surprising insights and penetrating questions about novels, plays, movies, and the interplay among them.

It is safe to say that this book might not have happened and certainly would not have turned out half so well without the timely intervention of Ivy Pochoda, who took time away from her own writing schedule to edit the manuscript. Her tough questions were as welcome as her praise, and her vision of what the book could be drove me to try to achieve those possibilities. I have been extremely lucky to find someone whose editing skills match her wonderful talent as a novelist. The entire team at HarperCollins has been a treat to work with, as always, but in finding Ivy to take over the project, they gave me a gift beyond measure.

To my longtime agent, Faith Hamlin of Sanford J. Greenburger Associates, I offer my profound thanks for the wisdom, toughness, and stability she provides. In the world of constantly changing editors, which is to say the world of publishing in any era, it is a blessing to have one person I can always count on for her steadfastness.

I am indebted to the various copyright holders who have lent permission for me to reproduce stills for this book: Woody Allen and Gravier Productions for *Midnight in Paris*; Columbia Pictures for *Lawrence of Arabia*; Getty Images/MGM for *The Thomas Crown Affair* (1968 and 1999) and *A Fistful of Dollars*; Shout! Factory for *Stagecoach*; Jesse Grant/Getty Images for photo of Johnny Depp; Warner Bros. for *A Clockwork Orange*, *The Matrix*, *North by Northwest*, and *Captain Blood*; Roy Export SAS for *City Lights*; and Paramount Pictures for *Shane*.

Finally, there are not words to express my love and gratitude to the person I describe in these pages as my Permanent Movie Companion. In addition to acting as my sounding board about movies, Brenda listens to my dubious ideas, puts up with my rants, gives me space to work, and generally smooths the road for me to be selfish in the way writers must be. Or at least this one must be. Without her, there are no books.

Contents

✴

Preface

❋

After the Credits Roll

OKAY, SO TWO PEOPLE WALK OUT of a movie theater. I know, it sounds like the setup for a bad joke, but work with me here. Call them Lexi and Dave. They toss their popcorn tubs and soda cups into the garbage cans, and as they stroll out into the growing darkness, Lexi says, "Overall, the movie is quite faithful to its original. So what'd you think?"

"Great," says Dave. "It's *Mad Max*. Big, loud, and crazy. My kind of film. You?"

"Great here, too. Not the story, although that was all right. More like the vision behind it. It was like a piece of art." Lexi thinks a moment. "A crazy, noisy piece of art."

"Art? I don't think so. Art is those foreign guys. Bergman,

Fellini, who's that Japanese guy? Maybe Woody Allen. You know, dull stuff."

"So you're saying that an action movie can't be a work of art?"

"What I mean is, who cares if it's *art* or not. It's a good story with lots of action. That's all that matters. Crashes, explosions, hot babes, flame-throwing guitars. What else is there?" Dave's a little exercised now.

"Um, everything? The speed. The way things looked—you know, how the action was staged, where the camera was when a shot was taken. I don't know, just the things that make the movie look the way it does. And the music, of course," says Lexi, trying not to sound superior. "You know, all that other stuff."

"I think you're making *all that other stuff* up. Like what?"

"Oh, I don't know," says Lexi. "Well, take the main villain. What's he called? Immortan Joe? He's like Darth Vader. You know, being helped into his mask and his breathing things, whatever they were. Although maybe he was more like Jabba the Hutt."

"If we're going there, I think the other dude, the one with feet like flowerpots and a silver nose—the People Eater—was Jabba the Hutt. He was gross enough."

"Besides characters, the film was a visual masterpiece. Who could come up with those crazy guys on poles? You know, the ones who swing between cars like wacko pole-vaulters or something. And the way it was shot. The whole movie, every scene or shot or whatever, looked perfect. Like a perfect version of itself. I don't know how to explain it. Art, you know. You either get it or you don't."

"Whatever you say," says Dave, laughing, as they climb into the car. "You think too much, Professor. I'll just stick to watching the movies. And you keep talking this smack, you're buying the whole pizza."

Welcome to the state of informal film criticism. We'll let our young people go on to the pizzeria unaccompanied, while we consider the implications of that conversation. They're both right, of course: Dave in asserting his right to watch movies the way he wants to, which is to say passively, treating them as simple entertainment, and Lexi in claiming that there just might be more going on than her pal acknowledges, even if he is not entirely sure himself what that something is.

We should stipulate here that the Max in question is *Mad Max: Fury Road* (2015), not the thirty-six-year-old original and not *The Road Warrior* and certainly not *Beyond Thunderdome*. Part of the difference is that the later version's budget could eat the original movie as an hors d'oeuvre and not spoil its supper. Simply put, George Miller had resources available that he could not have imagined in 1979. And he used them.

So here is the question: what else makes up "all that other stuff"? Which leads to another: does it matter? And to a third: should we care, and if so, why?

Those three questions deserve answers, so here they are, slightly rearranged. First, whatever constitutes "all that other stuff" matters absolutely. If you do something as simple as rearrange the furniture in a room, the scene will play differently because the characters can't navigate their way through the space the same way they did the first time. Instead of a right profile, you get the back of a head. Great, if that's what you want. And that is one choice in one scene. In *Mad Max: Fury Road*, which our young friends have just seen, there is a sequence where, in the midst of the gigantic chase sequence that forms the bulk of the movie, the heroes must pass through a bottleneck. Which becomes the eye of a needle, when tons of rock are brought down, leaving, after some cleanup, an aperture through which the trucks must travel that is essentially a circle in the rock at the center of the steep canyon. The canyon is controlled by a motorcycle gang that dresses like psychotic Ewoks, excels at extortion for passage through the needle, and stands watch on outcroppings looking for all the world like the Apaches in about half the movies John Wayne ever made. Furiosa (Charlize Theron) makes a deal with the bikers, but they go back on it, forcing her to flee with her human cargo while the bikers blow part of the canyon and impede the attack of Furiosa's enemy (and recent boss), Immortan Joe.

So here are some choices that have to be made in this scene: how many bikers will Furiosa negotiate with, where are the other bikers arrayed in the canyon, what possesses them to dress like furballs in the desert, what does the road through the canyon look like before and after the rockslide, and where are the other characters while the negotiation is going on. Every shot involves a hundred decisions. At least. Proof? Let's try another director. Here's Judd Apatow, about as unlike George Miller as anyone I can imagine, on NPR's *Fresh Air*, telling Terry Gross about directing *Trainwreck* (2015) and working with Amy Schumer, who wrote and stars in the film: "[I]n editing, you have to make a million choices. I mean, every second you could be on a different person's face, you could use a different joke, you could use different music, so there's so many things to debate, and overall it really could not have gone better." It doesn't matter if the movie is *The Seventh Seal* or *King Kong* (either one) or, well, *Trainwreck*; the principle remains the same: every shot demands a series of decisions and choices from the faces on-screen to the lighting to the filters on the lens.

Among the other choices to be made in a scene: people (location, number, proximity to the camera), framing, camera angles and distances, lighting, props, duration of shot, sound clarity, background music, and which shots come before and after. In other words, how many persons are present, what are they wearing (or not); do you shoot them collectively or singly, up close or from a distance at any given moment; what, if anything, is the music playing behind the action; how brightly is the scene lit; do they speak clearly or mumble; in short, how much and what sort of visual and auditory data can this scene convey before it breaks down from the load, and how little does it need to be viable? Second, should we care? We don't have to, as Dave's enjoyment tells us; he's just fine with what he saw and doesn't need to see more. After all, the multiplex isn't a film school, and we aren't being graded. Lexi, on the other hand, seems to care. She's noticing something about the movie that is independent of its quality: someone made this movie look and sound and feel the way it does. They may have made it well or badly, but they made it through a huge succession of issues to be decided and exigencies to be dealt with. More important, Lexi seems to want to care, and that is the thing that separates the two friends and from which we can draw a lesson.

Taking an interest in how movies are put together is a choice. You don't have to. Some movies may be improved by declining that option. Film, moreover, inclines us toward passivity: the experience of sitting in a theater with a larger-than-life presentational surface, the screen, on which heads can be ten feet tall, overwhelms us. It's easy to watch a giant screen without analyzing it. Not only that, but when movies these days are so action-packed and idea-thin, so escapist (and, to be fair, often so much fun), it's easier and fairly natural not to interrogate a summer blockbuster. What are you going to ask, "Why are they wearing spandex"?

Contrast that with reading novels or poems, where we can hold the information in our hands—literally. The very nature of the experience of turning pages and moving our eyes down lines of type involves an active participation on our part, which leads almost inevitably toward other levels of engagement with the text that are consciously active. Think of it this way: in a movie house, in order to stop participating in the experience, we have to consciously stand up and walk out, whereas in reading a printed text we are already actively engaged, so that to stop we need only close the book. Sometimes, not even that, as anyone who has ever been jarred awake by their book slamming to the floor can tell you. The point is, with print, we move from activity toward passivity when we stop. With film, the basic experience is passive, so any deeper engagement, including the ultimate act of film criticism—walking out of the theater—is necessarily more active and therefore a conscious decision. Nor is the choice to be a more active student of film an all-or-nothing selection. We can choose to notice aspects of a movie without becoming a film theorist. One of my sons, in fact, operates on a shifting scale: some films are worth the effort and some simply are not. He sometimes reports back that a movie was "pretty terrible but still funny." Which is fine by him in some cases. These are movies, you know, starring Adam Sandler or Rob Schneider. Or both. He's a really good film viewer, by the way, when he thinks the energy invested will pay dividends.

I have spent my career trying to interest students not merely in reading literature but in noticing how literature is assembled. Mostly, I have succeeded—or at least they have humored me while in my classes. Literary criticism, a fraught term if ever there was one, is not about who's better than whom, what novel or poem or play is the best. At least, that's not what it is in my classes. Don't get me wrong: I try to assign good works and skip the lousy stuff. But the real purpose of criticism, per Foster, is to take books and poems and plays apart so we can better understand how they're put together. What are the elements of this sonnet, that story, and how do they operate in the poem or story? You know, *all that other stuff*. Big stuff like symbols and images. Little stuff like the sounds of words and their placement in lines. Whatever the particulars, the real issue is the same: how do we become better readers—more attentive to detail, more involved, more attuned to nuance, more aware of the many levels of significance possible in a given work? Same thing with movies. Oh, sure, there are differences. No line lengths or meter or rhyme schemes, no narrator to figure out whether he's trustworthy or not. But not always all that different, either. There are still characters, still something like point of view, still images and even symbols. Plus lots of *stuff* that is specific to movies. It is not only possible but for some of us inevitable that we treat film as we treat other literary enterprises, that we study it to see how it works. We'll get into all that in a moment.

But before that, the big question. So why should we care?

Pleasure. Pure and simple: pleasure. Oh, sure, you can take this knowledge and use it to excel in classes or become a famous critic on your very own blog. You can even use it to become a pretentious burden to your friends. Not recommended, but that's your call. Of course, employing analytic strategies is fabulous brain exercise, and we can all use more of that, but it's really not the point. The best argument for learning to see more up on the silver screen is that it will bring you more pleasure. Don't you think knowing how *Star Wars* or *The Hobbit* is put together is pretty cool? Or that we can enjoy talking about something beyond the plot? That pleasure can take many forms, of course. Here are some that might appeal.

- Pleasure (1): if Lexi continues on the path she has laid out, she will learn to take more delight from her future movie watching than will Dave, for whom movies will always equal surface action—who said what and which events happened and what was funny and what sad, etc. There's nothing wrong with that, but there is more fun to be had. Learning to see more, moreover, takes nothing away from enjoying that surface action. There is a misconception in the culture that if we analyze the works we read or watch or listen to, we will kill our "simple" or "pure" enjoyment. Seriously? Then why do all those music geeks tear into the meaning of songs by Pink Floyd or Tupac or the Beatles or Pearl Jam or whomever to uncover every last shred of possible meaning? If so, then why would they do it? For that matter, do you really think they find the music less gratifying after that work than before? I've said this elsewhere, but it bears frequent repeating: no one, and I mean no one, takes more pleasure from reading than do professors of literature. True, they may seem to have smoke coming off their overheated brains as they consider five or six or a dozen different meanings, implications, and levels of signification simultaneously, but what may seem from the outside like the gnashing of gears sounds on the inside like a very contented hum. Far from spoiling your fun, you'll likely double or triple it.

- Pleasure (2): you can even take pleasure in lousy movies. Bad ones, you understand, use many of the same techniques as good ones. We'll look at some films of dubious quality as we go along just to make that point. Not only that, but as you become more accomplished as a critic, you can examine the lesser films to see just where they go awry (or perhaps work in spite of or even because of their flaws); occasionally, that's the only enjoyment to be had. The flip side of that coin is that you can also begin to see what great films have to offer that maybe escaped you when you were a less experienced filmgoer.

- Pleasure (3): knowing more is a great way to astonish your friends and confound your rivals, and who doesn't enjoy that?

Let's take a small detour to the pizza parlor, where Dave is wondering if he missed something about the movie. He's not convinced, of course—Lexi's observations weren't *that* persuasive, even if she is on the right track—but there was something about how much she seemed to enjoy the movie that caused him to reconsider the matter. Not that he's telling her. But he's thinking he might think about his next movie a little differently. See if any of that art business is going on. Nothing definite, you know, just maybe something that shows up if you pay a little more attention, watch for what's going on behind the action. Watch like she does.

You want to know what totally getting movies sounds like? Here's Anthony Lane on *Mad Max: Fury Road*:

> *That wonderful image* [of Max simply melting away into the crowd at the end of the movie] *allows Miller to draw back and survey the scene from on high. Such is the root of his near-mystical prestige as a creator of action films: a bright, instinctive sense of when and where to cut from the telling detail to the wider view, and back again. Those instincts were there in the first "Mad Max," which, for all its cheapness, picked up rhythm whenever it hit the highway, and they are resurgent here. They connect Miller not so much to the panicky despots of the modern blockbuster, like Michael Bay, as to directors of Hollywood musicals, and to the early choreographers of the chase, in the wordless days when pictures lived by motion alone. In "Mad Max: Fury Road," the Polecats—aggressors who arc from one vehicle to another, in mid-race, on the end of long stakes— are the descendants of Buster Keaton, who, in "Three Ages," fell from a roof through three awnings and clutched at a drainpipe, which swung him out into the void and back through an open window.*

That's pretty terrific. It has observation, understanding, attention to detail, grasp of film history all rolled up into one package. Lane, as his readers will attest, is a man who knows what he likes and what he doesn't (as with the Michael Bay dig) as well as why he thinks that way. I can't turn you into Anthony Lane. Heck, I can't turn *me* into him. Nor is that really desirable; even he would agree that one of him is quite sufficient. But what we can do is make you—make us all—a better reader of movies. More informed. More aware. More analytical. Which in turn will make your movie experience richer and more complete as you begin to see all the possibilities this marvelous medium has to offer.

So the question for you is, are you a Dave or a Lexi? Are you happiest not thinking about your movies, treating them as disposable commodities to be seen and then discarded? Or are you hoping to get a little something more out of your moviegoing, maybe find interesting things to say over your latte with friends? Would you simply like to be able to understand those aspects of films that you know are there but you can't quite identify? Most important, are you looking to really take ownership of your movie experience, to make those films truly your own? Then why don't we take a little trip together? Besides, you don't want to be left on your own; I'm thinking even Dave may want to come along for the ride.

A Note on the Text

In the history of the cinema, there have been thousands of films made worldwide. We won't mention all of them, but it may feel that way sometimes. This book will mention around a hundred movies, some of them only in passing. Even so, your head may sometimes spin. I'll try to explain enough so that you can get the point of the example even if you haven't seen it. If you're like most people, the older, classic films will be the ones you are least likely to have seen (unless you were a young person when they were around). By cutting almost as many films as I have included, I have tried to limit major discussion to just a handful of classic films representing several genres: *Citizen Kane* (experimental/art), *Shane* and *Stagecoach* and *The Magnificent Seven* (classic Western), *Once upon a Time in the West* and *Butch Cassidy and the Sundance Kid* (revisionist Western), *Annie Hall* (screwball comedy), *The Maltese Falcon* (crime/noir), *Body Heat* (crime/neo-noir), *Lawrence of Arabia* (epic), *The Lion in Winter* (historical/play adaptation), *Psycho* (horror/thriller), *The Gold Rush* and *Modern Times* (silent comedy), *Star Wars* (sci-fi), *Raiders of the Lost Ark* (action-adventure), *The Wizard of Oz* (fantasy), and *The Godfather* (gangster). Most of these are shown repeatedly on various movie channels, especially those specializing in classic movies (who knew, right?), and all are available via subscription services like Netflix. In a perfect world, they would all be available for streaming, but that's not where we live. The newer films are more varied in the hope that readers will have seen some of them so at least one or two examples will stick, and you can always rent a movie to get up to speed. In any case, I won't be giving any tests, so you're free to see them or not, as the spirit moves you. But I hope you will.

And now, for that last question (asked first): what is *all that other stuff*? Ah, well, if you really want to know, step inside.

Introduction

❂

A Language All Its Own

LET'S SUPPOSE YOU WERE TO—what? . . . invent? create? stumble upon?—an entirely new medium. You know it's new because the technology has never existed before. Think movable type. Radio. Hypertext. Think above all: pictures that move. Suddenly you have the capacity to render people, creatures, objects, everything, in motion just as they are in real life. What an invention! Think of all the possibilities! Think of everything you could do! There's just one little thing:

What is it?

That seemingly innocent question has bedeviled the movies since their inception. For most of the century or so of its existence, the cinema hasn't known what it is. Or rather, those in charge haven't always known, nor have the rest of us. Is a

movie more like a play or a novel, more about story or spectacle, more reliant on dialogue or action? The truth is, it's none
of the above, as well as all of them. It shares qualities with the
literary and visual arts, employs sound as well as pictures, has
elements of dramatic presentation and staging even while it
makes narrative selections like fiction. What sometimes has
gotten lost in the discussions of film is that it doesn't matter
what it is *like*. What matters is what it *is*.

That is the crux of the matter. Those shared qualities mislead
us into thinking that film is one of those things with which
it shares similarities, that it is something other than what it
actually is. Movies are movies. They are not novels, biographies,
short stories, dramatic plays, comedic plays, musical theater,
epics, comic books (although one could be excused for thinking so these days), confessions, photography, painting, or holy
texts. Film can, and often does, make use of all these other
forms from other media. It shares certain qualities with each
of them, even overlaps tendencies with a number of them. But
it is none of them. It is itself. It has expectations, procedures,
rituals, and logic peculiar to film. Above all, it speaks its own
language, which, like every language, obeys a grammar, or set
of rules, that is particular to this language. We need to understand the rules of that language, the *grammar of film*, in order to
fully decode the language and understand what movies do and
how they do it.

Maybe we should start with an element so basic that we're
in danger of overlooking it. What does film have that no other
medium (up to its creation, at least) possesses? Story? No that's
all over the place. Characters? Ditto. Visuals? Plays have those.
So what's this singular item? A camera. Okay, yes, photography.
But that camera can only take stills. This one can record, as
we understand, images that *move*. It can also freeze them. But
movement is what it does best. And that camera has a lens,
a component for "seeing" the action. The lens has two main

functions, but we normally speak of them as a single task: focus. On the one hand, to focus is to bring clarity, to allow the film in the camera (or the digital successor to film) to retain a sharp image—or a fuzzy one, or a grainy one, or any of a hundred other variants, but an image in any case—on each frame. On the other hand, to focus is to select and therefore to exclude: the lens apprehends just so much of the available scene and no more. This quality is huge in establishing what is special about cinematic language. If you're watching a play, for instance, and six characters are onstage for a scene, all six are available for your attention. True, some will be farther upstage or downstage, which tends to control our eye, or they may be more central or farther out toward the wings. But the bottom line is that each of them is present. An unscrupulous actor can invent a bit of business, like fiddling with a vase or making faces or gesturing, which can move him from a peripheral role to a center of attention not warranted by the script. He might be looking for other work tomorrow, but he can manage it tonight. Not so in a movie. Of those six characters—still all "present" in the scene—the only ones we see on-screen are the ones on whom the lens focuses. It may show us all six, or five, or four, or three, or two, or one. In any combination, in the cases of more than one. If it only shows us one, it may be the person performing the action or one of the others. How different it is to see the speaker or to see the listener! It may even show none of them but something else entirely—a ticking clock, a cocker spaniel, you name it.

So film shows action, even when the action is minimal. But it does more: it selects the action to show. Not just who or what is in a shot, but how close or far, from what angle, and for how long, among a host of other decisions.

Those decisions matter because the way a movie shows action is what causes us to care about it. **Film is the only literary form in which the text itself moves.** I can hear the objections now. Yes, there is movement in drama, but where does it take place? Onstage, in performance, right? By its very nature, dramatic performance is transitory, of a single moment. When you see and hear the reading of a line from, say, Arthur Miller, it's there for the time it takes the actor to speak, and then it is gone. It will never exist again in quite the same way. The thing that remains, the script, is the thing we can study. That is the text of a play. The text of a film, on the other hand, *is* the film itself.

What about the screenplay? That's a script, just like a play.

Good question. Good answer, too, except for the word *just*. It's sort of like a dramatic script. The difference, however, is huge. A play exists as a written text out in the world for a host of interpreters to produce as a work in performance. With movies, to the contrary, the screenplay forms not the definitive text but merely the template for a finished work that may differ substantially from the original words on pages. That work is a visual and (often) auditory construct that itself stands as the final text. That's the thing that can be studied and analyzed. We say, "Let's go see a play"; we do not say, "Let's go see a screenplay." That's a distinction whose importance can't be overstated. Many of us will have read plays in school; the vast majority of film fans will go their entire lives and never see, much less read, a screenplay. A text, in turn, has a specialized language with its own set of rules. How those rules work to direct that language will be our subject here. We're going to become fluent in a new language: Movie.

To demonstrate these two special properties of film (don't get too cozy, there are plenty more), let's try a thought experiment. Here's the first scene you're shooting in your directorial debut. We have a scene with six people dealing with a tragedy. A teenage boy has just been in a car accident, which may or may not have been suicidal, and lies hovering between life and death. The scene is at the hospital. Two of the characters are the parents of the injured boy; the other two adults are the next-door husband and wife, and she has been having an affair with the husband in the first couple; the final two are the teenage son (and best friend of the injured boy, who told his pal about the affair immediately before the wreck) and preteen daughter (who knows and suspects nothing) of the neighbors. You want to shoot twenty seconds of film in which wife number two says to her lover (husband number one) something to the effect that "you shouldn't blame yourself."

So here's the question, Mr. or Ms. Director: what are you doing with the camera during those twenty seconds? I can think of a couple of dozen possibilities for what or whom to include involving one or more persons (or objects) in the room, and every one of those will convey a different meaning. Just think, for example, how differently the shot plays if you show the adulterous wife as she speaks along with her husband (who doesn't know), versus her and the wronged wife (who does). Or the angry boy alone, versus him with his unaware sister.

Okay, got it? Made your decision? Excellent. Twenty whole seconds figured out.

Now, for a two-hour movie, repeat 359 times.

And remember: this is only the visual aspect, and only one part of that aspect at that. There's sound to deal with, too. We have a lot of options in that arena. Do we have Robert Altman–style talkovers, where we only sort of hear the main conversation because we're also hearing all the sidebar discussions, or do we handle dialogue the old-fashioned way, in which all voices that aren't the main ones fade into the background? And what of music? Yes or no? Loud or soft? Foreground or background? Remember, again, that this is only one moment out of roughly two hours. The challenge is a little humbling, isn't it? Now, before we hand over your director's chair, let's see if we can figure out what film is and how it works its magic.

How about a real-world set of decisions as an example of this process of choosing? One of the staples of the cinema is the movie fight, and one of the best among fairly recent examples is from *The Bourne Identity* (2002). The key scene for our purposes is the fight in Jason Bourne's (Matt Damon) Paris apartment. Bourne, still unclear about his identity, has returned to his home driven by Marie (Franka Potente), who has accompanied him upstairs. He makes a phone call and finds a troubling piece of information: one of his aliases is dead and lying in a morgue. Don't you hate when that happens? Something about the phone call and some noises he can't quite identify puts him on his guard, and he picks up a kitchen knife. When Marie emerges from the bathroom and talks to him, he leans against the doorway and drops the knife point-first into the wood floor, hoping not to alarm her. Something draws his attention to the double French windows of his study, and as she distracts him, a hit man swings through the window blazing away with an automatic weapon. From there a truly amazing fight scene develops as Bourne, the perfectly trained assassin, meets his double, another killer trained by the same program. They mirror each other's moves, know what to watch for in the way of openings. The chief difference is that the other guy, Castel (Nicky Naudé), has the weapons—okay, Bourne has a Bic pen, which he uses to great effect, but come on—and our guy has to win, else no movie.

The fight choreography is outstanding, of course, or we wouldn't be having this discussion. But what really makes the scene is the way the shots are framed and cut. We begin from complete stasis: Bourne standing still at the window, then Marie speaking from another doorway, then to Bourne at the window but looking over his shoulder at Marie, and then the window explodes and all hell breaks loose. The shots go something like this:

1) Bourne standing at window

2) Marie speaks

3) Bourne by window, looking away

4) Castel bursts through window, gun blazing

5) Marie, horrified

6) Bourne grabs Castel, takes out his knee, and both fall to floor, gun still blasting away

7) Bourne and Castel wrestle over the rifle

8) A jagged line of shots penetrates the ceiling above them

9) Bourne disarms Castel

10) Gun slides away from the fighters

11) Castel gets Bourne in a headlock

12) Bourne frees himself with a knee and a pair of elbows

13) Castel knocks Bourne across the room with a spinning leg drive

14) Bourne slides across the floor, picks himself up

15) Bourne, shot from behind, moves toward Castel, who moves toward him

16) Castel, shot from behind, engages Bourne

17) Two-shot (two persons in the same frame) of the men landing blows

18) Two-shot of Bourne and the frightened Marie, who is the one in focus

19) Castel moves through the frame, blotting out Marie as he lands a blow

20) Two-shot from behind Castel as Bourne parries

21) Shot of Bourne's shoe buckling Castel's knee

22) Castel on floor, rolls to a knee, pulls out a wedge-shaped push knife

23) Marie (single) shouts "Jason" as a warning

24) Three-shot from behind Castel, with Bourne in front of him, Marie beyond Bourne

25) Two-shot of upper bodies engaging, then just legs, then upper bodies as Castel slashes with knife

26) Single of Bourne dodging knife, then landing a punch as he retreats from hallway into study

27) Two-shot as Castel's head snaps back, then he stalks forward to engage again

28) Two-shot from side of Bourne parrying the slash, then grabbing Castel's arm

29) Two-shot with camera circling the combatants as they look for openings

30) Two-shot of Bourne attempting to disarm Castel, who throws him to floor near desk

31) Single of Bourne on floor and trying to gain his defensive posture, Castel entering frame

32) Castel advancing, from Bourne's point of view, then Bourne's feet driving him back

33) Single of Bourne kipping up to his feet

34) Single of Marie, amazed and aghast

35) Single of Castel, blood in his eyes, clambering to his feet

36) Single of Bourne at desk, his hand fumbling among papers and cash for the Bic pen, finding it, and uncapping it behind his back

37) Shot of Castel in full-attack mode

38) Single of Bourne dodging knife, then stabbing Castel in forearm with pen, removing it, and driving him across room with a blow

39) Castel recovers as Bourne advances (he is now the aggressor); the camera circles with him, which brings Marie, still in doorway, into the shot

40) Castel kicks wildly, misses, then swings wildly with knife, missing again; Bourne lands blow, then grabs knife arm and drives pen into knife hand between the middle knuckles

41) Shot of knife falling to floor, Bourne sweeping it away with his foot

42) Bourne drives Castel backward across desk with a kick; Castel tumbles to floor

43) Two-shot from behind Bourne of Marie looking completely daunted

44) Single of Bourne in ready pose

45) Single of Castel kipping up to his feet, looking more mechanical than ever, pulling pen out of hand

46) Two-shot of Castel charging Bourne wildly, Bourne parries, stomps Castel's shin, breaking it, then breaks his arm and drives him to floor

47) Single of Castel landing on herringbone wood floor looking very bad indeed

48) Single of Marie looking decidedly ill

49) Shot from over Marie's shoulder of Bourne stripping Castel of his kit bag, then throwing it to Marie to look through it for clues

50) Single of Marie dropping back and moaning at the horror she is experiencing

51) Shot of Bourne pointing at bag and barking orders to empty it

52) Shot of Marie emptying bag

53) Two-shot of Bourne demanding to know who Castel is and who sent him while slamming his head on floor

54) Single of Marie looking at papers, which turn out to be wanted posters for Bourne and her, while we hear Bourne's questioning go on

55) Marie shouts, "He's got my picture," as shot cuts to Bourne, still leaning over Castel, who is nearly out of the bottom of the frame

56) Single of Marie, terrified and angry, advancing on the hapless Castel

57) Two-shot of Bourne lifting Marie away from Castel

58) Three-shot as she escapes and kicks at Castel, Bourne again dragging her away

59) Single of Bourne telling her to stay clear and that he will "do this"

60) Two-shot from behind Bourne, with Marie, which becomes three-shot with no cut as Castel rises into frame

61) Three-shot from over Marie's shoulder past Bourne to Castel, now standing but suddenly turning and crashing through the window and over the balcony railing to his death

62) Single of Marie, her hair across her face, unable to form a word

63) Single of Bourne's back as he goes to window and looks down on carnage, then checks his watch and moves decisively.

We'll leave our two protagonists there, the fight ended. For now, enough to credit them with putting on a splendid experience.

That's 2:17 from the moment Castel enters the first window to the time he goes out the other. That's 58 shots in 137 seconds, or 2.36 seconds per shot. Put another way, a whole lot of quick cuts; so many, in fact, that the eye and brain are tricked into thinking that we're seeing the fight in continuous shooting. But of course we're not. A continuous shot would be considerably less effective than this rapid-fire series. And would play slower.

What matters for our purposes, however, is what lies behind

the scene: every single one of these shots—and the cuts that begin and end them—represents a choice. Actually a series of choices ranging from which of the three participants appears to how he/she/they are shot (who's in the foreground and who the background), how much of which character (twice, for example, we see only a sliver of Marie's hair, the whole back of Bourne's head, and the upper half of Castel facing the camera), where the camera's focal length falls, and how much of the action the lens will see, and when the shot ends. I mentioned earlier the way the camera circles the combatants in one shot. No one makes that choice by accident; you have to stop filming and make specific preparations to shoot that one. Later, in the climactic moment of the fight, we don't see *Bourne* stomp *Castel* on the shin. Rather, we see Bourne's foot stomp Castel's shin, and we take it on faith that the rest of the men's bodies are attached. In the following moments, Bourne is brutally interrogating the prone Castel, slamming his head (or something) into the floor as he demands, "Who are you?" I say "or something" because we don't actually see him do it. His violence is off-screen, and what we see is Marie's horror not at his actions but at her realization that their assailant has carried wanted posters with photos of both of them for identification purposes. That decision to shoot her and only hear him doesn't so much reduce the brutality as make it auditory rather than visual; if we were looking at it, we wouldn't notice the *sounds* of violence, distracted as we would be by the sight of it. Not to worry, though: our imaginations can supply any needed pictures and all the disgust that might apply. We viewers are good that way.

So, decisions, decisions, decisions. Which characters, in what spatial arrangements, from what angles, with what lighting, from what distances, with what focal lengths, as they perform what actions? For director Doug Liman, along with cinematographer Oliver Wood and editor Saar Klein (because what we're talking about here is in large measure editing), this scene represents sixty-three final choices from among hundreds—at a minimum—of competing possibilities. We should pause right here for a bit of clarification. The final look of that scene rests almost entirely in the hands of the editor. The director will have decided what to shoot and how to shoot it—how many takes, from how many and which angles, at what distance, and so on—and the cinematographer's job is to carry out those decisions with the camera. The result might be anything from several minutes to an hour or more of film, depending on how many takes are involved. From there, the editor will cut film (or make the digital cuts) to achieve the effects he or she and the director are seeking. Some directors are more involved in the editing than others, but the job of taking a scene from long strings of film (I'll use this wording even though we both know that in most contemporary films no "film" is employed; it's easier this way) to however many shorter snippets—and determining what length those short pieces may be—falls to the editor. For instance, in the shot in which Bourne stomps Castel's shin, there would have been several alternatives to the extreme close-up of the foot and the shin. They might have been anything from full-body shots of one or both all the way down to the final selection. They could have been shot from a variety of angles, catching one or the other character facing the camera. What Saar Klein chose was this particular reduction of the whole act down to just the parts of the body involved in the business. Was it a tough decision? We'll never know. What we do know is how the choice turned out in the final cut. Which ought to be enough.

As the director, you now have three minutes safely in the can. Practically finished, right?

Okay, that's a whole bunch of information about the scene, but here's the big thing we can take away from it: in the way it releases information, it is unlike any other literary form. Fight narrative, from Homer to Chuck Palahniuk, follows essentially the same pattern—"and then ..."—whether the form is oral, as in *The Iliad*, or written, as in *Fight Club*. In fact, when I used to teach the former work, one of my favorite moments was to stop in the midst of an action sequence to note that sports reporting has changed remarkably little in 2,500 years. In a work that in so many ways remains alien to contemporary readers, its narration of action, whether a fight between two heroes or the horse race during the funeral games for Patroclus, could with only a few surface changes have appeared in *Sports Illustrated*. That's because narrative is almost necessarily linear, not because *SI* had a policy of hiring classicists. It is in the nature of words that events succeed one another and that information can only arrive one bit at a time. On the stage, of course, we can receive information from multiple sources, from movement and sound and color and speech, but it occurs all at once. All the action in a given moment is available to the audience simultaneously. Film, like oral or print narrative, is essentially linear. Frames succeed frames at a predictable rate; actions beget actions. At the same time, the rate of information is much quicker than older forms, and it includes a good deal of simultaneity: we can see and hear things, even seemingly unrelated things, in a given moment. Like drama, it *presents* action directly, as opposed to telling us about that action. We don't read that a shot was fired; we see it fired. But unlike the drama, we do not necessarily see all the action available in a space at once. The Bourne fight shows that clearly.

This scene is all about, along with the razor blade and tape, or their modern, digital equivalents, the camera. In this scene, that miraculous device tells us what matters, selecting and editing those bits of information on which the director wants us to train our attention. As Robert Scholes and Robert Kellogg told us back in 1966 in *The Nature of Narrative*, film is a narrative, not a dramatic, art. That's because of the selective nature that the camera brings to its task, choosing what stays and what gets excluded, and selection, rather than presentation, is a prime element of narrative. Their assertion is mostly true, most of the time, which is why it has never worked very well to simply film a stage production: the result looks, well, stagy.

But this essentially narrative medium is also not a novel or short story. Take that Bourne fight we just looked at. In a work of prose fiction, the writer also selects actions and responses to bring to our attention, but that selection requires an intrusion of the narrative voice beyond speech and action, and those actions and responses cannot be managed simultaneously. Not only that, but to give on the page the range of emotions displayed in a handful of seconds of screen time would require a hundred or so words at a minimum. The release of information in fiction is layered, sequential, released over time, which results in a different experience.

Here's what novelistic narrative does with a fight. This one, too, is from *The Bourne Identity* (1980), by Robert Ludlum. Not the same scene; that one is not in the book. Bourne has been taken prisoner by killers, his left hand (the bad guys think both) has been smashed, he has been forced into the backseat of a car, and he is being stripped by a large thug.

> The car sped down the Steppdeckstrasse and swung into a side street, heading south. Jason collapsed back in the seat, gasping. The gunman tore at his clothes, ripping his shirt, yanking at his belt. In seconds his upper body would be naked; passport, papers, cards, money no longer his, all items intrinsic to his escape from Zurich taken from him. It was now or it was not to be. He screamed.
>
> "My leg! My goddamned leg!" He lurched forward, his right hand working furiously in the dark, fumbling under the cloth of his trouser leg. He felt it. The handle of the automatic.

"Nein!" roared the professional in the front. "Watch him!"

He knew; it was instinctive knowledge.

*It was also too late. Bourne held the gun in the dark-
ness of the floor; the powerful soldier pushed him back. He
fell with the blow, the revolver, now at his waist, pointed
directly at his attacker's chest.*

*He fired twice; the man arched backward. Jason fired
again, his aim sure, the heart punctured; the man fell over
into the recessed jump seat.*

This passage has enough action to satisfy any thriller junkie's
need for a quick fix. At the same time, the differences between
it and the earlier film scene are fairly clear. In its favor, the
novel can tell us about internal mental states. Not so easy
in film, where everything must be external. We may discern
what's going on in a character's head, as with Marie's horror at
finding herself on a wanted poster in the assassin's bag, but we
can't find out directly, unless the movie resorts to the clunki-
ness of a narrator. And we can imagine the action from the
description, if you regard the use of imagination as a plus (I
do). In fact, we have to imagine it, since it is described and not
shown. On the big screen, we *see* the action happen, whereas
on the page we must become co-creators: if we don't imagine it, don't see it for ourselves, it doesn't work. We become,
in ways that we rarely do in film, co-creators of meaning. We
don't, for example, know for certain what Jason Bourne looks
like. In the movie we do: he looks exactly like Matt Damon.
One advantage of the film version of a scene, on the other
hand, is that the automatic Bourne reaches for won't become
a revolver by the time he fires it (barring some monumental
blunder by the prop department), as it does in this passage. I
never said it was a great novel.

So yes, film is a different medium with different attributes from fiction, one of which is the presentation of time. As soon as filmmakers discovered this property of their new toy, that time can be measured without words, clocks became very popular—ticking, stopped, grandfather, electric, mantel, or wall-cat. A parent is worried—show the clock. A bomb is set to go off—show the clock. A hostage release is being negotiated—a thousand clocks. There were probably more clocks displayed in the first ten years of Hollywood than in the entirety of fiction and drama combined. But what if you're making a movie of *The Iliad*? No clocks? No problem. You could probably show a sundial, but that's a little obvious. But you could certainly show shadows lengthening or shortening. You could show the movement of celestial bodies across the sky. The cosmos as clock.

The other thing they discovered almost immediately was the opposite of the shot, the cut. Using a variety of devices, they could take us out of the current shot and into another one at lightning speed. And of course, if you can make one cut, you can make thirty-seven, by which point you will have created a montage, French for a-bunch-of-things-happening-in-rapid-succession-connected-only-by-juxtaposition. Or something like that. You've seen them, although not at the breakneck speed of classics like Sergei Eisenstein's *Battleship Potemkin*. We get a montage of Phil's (Bill Murray) endlessly repeating day in *Groundhog Day* (1993), in which among other images we see the clock roll over from 5:59 to 6:00 again and again; we are spared a graphic depiction of sex by the rainbows-and-unicorns "Take Me to Pleasure Town" montage sequence in *Anchorman 2: The Legend Continues* (2013). The montage became so popular so quickly at the start of the cinema age that almost as suddenly it became a cliché, and in the latter half of the twentieth century it largely vanished—except for the 1980s, when it enjoyed a sudden vogue in rock music videos. And *Rocky* films. Modernist fiction thrilled to the possibilities of the montage, but in novels the device takes much longer to develop and reveal itself, because prose is linear, not simultaneous. As with many things, the montage has enjoyed something of a comeback, even if its jumpy, headlong progression has been slowed with the passage of time.

At the same time, the montage revealed another characteristic of movies: they are sequential and hence linear. While a filmmaker can jump from place to place, jumping from time to time is problematic. True, he can portray a time traveler pretty well, but those leaps are really leaps of space. What's hard is moving a character back in his own life; even five minutes can be confusing. Maybe especially his own life. In general, movies move one direction in time, and any deviation from that path proves hard to follow. I think it has to do with images coming one after another, that our brains don't like it when an earlier image succeeds a later one.

But back to what film is and what it's like or not like—let's make a short catalog. Like drama, film is presentational. That means you can never tell us about a character; you have to show your work. So maybe that's like geometry class, but never mind. Part of that presentation is visual: the audience actually sees the action. Another part is auditory; we hear both dialogue and incidental sounds, from heel taps to full musical scores. In fact, there is an entire industry segment devoted to sound, and a specialized person, the "Foley artist," named for one of the first geniuses of the craft, Jack Donovan Foley, who matches sounds exactly to the action, which is no mean feat. No need for one of those in a novel. But film is also narrative in the way it selects information to reveal or conceal. In that way, it is selective. So that distinguishes it from drama and moves it a little closer to the novel. Yet it is still far from the novel because it employs a different, completely modern technology, the moving picture camera, and uses as its basic unit of meaning the shot, which is a still frame (or a group of frames comprising a single picture) from among the 24 (or 18 in earlier times) frames being shot each second. And because those shots contain both sight and sound, they present information simultaneously. Here, then, is a list of constituent elements of film. It is:

1. Presentational

2. Visual

3. Auditory

4. Narrative

5. Selective

6. Dependent upon a new technology, the camera and film

7. Based on the shot as its basic unit of construction

8. Reliant on cuts, fades, dissolves to shift from shot to shot

These specific considerations, however, are for later. For the moment, it's enough to understand that film, like any art, employs a specialized language. That language contains a number of different elements: visuals, sound effects, musical background, the play of light and dark, timing, spatial arrangement, action, and, often, speech. Parts of that language are shared by other arts, but the mix, the entirety of cinematic language, is particular to that one art form. Above all, those several elements work in very specific ways, following a set of rules—a sort of operating system for the medium—that we can analyze to break the large picture down into a series of manageable smaller ones. The only way we can understand that art form is to examine it in detail and to master those rules—the grammar—of that language. Don't worry, we'll get to them as we go along. Part of the reason you didn't master that *other* grammar was that it was all jammed down your throat at once. Five parts of speech in one class period? Puh-leeeease! Also, it was way more boring than this one.

There are rules and patterns that apply to all genres of literature and others that are specific to an individual genre. I've talked about the universal elements in *How to Read Literature Like a Professor*, things like how we interpret rain or snow, winter or summer, immersion in water or meals shared with others. And in *How to Read Novels Like a Professor*, we explored those elements that are specific to book-length works of fiction in prose. If it rains in a movie, we can draw on our knowledge of how rain operates in "The Rainy Day" (a Henry Wadsworth Longfellow poem), *A Farewell to Arms* (a Hemingway novel), or "The Sky Is Crying" (an Elmore James blues song made famous by Stevie Ray Vaughan) in order to understand it. But if we want to understand how scenes work, we really can't look to stanza structure in Longfellow's poem or chapter organization in Hemingway's novel. In order to understand how scenes work in *The Imitation Game* or *Selma* (both 2014), there's no way around it: we're going to have to study the special dialect of movies.

If you wish to understand the language of film, to master the grammar of that language, here's rule number one: **Movies are motion.** I know, sounds pretty dumb when you say it. We *all* know that, right? Well, yes and no. We have observed it all our lives, but until we have said it out loud or put it down on paper, that simple truth has not risen into our conscious minds.

It's a little like the law of gravity: intuitively, people knew it before Newton spelled it out for them, and once stated, pretty much everybody could assent. After all, they *knew* something caused objects to fall down and not up. Still, it needed saying. I am not claiming to be Newton (you will have figured that out already) or that this statement is original to me. Everyone who has thought about movies has reached the same conclusion. But we need to start somewhere.

We could expand that first principle somewhat: movies are motion, depicting events in time and space in which characters, objects, and the devices for recording them may be in motion, in any combination. The first element is pretty clear: people move. Think of John Travolta's Tony Manero in *Saturday Night Fever* (1977) dancing his way down the street. Heck, think of Travolta anywhere in that film. Or Mark Hamill's Luke Skywalker in his X-Wing fighter whooshing in on the Death Star in *Star Wars* (1977). In that case, we have the object in motion as well. Sometimes, though, people are static and things move. Consider the train pulling into the station. We've all but lost the magic of that moment with the decline of railways, a moment first employed by the Lumière brothers (1896) to frighten their audience and launch the cinematic era that was reworked in what seems like half of all Westerns, but the arrival of a train at the station was, for a century and more, a really big deal in real life. Thank heaven for Harry Potter, whose films represent one of the last regular appearances of trains and their stations. In film, that arrival usually signified the start of some new action (or, once in a while, as in *Anna Karenina*, the final action). When the train pulls into the station bringing Charles Bronson, his guns, and his harmonica in the opening of *Once Upon a Time in the West*, the arrival itself represents almost the first action: the three gunmen waiting for him are paragons of stasis, their lack of movement exaggerated to make the wait seem even longer than it is. When the train pulls out again, revealing our protagonist emerging from a gout of steam like some sort of Greek god, we know we're about to get action aplenty.

Sometimes, though, the action rests entirely with the camera, when it pans over or zooms into or out of an essentially static shot. If, for example, the director needs to show a mural, or a building's exterior, those are obviously not going anywhere, so the camera is going to have to be the mobile feature in this equation. Documentarians rely on this sort of motion: without the ability to drag the lens across a Mathew Brady battlefield photo or a Confederate musket, Ken Burns could not have made *The Civil War* and might have had no career at all. On a more basic level of dramatic filmmaking, the establishing shot—that initial picture of a city or a dwelling that "establishes" where we are in this imaginative universe—more often than not employs a mobile camera to survey a static scene. I talk elsewhere about the beginning of Orson Welles's *Citizen Kane*, where the camera moves through the bars of the gate that otherwise prevents admittance to the title character's mansion and then stalks its quarry until finally it arrives at the only lighted window in its field of view. Obviously, the monstrosity is not going anywhere, so the camera must go to it. Welles uses techniques of camera movement repeatedly, whether he is dollying (running the camera forward or backward or even parallel to the object being shot along a track on a small rolling cart or dolly), zooming (drawing closer or moving farther from an object or person by means of changing the length of the camera lens while keeping the camera itself in a fixed position), or panning (moving the camera from side to side from a stationary point to take in visual information laterally). In one of the most celebrated shots, the camera sweeps along the vast warehouse in which Kane's innumerable trophies, discoveries, and purchases are packed to bursting, as if to catalog this

Museum of Crazy. Whatever the nature of the camera movement, however, there's a basic principle here: **If the scene,
whether moor or mountain range or Monument Valley,
refuses to move, then move the camera.**

Often, we're getting motion from all three components, as
in Alfred Hitchcock's *North by Northwest* (1959), when in the
most famous scene, Roger Thornhill (Cary Grant) is pursued
by a sinister crop-dusting plane. The plane swoops and dives
and strafes, Thornhill runs and dives and rolls, and the camera
tracks and moves with him. In this case, it sticks reasonably
close to Roger's viewpoint on events, so that the plane or the
approaching fuel truck, which proves to be his salvation, is seen
first at a distance and then growing larger. The truck runs over
Thornhill and, in fact, over the camera. When he first sprints
out into the road, the camera observes him taking up position
in the middle of the lane—not from the distance of the truck,
but from a slight way off. Then, as the tanker gets closer and
closer, the camera *becomes* Roger, so that we see only the truck
getting larger and larger and suddenly, very large indeed. We
have the sense of being bumped by the almost-stopped rig,
and then the camera pulls back to reveal him, unharmed, lying
under the cab. Peter Jackson used many of the same techniques
years later when he showed Frodo Baggins fleeing or hiding
from the Ring-Wraiths. Nothing good is ever forgotten in
Filmland.

So, then, because it can't be said too often, here's the first rule
of cinematic grammar again: **Movies are motion.** It's right
there in the name: motion pictures. Whatever else we may say
will rest on this foundation, that film is the only literary art that
relies on capturing, storing, and presenting movement. There
may be moments of stillness in the midst of all that activity
and commotion, but they are made memorable through the
contrast with the near-constant—and expected—movement.
Once we understand this first precept, the rest is easy.

Reading
the
Silver
Screen

1

Seeing Is Believing

IF WE'RE GOING TO LEARN TO READ MOVIES, the movies are going to have to give us a little help. Provide some clues. Hints, allegations, evidence. How, for instance, do we tell the good guys from the bad guys? And hat color may not always be the most reliable indicator. Sure, Darth Vader dressed all in black, but so did Joaquin Phoenix as Johnny Cash. Besides, the Storm Troopers were all in white, and they weren't exactly pillars of society. So no answer there, although the principle is right: if we are to know about characters, they have to show us. And not just about good or bad but about degrees of goodness, about change or growth or anything we might care about in the character line.

How do we know how to feel about a character? Let's say

that we're supposed to like someone, or at least have sympathy for him. Except that he's a professional killer. He may be doing it for the right reasons, but there's no getting around the fact that he makes his living by making other people die. That's the problem Clint Eastwood sets himself in *American Sniper* (2014), the story of real-life war hero and murder victim Chris Kyle. One of the challenges here is to show Kyle (Bradley Cooper) as someone who suffers and grows through the course of his experience—even if his outward presentation is of a soldier who is closed off and emotionally stunted. We suspect that's just a mechanism to live with himself, but we don't know that. Or we might not know that but for a pair of scenes. Early in the film we watch his first kills. A mother and her young son, who is maybe nine or ten years old, step out into a street in Fallujah, Iraq, as Kyle watches from a rooftop. He notices that something may be wrong because of how the mother is walk-ing, as if she has something pinned under her arm. That some-thing is a Russian antitank grenade, which she hands to her son for him to carry close to the advancing Americans before throwing it. Just as he raises it to throw, Kyle fires once, kill-ing him instantly. The mother runs forward and picks up the grenade, with the same result. Two shots, two kills: a mother and her child. Not the most heroic of beginnings. We have watched his face through this—watching his face is something the movie does compulsively, since on matters of emotion and inner life he is inarticulate—and he betrays almost nothing. This is his job, and if it is sometimes unpleasant, that's just the way things are. Only when his spotter/bodyguard crows at his prowess and Kyle tells him to shut up do we understand the cost of this act for the shooter. Contrast this with what is prob-ably the turning point for Kyle, his second scene with a child in his sights. Shortly before his climactic confrontation with the rebel sniper Mustafa, Kyle has shot a man aiming an RPG at a U.S. Humvee, and an even younger boy, no more than eight, runs over and tries to pick up the weapon. In any other context, his struggles with the outsize launcher would be comical, but in this case they are potentially deadly. Throughout his wrestling with the gun, Kyle is imploring him first not to pick it up and then to drop it, growing more and more agitated (and crude in his language) as he goes. Cutting between the boy's laborious lifting and Kyle's stricken face, we understand that this time he is fully aware of the implications of taking the life of a young child. When the child finally manages to shoulder the launcher, one shot shows Kyle almost in tears at the prospect of what comes next, the next his finger slowly tightening on the trigger: Kyle cannot save himself from the situation. What does save him is the boy, who abruptly drops the weapon and runs away. When the film cuts back to Kyle, we see him on the verge of tears, hyperventilating and seeming to fight an urge to be sick. There is even a moment when his eyes seem to be focusing on nothing at all. It is a great performance by Cooper. He has never looked so terrified in the midst of battle as he does in this moment when no shot is fired. Now we know something no words could tell us: this is a man who has to leave the war before it destroys him. He's not quite done yet, but he desperately needs to be. The scene also tells us that this is a man who has not lost his moral compass, who has grown to the point that we can admire him as a warrior and sympathize with his humanity.

Oh, you want to talk bad? How's this for bad? There's a scene in *Shane* (1953) where one of the dirt farmers, tired of being pushed around, gets into a confrontation with the main villain, Jack Wilson, the hired gun brought in by the big rancher to terrorize the newly arrived farmers. Wilson, played by Jack Palance before he ditched the "Walter" in front of his name, is tall, lean, and spotless, standing securely on the rough-hewn gallery in front of the saloon. The sodbuster, Stonewall Torrey, played by Elisha Cook Jr. (who had already been the hapless would-be tough guy Wilmer in *The Maltese Falcon*, where he is ridiculed and humiliated by Humphrey Bogart's vastly tougher Sam Spade), is small, slight, disheveled from his labors, and slipping in the muddy street. From the beginning, we know two things: there's going to be a fight and the combatants are grossly mismatched. Stonewall is not only tiny (even his posture emphasizes his lesser physical gifts) but also in an inferior position—lower and with bad footing. He doesn't know what he's doing. Wilson does.

It's even worse than that. With the unerring sense of a predator, Wilson understands and manipulates his victim's uncertainty and fear. He baits him about his name, about being southern "trash," and about how even the heroes of the Confederacy—Stonewall Jackson, Robert E. Lee, all of them—were nothing but trash. He pushes Torrey until the shoot-out is inevitable. But while he's been doing that, he has been doing two other things: pulling on his leather glove to ensure a secure draw, and smiling. He knows where this is leading. He should; he's leading it there. And he's enjoying it. Because he, like we, knows who will win. When he pushes the final button, Torrey draws, but then does something very telling: he hesitates. When his gun clears the holster, Torrey pauses, suddenly realizing his error. The revolver lowers slightly, then rises slightly, as if maybe he thinks he must go forward with it but doesn't want to. Wilson is in no danger and with a word could stop the showdown. That's not his purpose, however, and he shoots. Once. Effectively. And smiles again. His work is done. Almost. As Stonewall's friend Swede comes slip-sliding over to collect the body, Wilson freezes him with a stare, then turns, pushes the butt of his Colt subtly out—I'm ready, and

Figure 1. Wilson's amused spectators really make the scene.
Courtesy of Getty Images Paramount Pictures.

the revolver is ready too, in case you haven't noticed—and walks back into the saloon.

And now we know everything we need to know about Wilson.

There's an old truism in fiction writing classes: show, don't tell. Actually, it's not *that* old. Nobody told Dickens, from the look of his novels. Or Tolstoy. Or Cervantes. But old as in, since the beginning of creative writing classes. As in, since Hemingway or thereabouts. And if the truism is true of fiction, it's much truer in film. Unless the audience actually *sees* something, it doesn't exist. Don't tell us, or have another character tell us, that someone is kind to animals; show her feeding the stray dogs from her own inadequate food stores.

So what do we learn about Jack Wilson in his killing of

Stonewall Torrey? That he aims to win. That he knows how to gain and use unfair advantage. That he is utterly ruthless and without mercy. That he's very good at his job. And that he really enjoys it. That's important. For Shane to be justified in going after Wilson when the time comes, Wilson needs to be a genuinely bad guy. He can't just talk a bad game; he has to *be* bad. A bully. Someone willing to take unfair advantage. Someone untroubled by murdering "just another sodbuster." Someone who will deserve what he's going to get. And he's all that.

Now, before anyone has a chance to forget this, let's say it again: **Film is a visual medium.** Beyond that, we can add this proviso: **in which the visuals are in motion.** Yes, it has, or can have, other elements involved. It can employ sound, for instance. There is usually narrative. The images can be in color or black and white. The movement can be live-action or animated. And so on. But the bottom line is that film involves *pictures that move.* As a culture, we've become so inured to the phrase "moving picture" that it hardly even registers what a miracle that is. There is no one alive today who was alive when pictures couldn't move. Not one single soul. But there was a time, and not so long ago, when pictures did not move, and a slightly earlier time when they took days or weeks to create. Not much change, aside from the materials used, in the thousands of years from cave paintings to *Whistler's Mother.* The transition from painting and drawing to photography and thence to cinema is, in the scope of human history, a nanosecond.

Which brings us to the second part of the equation that is film: its audience is human beings. Two factors are key in our being able to comprehend movies. The first is that sight is far and away our strongest sense. The second is that, unlike canines and felines and various other neighbors in the predators' club, humans had to learn early on in their history to use their brains to make up for their pathetic inability to overtake any quarry quicker than, say, a rutabaga. Endurance, stealth, memory, patience, strategy, teamwork: those are the skills that made humans efficient predators. They also, aside from the first one, involve development of perceptual and analytical skills that make us very good at creating and decoding visual storytelling. When Charles Foster Kane drops the snow globe and utters his famous last word at the beginning of his movie, we are capable of hanging around till the end in the hope of discovering what he meant when he gasped out, "Rosebud." So capable, in fact, that we might burn the place down if not given the answer. Aside from theater safety, that ability has other uses. One I have elsewhere misnamed the Indiana Jones Principle: if you have an otherwise fearless hero and he needs to have a weakness at a critical moment later on, you have to show that weakness early. That's why Indy freaks out at Reggie the snake in the cockpit of his seaplane in *Raiders of the Lost Ark*, because after a while, he's going to meet what seems like every snake in the world. At that point we understand why he is so paralyzed and what he has to overcome in order to move forward.

This is pretty much the principle of Chekhov's gun. That master of another visual medium, the stage, Anton Chekhov, said at various times something to the effect that, if one is going to display a gun in act one, it has to go off in act two, or else it shouldn't be shown at all. He of course meant this as a warning to the writer: don't introduce extraneous visual information, especially not of the sort that carries powerful expectations. If an early scene contains a racquet, the audience will not inevitably leap to the conclusion that someone is going to commit tennis. On the other hand, we *expect* guns to go off, so if one doesn't, we have wasted a lot of anxiety over a false lead.

This principle cuts both ways: (a) if we don't see it, a thing—a quality, a fact, even a person—simply doesn't exist, and (b) if you show us something, you had better make use of it.

We need to see, for instance, not merely trouble but the coming of trouble. In *Stagecoach* (1939), the trip has already proven arduous when they stop for the night at a way station. While the travelers are resting up overnight for the rest of the journey (and one of them is giving birth), one of the Apache women slips off into the darkness to alert her tribe that the coach will be rolling without an escort. In other words, easy pickings. Why? Well, from John Ford's less than enlightened view, to cement the story of Indian perfidy—can't be tamed, can't be trusted. Not the noblest reason, I admit, but the past is the past. Beyond that, however, there is the practical matter that in a bare-bones existence, it wouldn't make sense for raiding parties to randomly circulate up and down Monument Valley in vague hopes of finding unattended targets of opportunity. They may be on the warpath, but they're not stupid. And finally, in showing us the woman sneaking away, the movie shows us the approach of danger: the Indian attack, after all, is the thing we all came to the theater to see. Half a dozen or so crabby misfits in a cramped conveyance is hardly anyone's idea of good viewing. Those same squabbling few become hugely interesting when the first arrow lands. The woman's action, therefore, is a promissory note on future thrills and alarms.

Or let's say you want to convey the desperate situation in a mining camp, as Charlie Chaplin does in his silent classic *The Gold Rush*. Let us further stipulate that, like him, you can't use words, aside from those few that will fit on an *intertitle* (those title cards that appear periodically). You can have the Little Tramp, Chaplin's iconic character, chew on a shoe sole, to no avail. And you can have his huge cabin mate, delirious from hunger, chase him around and around the small, bare table. But if you really want to seal the deal and convey just how far gone they are, you can show Charlie appearing to be a drumstick to his starving friend. That image not only conveys the depths of their hunger, but is also screamingly funny.

So what does all this mean? Chiefly, that we are dependent on visual data, that we are very good at processing that data, and that we cannot only store it for a long time in memory but call it back when needed. All of this is excellent news for filmmakers, who would go broke if their main audience lacked this very special skill set.

Sometimes the basic truth about seeing and believing takes on a new twist. We've all had the experience in some horror film or thriller in which a character we had left for dead suddenly proves to be a lot less so. You can plug in your own movie experience here. For me, it took place in a school gymnasium where twelve hundred of us were watching *Wait until Dark* (1967). Audrey Hepburn's blind Susie has been terrorized for a couple of hours first by henchmen of the awful man Roat (Alan Arkin) and then by Roat himself after he kills the henchmen just to cement his bad-guy credentials. She has taken out every lightbulb in the place, missing only the bulb in the refrigerator, whose door has been blocked open unbeknownst to her. In a moment of great courage, she stabs Roat when he takes her into the bedroom to kill her, and we think he's a goner. But back in the kitchen, by the light of that one, feeble bulb, he lurches at her and grabs her ankle and . . . six hundred girls (and more than a few boys, to be fair) screamed as one. I'm pretty sure the gym moved a few inches off its foundation, and my hearing has never been the same. But I learned the lesson every good film reader must learn:

check the pulse. In the world of cinema, no sale is ever final. As you know if you've watched Friday-the-Thirteenth-on-Elm-Street-at-Halloween-with-Chainsaws.

So here's a helpful policy: unless you're quite sure a corpse actually is one, lots of bad stuff can happen. Also occasionally good stuff. Few things in Hollywood are as unpredictable as the condition of the nearly departed. We viewers need to pay particular attention and make sure the stake does indeed go through the heart. Not that horror flicks have a monopoly in the fake-death department, as anyone watching a glowing white Gandalf ride to the rescue after falling to seemingly certain doom in *The Lord of the Rings: The Fellowship of the Ring* can attest.

Once in a very great while, a sequel may be required. Case in point: everybody's favorite buddy combo, circa 1970, Paul Newman and Robert Redford. So much blue-eyed blondness that it hurt. But mean old George Roy Hill (the director, not the heavy) had killed them off in *Butch Cassidy and the Sundance Kid*. That sort of thing makes sequels awkward. But then there's all this money out there just hanging on the Redford–Newman tree, and nobody in Hollywood is going to let all that greenery die unmolested. You can just about hear the gears spinning on that conversation:

"Yeah, we'll bring them back, see."

"But they're dead."

"Okay, so—same guys, different names. Different place, different time."

"But bank robbers again?"

"No, that's the beauty of it. Grifters this time. Still crooks, but likable, you know? And in . . . Chicago. Yeah, Chicago."

"In the Depression."

"Right, sure. They'll be just like before, but different. And we'll get Hill to direct again."

And so they did. And they knew there'd be criticism, so they even came up with the world-champion tagline: "This time, they just might get away with it." Perfect.

And it almost was, ultimately winning seven Oscars, including Best Picture.

But it also had the big belly-drop. At the culmination of the "Big Con," the sting of the title, just as the two con men have separated Doyle Lonnegan (the convincingly dangerous Robert Shaw) from his half-million Depression dollars, they're interrupted by the feds bursting in to arrest them—or at least Newman's Henry Gondorff. The main G-man, Polk, lets Redford's Johnny Hooker go and thanks him for his assistance in the case. Incensed, Gondorff shoots Johnny in the back, prompting Polk to plug Gondorff. Blood trickles from Johnny's mouth and Gondorff's chest, and amid the horror and shock, Lonnegan is swept away from the crime scene by the local corrupt policeman, sans money.

Oh, no! We didn't like this ending the last time. Hopes dashed, the sick feeling of Butch and Sundance running into a hail-of-bullets-freeze-frame returns. Except . . .

Except "Polk" is no G-man but one of Henry Gondorff's old associates. He gives our two heroes the all clear, and they rise from the dead—or at least the floor. Smiles all around, wipe away the stage "blood," and let's share the dough.

But isn't that cheating? Sort of a trick ending, isn't it?

There's a trick, all right, but it isn't on us. There are a million trick endings in Hollywood, and those would be cheating. No preparation for the outcome, completely against logic, strictly pull-it-out-of-the-hat stuff. But not here. The beauty of this ending is that it grows right out of the action of the movie. One of the characters even says that Lonnegan will never rest if he finds out he's been duped. That means our boys would have to disappear completely and that the heavy must never know he's been cheated. Well, you can't get more disappeared than dead. And the true Big Con here isn't the money, it's the vanishing act. The money, though, is a nice addition.

For a visual medium, the movies send an odd message: don't trust what you see. Or what you think you see. In the neo-noir crime thriller *Body Heat* (1981), we see—or think we see—Matty Walker (Kathleen Turner) get blown up by a bomb identical to the one that her lover, Ned Racine (William Hurt), used to dispose of her husband's body. In the subsequent developments, Ned is tried and convicted for the murders. While languishing in prison, he suddenly realizes he's been set up, that he was marked as the fall guy from the start, and that Matty has meticulously planned her scheme from before the time of her marriage. It involves switched identities and another cold-blooded murder as well as the destruction of Ned's life, but suffice it to say that the scheme has worked to perfection. And that Matty is alive and sipping umbrella drinks on a beach. We'll have more to say about the movie as we go along, but for now it's enough to say that our certainty, and Ned's, for he is a witness to her "death," turns out to be a lot less certain than he or we had thought. This device of seemingly assured death has been a device in scores of movies down the years, and its success almost always relies on us seeing almost everything we need to see. We just lack that last bit of detail. Someone takes off his clothing and swims into the sea, but we don't see him drown. Someone walks into traffic and disappears. In this case, we see Matty walk around the booby-trapped storage shed and assume she has entered it, but of course she hasn't. Our minds supply information that our eyes have not actually seen. In the movies, many old tricks just keep working.

We've been talking dead people here, but the rule is more general. Movies exploit not what we see but what we think we see. Naturally, no one *really* dies in a made-up movie, but lots of characters die, or seem to, only sometimes they don't. And often, we're not in the know that they're somewhat less dead than advertised. Film is based on deceiving the audience, not only making it believe in events that never happened to persons who never existed but also duping it into thinking one thing is true (within the context of the film) when, often, the truth lies with its exact opposite. So the check-the-body rule broadens out to something like this: nothing is certain unless visually corroborated. In other words, **Make sure you see what you think you see.**

Otherwise, who knows what *your* shrieks will sound like?

2

The Camera Does
the Thinking for Us

EVER SINCE THE LUMIÈRE BROTHERS filmed that train pulling into the station, movies have been intimately tied to their historical siblings, planes, trains, and automobiles. In fact, those were the title words of the John Hughes–directed Steve Martin–John Candy comedy (1987), and it really did deal with vehicular mayhem. Beyond that one instance, from *The Great Train Robbery* to *Easy Rider* to *Thelma & Louise* and on to the Fast and Furious franchise, filmmakers have been in love with shooting speed. One of the reasons for that fascination is that moving vehicles can convey so many different messages: power, fear, elation, revenge, urgency, criminality, heroism—you name it. It all depends on context and camerawork.

Those forms of conveyance are expanded in *Marvel's The*

Avengers (2012), which is about a group of superheroes who take saving the earth into their own hands. A pair of vehicular scenes demonstrate the importance of the camera in telling stories. In the latter film, we only see the alien invaders' movement from the outside. We watch them from behind as they emerge from the wormhole over Manhattan (best not to ask; just go with it), then flip to our side of the wormhole as we watch their swift advance on us. The one position the camera never occupies is the viewpoint of an alien. They are the Other, the Threat, and the film keeps them firmly in that situation. When Tony Stark (Robert Downey Jr.) flies as Iron Man, on the other hand—and his suit of armor is itself a conveyance—we see him inside the suit, his face partially covered by technical features of what the suit empowers him to do, as well as see parts of his flight from inside the armor. We do care about Stark, as we do about the other Avengers; there's not much point to the movie if they remain emotionally distant. To give us that point of identification with them, director Joss Whedon employs a subjective camera, not exclusively but frequently enough to get his point across.

The subjective camera is, if anything, more powerful in the kidnapping scene in *Slumdog Millionaire* (2008), in which director Danny Boyle has everything in motion: people, things, cameras, so that the action is a blur of movement. Jamal (Dev Patel in his breakout role) has taken a train to the appointed station at the appointed time, as he does every day, in hopes that his beloved, Latika (Freida Pinto), will arrive to run away with him from her abusive gangster lover. As we watch him on a balcony beneath a clock and holding on to the railing—powerful images both of his mind-set and situation—his body language tells us that this is a repeated and largely hopeless activity. But then Latika appears, sort of, as an image caught between trains hurrying in opposite directions, static between the speeding cars and the milling crowds of people on the platform. Rising from his crouch, he can barely see and call, somewhat futilely, given the din of the station. For one brief moment, the two lovers become still points in a turning world. But then Jamal spots his brother Salim (Madhur Mittal), now a trusted lieutenant of the gangster, along with his posse of toughs, rushing her way. Jamal calls to Latika to run, which she does, dodging through cars of a stationary train, while the gang members chase her as the crowd and train continue moving in the background. Salim catches her by the hair and drags her out of the railway car, then he and his three pals manhandle her back through the crowd. Meanwhile, Jamal is running on a parallel platform, trying in vain to reach her before they can drive away. Both her rough treatment and his sprint against the flow of the crowd—always a good technique for conveying speed and urgency as well as frustration—are shot with jumpy handheld cameras (this is one time when you really want to pretend that Steadicam technology was never invented)—hers from behind to emphasize helplessness, his from the side to push his desperation. He arrives too late for rescue and only in time to watch helplessly as she screams his name and a very large knife blade is drawn across her cheek, branding her permanently, it would seem, as property of the gangster. The scene, which neatly encapsulates all of Jamal's frustrations, succeeds not despite the chaos introduced by the way it is filmed but because of it.

Taken together, these two movies demonstrate how camera placement and stability affect our sense of the characters' experience. First, *how* something is shot matters as much as what is shot. The jerkiness of the handheld camera can suggest the instability of a character pursuing a target or fleeing danger, the hazards of moving through a crowd or a forest, or a sense of confusion or disorientation. For this reason, a subjective camera is a frequent technique in horror films. The objective camera, on the other hand, can produce a sort of documentary fact:

the audience is watching at a safe distance (even if the arrival of alien craft doesn't feel all that safe) and seeing the action as contained within a stable frame. The objective camera is by far the more common technique in film, and rare indeed is the movie, the indie-horror hit *The Blair Witch Project* (1999) being a notable exception, that relies mainly or entirely on subjective camera work.

We humans have long struggled to achieve the sort of scope and scale that film makes possible. Novels can do certain things really well, but they sometimes take a thousand or so pages to do so. Not often, happily, but it happens. Theater has been trying since the Greeks to tell big stories in small spaces, as you no doubt know. If you've been to the theater lately, especially if that theater is on, oh, I don't know, maybe Broadway, you may have seen some remarkable things. People flying. Characters disappearing and reappearing out of thin air. You know, magical stuff. Now, this has been going on for a while. As in, a four-hundred-year while. They've been flying for at least a century, since J. M. Barrie brought us Peter Pan. Was that the first? Not being a theater historian, I can't say, but it's far enough back to prove a point: the stage can be a lot like the movies.

We can go back to Shakespeare and get even more examples of what we might think of as drama on a grand scale. The Globe Theatre had seven different possible playing areas: on the first floor the main apron or "thrust" stage jutting out into the audience space, and where most action took place, and a curtained space behind it that acted as an inner stage (useful for displaying caskets or depicting a monk's cell); on the second floor a center balcony (Lady Macbeth walked here) and a chamber, the "Lords' Rooms," where actual nobility sat to watch the backs of the actors and in which Hamlet may have confronted his very confused mother; then a window balcony on either side which undoubtedly harbored Juliet, and the Heavens, an area usually hidden from view where cannonballs could be rolled to suggest thunder. So, there were lots of places to position actors and numerous ways to make the action much more continuous than it is on most modern stages. The possibilities of the Globe are often called "cinematic," which they were, from a certain point of view.

Except that the stage can never be cinematic. Not really. For all the possibilities that a multilevel, multistage theater provided Old Will, his plays in his playhouse could never be like movies. Nor could J. M. Barrie's, nor George Bernard Shaw's, nor Eugene O'Neill's, nor Andrew Lloyd Webber's. Of course, all of them have had works that became movies. Not the same thing. Because for all their brilliance, their chosen mode of presentation lacked the single item that set film and drama apart: *the camera*. Not the part that stores the film, although we'd not get far without that. No, the meaningful part of the camera, from our perspective, is the lens. That little item provides something that no stage can ever offer.

Selection.

Since it is ever my wont to abuse the Bard, let's take a single scene, with Hamlet in his mother's, Gertrude's, chamber (that's Act III, scene iv for those of you keeping score at home). Hamlet has just proven Claudius murdered Hamlet Sr., at least to his own satisfaction. He has gone to the King's chamber to run him through but, inconveniently, finds the King at prayer—not the best time to kill a man and send his soul to Hell—so he runs on up to Gertrude's room. Polonius, the meddling fool who advises the King but is also the father of Hamlet's sweetie, Ophelia, is foolishly meddling, trying to get Gertrude to spy on her son. On hearing the prince approaching noisily—nothing like shouting "Mother, Mother, Mother" to alert your enemies—Polonius withdraws behind a wall hanging—the famous and fatal "arras." Hamlet enters and mayhem ensues. The interview between mother and child is loud, confused, violent in word if not deed, sexually charged, and alarming, at least to Gertrude. She is legitimately afraid she is about to be murdered, and her cries prompt sympathetic shouts from Polonius, and those buy him a sword right through the arras, as Hamlet mistakenly assumes that only Claudius would be in the Queen's bedroom. More shouting and weeping from Queen and Prince, followed by a visit from the old king's ghost, whom only Hamlet can see; he's terrified by the ghost, she by her son's erratic behavior. It's a lot of fun.

So here's the thing about that scene: where and how you see it matters a lot. If you watch it as a play—and nearly all of us have—you see it all at once: Hamlet, Gertrude, the bulge behind the arras (or lump at the bottom), and, once he enters, the ghost. The two principals have more or less equal claim on our attention at each moment, with adjustments for movement up- or downstage by one or the other. We see Gertrude's reactions even as we see Hamlet provoking them with his wild words. If we see it by way of a film, not so. In the Franco Zeffirelli *Hamlet* (1990), starring Mel Gibson and Glenn Close as son and mother, we see the two of them in the frame at the same time precisely once, for half a second as she slaps him, before the murder of Polonius. That's around two minutes of single shots. Here's something of how it goes:

Hamlet speaks (long shot)
Gertrude reacts, speaks (medium close)
Hamlet says something outrageous (close shot)
Gertrude looks horrified (close shot)
[More in this vein]

Zeffirelli is no dope; whether we like how the scene is shot or not (I happen to, but your results may vary), we understand what he's up to. He knows that an essentially static scene needs activity, and if the characters aren't moving around a lot, the camera can provide it. Moreover, the quick takes and frequent cuts of the scene elevate our sense of being unsettled, which is something everyone in the play feels as well. Movies are action, as we've noted before, but they're also movement, which is not quite the same thing. No matter how little action there may be in the blocking of a scene—how it's laid out and performed in actual space—we have to feel that it advances the plot or character or meaning or theme or all of the above. In this case, the cuts themselves carry meaning. Of course, the dialogue and action also carry meaning; how can they not when someone winds up dead on the floor? But in those jumpy switches from mother to son and back, the director and cinematographer are furthering our sense of their estrangement, their psychic distance from one another. We can understand that from the elements Shakespeare provides, and we do whenever we see the play staged, but we *feel* them in a different way because of the sudden switches the cuts provide.

Why is this possible? Because at its base, the language of film is different from that of the theater. Its grammar is one of selection, not of presentation. By contrast, the theater has no choice but to present everything happening onstage at any given moment. In the same way that the choice of a narrative point of view in fiction determines what kinds of information can be conveyed and the author, through the narrator, determines how much information to share, so the camera's placement and focus, along with the cuts, determine what we will see and how we will see it, hence the Scholes and Kellogg assertion that film is a narrative rather than a dramatic art. After several decades to consider the matter, we might well decide that it's a hybrid, a narrative form that employs dramatic materials. We can come back to this question later. For now, we're chiefly interested in the first part of that equation.

Since I already mentioned characters speaking, let's consider the possibilities. Onstage, the blocking of a scene is everything: since we will process the presence of everyone in the scene simultaneously, what really matters is proximity to the audience (who is upstaging whom?), or maybe height or elevation (is the speaker on a platform or in a pit relative to his auditors?), or perhaps colors (is someone kitted out more brightly than everyone else, thereby stealing our attention?). Even then, the tricks may or may not work. If the key character is in a red dress and I'm color-blind, I won't get the point. Not only that, but nearness may matter more if the viewer is seated in row C and not where I customarily find myself, row W. So which character's experience of that scene is most critical? And how do we determine that fact? In a movie, on the other hand, the director and cinematographer can make sure we get the point. Just think of the possibilities. The camera can, at any given moment . . .

- focus on the speaker

- focus on the primary listener(s)

- focus on the secondary listener(s)

- use a wide lens to include speaker and listeners

- use deep focus to bring both into the frame with relative clarity

- use shallow focus to include both but focus primarily on one over the other

- use shallow focus but change from one to the other

- cut quickly or slowly from speaker to audience

- focus on any portion of the speaker's or listener's anatomy—the object of contemplation can be a foot just as well as a face, you know

- alight on some creature or thing that is not part of the dialogue—a passing cloud, gathering storm, or donkey in a pasture

- any combination of these

- none of the above

I know I missed some possibilities, but that's a pretty substantial list. The point is, as readers of the movie, we find that whatever the camera lingers or flashes on, the lingering or flashing offers us as much information as the thing shown in whatever fashion. As mere viewers, we are not required to notice the choice, only that we're seeing more of, say, Peter O'Toole than of Omar Sharif.

Since we've talked about royalty already, let's return to them. In *The King's Speech* (2010), director Tom Hooper leads us through the trials of speech impediment and speech therapy, the old king's death, the abdication of Edward VIII to the transformation of just plain (Prince) Bertie into King George VI, and ultimately forward to the eponymous address. This is no ordinary speech, but an address to the nation—to the empire, really—on the occasion of Britain declaring war on Germany. He has to rally the people, *his* people, to the cause of defending the nation. This is why the Brits keep their monarchs around, so someone above the political fray can speak on really, really big events. So the King (Colin Firth) must speak. Without his stammer. To do so, he is coached by his therapist, Lionel Logue (Geoffrey Rush), while listened to by a dying-by-degrees Queen (Helena Bonham-Carter), his brother David

(Guy Pearce) and wife, the former Wallis Warfield Simpson (Eve Best), and a significant portion of the billion or so subjects of the Crown. This will be no stroll in the park. It takes everything the King and Logue can muster to get through the ordeal, the first of many such partnerships over the next five years. The process of selecting what or whom to show is masterful. Hooper—or more properly speaking, Hooper via editor Tariq Anwar—gives us absolutely as much of the King suffering and fighting his stammer as we can bear. Maybe just a touch more. It is required viewing, of course, but extremely painful. So what else can one show? Everything. The scene begins with the door to the recording studio being closed by a servant in the outer room, as if to say the King is now trapped; there is no escape from this ordeal. Which leads to:

1) The King, looking down, then speaking Logue's name

2) Logue, looking deferential

3) Back to King George, breathing deeply, anxiety evident

4) Logue full face, encouraging, "Forget everything else. Just say it to me."

5) George, anxious

6) Logue, positive, gentle

7) George, breathing deeply in preparation

8) Two-shot (one of the few) of the men on either side of the large microphone, Logue counting down with his fingers. On "one," he points to George

9) Single of George, beginning to freeze

10) Logue, gesturing the first cue and mouthing the words

11) George, locked up in terror, he hesitates, swallows as if to speak, cannot

12) The Queen, with Churchill behind her, her eyes clenched, holding tight to her daughter's hand and the chair arm, showing obvious horror at the silence

13) Robert Wood (Andrew Havill) in headphones, waiting for some sound

14) Logue, patiently waiting, but nervous

15) George, struggling, mouthing, finally getting out the first words

16) Logue, leading into the next line

17) George, struggling through the lines

18) The gathering with the Queen in palace

19) The BBC studio relaying the message to various parts of the empire, George's voice superimposed, the camera panning to take in the entire operation

20) George, struggling to get the words out

21) Logue coaching him to take his voice down

22) George getting out "this message"

23) People in an English pub

24) George fighting his way through the speech

25) Logue coaching the next move

26) George getting out the end of the phrase, "at war"

27) Logue nodding—very good

28) Two-shot, Logue and George explaining how they searched for peaceful solutions

29) George, carrying forward, painfully

30) Logue mouthing the next words

31) Two-shot from over George's shoulder circling briefly to profile of the two

32) Wood listening on headphones with colleagues

33) Two-shot from over Logue's shoulder

34) Logue nodding approval

35) A mother and sons in living room

36) George continuing

37) Workers gathered around radio in factory

38) Servants below stairs at palace, listening

39) Gentlemen at their club

40) Two-shot from over Logue's other shoulder, Logue giving vigorous hand signals

41) George continuing

42) Logue punctuating the final phrase before it is said

43) Duke and Duchess of Wales alone and close together on sofa in large room, large bay windows expanding the sense of space around them; camera slowly zooms in on the pair

44) George struggling but picking up steam

45) Logue watching pleased but impassive

46) Crowd outside palace listening to loudspeakers

47) George's mother listening alone, approving

48) George, medium shot, pushing on, finding his rhythm

49) Soldiers around a field radio

50) Close-ups of Archbishop of Canterbury (Derek Jacobi) and Churchill (Timothy Spall) behind the Queen

51) Two-shot from behind George's shoulder—in the homestretch

52) George, close-up again, in his final phrases, first in profile, then full-face

53) The Queen, finally breathing, young Elizabeth smiling tentatively; Churchill and Archbishop nodding in approval

54) Close-up of Queen smiling

55) Workers in BBC room clapping

56) Logue praising simply

57) George sighing in relief

58) Two-shot, George rushing to get his suit jacket, Logue going to shut window

59) George putting on jacket

60) Logue putting away his glasses, then making a comment to break tension

61) George in profile, responding in kind

There's a basic split between presentation and narrative selection at work here: the actors' training and instincts are grounded in theatrical practice, which is a presentational act, while the selectivity begun with the lens itself and completed in the editing room hacks away at the actors' efforts. This goes back to that discussion of the role of editors when we were looking at the Bourne–Castel fight scene. Neither you nor I was present when the scene was shot or edited, of course, but it would go something like this: Hooper would have set up the scene to capture the relevant faces over the course of however many takes were required to get the right looks, the right feel, the right emotional heft for the scene. In postproduction, that period after principal photography when a mass of recorded film or video is transformed into a movie, he then turned all those shots over to Anwar to cut—to sort through, select, trim to length, place in order, in short to transform into the scene we witness in the final cut of the movie. Some directors may be present for the editing process, some may only look at the final results to okay the work, and the majority likely fall somewhere between those poles, checking in occasionally but mostly leaving the editor in peace. After all, there is no reason to expect that, just because someone has the vision, temperament, and organizational skill to direct an army of actors and other specialists in the creating of a movie, he or she also has the technical skills or disposition to splice together film or digital files as well as someone whose entire being is tied up in that activity. There may have been twenty different options for arrangements of shots within the scene that could command our rapt attention. Or hundreds. Or hardly any. We do know that, in the present instance, there was at least one. Which is a reminder for us to focus on the way in which selection can control our reactions.

———

In the last chapter we looked at a scene from *American Sniper*, to examine the importance of seeing the character's face to learn what's beneath the surface. There's another scene shortly after that demonstrating something very different: how much we can learn even when we can't see very much at all. In the big final battle scene, Kyle has taken out Mustafa at superhumanly long range. In doing so, however, he has alerted the rebels as to the Americans' location, and a huge, chaotic firefight ensues. Air support, contending with an approaching dust storm, has failed to hit its target, and the ground support was too far out when Kyle took the kill shot, so it's racing to get there in time. In the midst of all the noise and dust and danger, he calls home on a satellite phone to tell his wife he is coming home. The exfiltration team arrives, and the squad fights its way off the rooftop they have occupied, with Kyle providing cover until everyone else is down. Once outside, the scene is a mass of ghostly forms, compliments of the dust storm. We see running shapes, then a rebel taking aim only to be shot by Kyle, and then Kyle apparently shot in the leg and falling to the ground. The scene cuts to the exfil vehicle with the next-to-last soldier, Dandridge (Cory Hardrict), being pulled to safety and the doors shutting. Only as they begin moving does he realize that Kyle has been left behind and insists on waiting for him. From that point on, everything is indistinct: Kyle getting up and limping toward the truck, Dandridge sticking his head out of the truck and calling for his comrade, Kyle getting closer and closer but slowly, something—a gun, maybe?—being jettisoned, and eventually, Dandridge pulling Kyle into the truck. Only when the camera tracks back through the storm can we see with certainty that the thing thrown away was indeed the sniper rifle, which, Kyle having killed Mustafa, he no longer needs. The next shot is of Mustafa lying dead in his sniper's lair, confirming what we know: Kyle's war is over. Here's the beauty of that scene: we can't see everything clearly, but we don't need to. The film supplies shapes, colors, and movement, along with such nonvisuals as speech and sounds; our minds are fully equipped to do the rest. What we encounter in the scene is the outward manifestation of what is called the fog of war—the chaos and confusion that overtake the senses in the midst of battle. We may have encountered it in the firefight leading up to this moment, but the sandstorm-shrouded exfil makes us feel all that mayhem. We've been talking about how the camera controls what we see, which we usually take to mean very precise selection of details, but here, the filmmakers are asking us to supply the missing elements—in other words, to see what isn't really there to be seen—and we happily oblige. This is the unspoken collaborative element of the movies: the audience has a hand in creating meaning. Sort of makes you proud, doesn't it?

What can we take away from this scene? From this movie? Let's consider our old pal Dave, who only watches movies, he claims, for the action. This baby's got plenty of that. Dave, we know, has loved the firefight with its manic activity and noise. But he's been thinking lately if maybe Lexi's onto something. What catches his attention is this sudden shift from a sort of ultraclarity in the rest of the movie (which he understands makes sense in showing us the life of a sniper) to this clouded view of Kyle dragging himself toward rescue. And what might in another movie strike him as too "artsy" makes complete sense to him here.

"I get it," he tells Lexi. "You know, there's all this confusion and just, like, dust and stuff. And we can't see much of anything. But we know it's there. That's kind of where he was all along."

"He?"

"You know, the sniper. Chris Kyle. It can't be easy to do a

job like that. To do the right thing, you have to do the wrong thing. Really terrible stuff, but to keep your guys safe. That has got to mess with your head. I don't think I could take it."

"Well, did he?"

"No, not so much. Maybe if he'd had more time. He seemed to get better, but . . . Besides, can you ever be really okay after all that?"

"I doubt it."

"But it's a really great scene. You know?"

"Yes, I know. So it's not just a sandstorm, it's a theme?"

"I don't know if I'd go that far."

"Keep working at it."

When we read a novel, the relationship seems pretty simple between the audience, the material, and the maker. There's this *thing*, the book, and the book obviously had an author, rarely more than one, and we're holding it, so we're the audience. We can break this down into three elements: medium (the physical or electronic book); the creator of that medium, the author; the receptor (us, the audience). The author can select what information to present, in fact often does that selection in the act of choosing a narrative point of view. A first-person narrator, for example, can't tell us directly about an event at which she wasn't present. At the same time, we usually have a wealth of information about a given scene and that provides a lot of material to work with.

When we watch a film, by contrast, we're seeing what the camera has selected as the center of our attention. And it's a very exclusive device. If it wants us to see only Sundance, we can't expand the frame to bring in Butch, even if he's only inches away. We glimpse *Psycho*'s Janet Leigh, then a shady figure, then Janet, then a knife, but never all together—which turns out to be fine. The point is, in real life, or in the theater, we would see whatever was there, while the camera culls, selects, presents, reveals, and hides. Want to see more? You'll have to make your own movie. They've given us all they're going to give.

3

Shot, Scene, Sequence!

IF WE'RE GOING TO TALK ABOUT MOVIES, and I suppose we are or you wouldn't still be reading, we need to establish what it is that we're talking about. In discussing fiction, we spend a lot of time talking about the narrative strategy and voice and the point of view being used. If it's poetry, there will be a lot of talk about meter and rhyme scheme and form. Movies are neither of those genres, however; they are a visual medium in which the basic building block of meaning is also visual. Most of us know that, of course. We just don't know the specific terminology. When we try to talk about what we witness on-screen, we have one word available. Occasionally, it is the right one, but too often it isn't adequate to the task:

Scene.

Don't get me wrong; it is a perfectly sound word. A technical word, so that's also good. Our application of it, though, sometimes leaves a lot to be desired: "You know that scene where he just stares into her eyes"; "That scene in the bank where all the tellers break out into a tap dance"; "What about that scene where the robbers come out of the drugstore, and then the police chase them, and eventually they get cornered in that old barn?" If all those things are scenes, we have a problem with our technical vocabulary.

Happily, they're not. One is (the second), but the others are something else.

Films not only have to have chemistry; they're like chemistry. Now, relax, there won't be any lab reports. But we learned in chemistry class that our world is made up of some very basic building blocks. Reduced to its most essential (I almost said elemental) level, there is nothing in the maple tree in front of me that resembles a tree in miniature. Rather, there are billions of extremely tiny things that are no expression of treeness, yet together they make this fine example of *Acer saccharum*, the sugar maple tree. And we know that those things are atoms, the most fundamental of meaningful items in the physical world. There are particles smaller than the atom—protons and neutrons and electrons and quarks and some things they discovered after some of us took chemistry and that sound, frankly, more than a little made-up. And those atoms, of hydrogen and oxygen and carbon, say, can combine into *molecules* to create some interesting and useful properties, one of which may well be to express treeness. Okay, there are some intervening stages between a hydrocarbon molecule and the spreading chestnut, or in this case, maple tree, and those matter, too. But we don't get there without those really basic units and their habits of combining with each other.

Movies have those, too, with the added advantage that their building blocks are actually visible. And the most basic unit in a movie is not the scene; it's the shot. When we lay out the atomic theory of film, shots are atoms. There's nothing smaller that carries meaning, and shots combine with other shots to create still more meaning. Actually, there is a smaller unit, a sort of subatomic particle (to continue our chemical analogy): the frame. A frame is an individual rectangle of film containing a single image; put a couple of dozen of those in a row and you have a second of film. Obviously, there is meaning in a single image, but it is only when we string a sizable number of them together (remember: twenty-four frames per second) that we have something with real meaning. That's the shot. Then if you put enough of those together in the right order you get a movie. Simply stated, a shot is what the camera captures at a given moment. It can be static—John Wayne in *Stagecoach* (1939) holding his empty saddle and his Winchester in soft focus—or it can be dynamic—Steve McQueen's Mustang in *Bullitt* (1968) flying over the lip of a San Francisco hill. Syd Field, in his classic screenwriting text, *Screenplay*, writes, "A shot is what the camera sees." In *Understanding Movies*, Louis Giannetti says that a shot is "a single unedited strip of film," which is a whole lot like "what the camera sees." Take my word for it, they all say very much the same thing.

Which brings me to my next point, and for us to get to use that one word we know. Field goes on to say—in fact, everyone goes on to say—that "[s]cenes are made up of shots." Ah, scenes! How many shots? How long? How long—or short—can a scene be and still be a scene? There are no absolutes here. Heck, there aren't even approximates.

This is Screenwriting 101: the scene is the essential building block of movie meaning. But we're not learning to write movies here but to read them. We're in Screenreading 101, where the principles are largely the same. The scene is not the smallest unit in the chain, as we've seen; that's the shot. Nor is it the longest, which, excepting the movie itself, is the sequence.

*Figure 2. This is how you make an impression. Shot of John
Wayne as the Ringo Kid. Photo courtesy of Shout! Factory.*

Scenes are made of shots, and they in turn accumulate into
sequences, and sequences make movies. One of the oddities of
film is that it is a *continuous* medium made up of *discontinuous*
moments, a moving picture in which not one of the individual
pictures moves. Kind of makes your head hurt, doesn't it? A
scene can be made up of a single shot or, as sometimes happens, hundreds of them. Yet none of those individual shots is
the real deal. It's only when they are assembled into a scene
that they mean anything. Those scenes, those units of meaning,
are then grouped with like scenes, if any exist, to form short-
story units, or sequences. On those, more anon.

In stage drama, a scene is usually described as a unit of the
play that takes place in the same location with the same characters present. If you're getting really technical, that means that
each time a character enters or exits, it would be a new scene,
but for most purposes, we take that to mean the same general

group of people, so it's still the same scene when the messenger from Mercia arrives and when he leaves again. That mostly works for film, except that location can be a lot more mobile when we're not tied to a theater. In the movies, a scene can be a shouted conversation between two characters while they're careening down the mountain on bikes or a single image of a character for a fleeting moment. The big difference between the two media is that the theatrical scene is something we process simultaneously. What I mean by this is that there is no selection on the part of the director to direct our complete attention to a single part of the action. Oh, sure, he can move characters farther up- or downstage, and we'll *probably* give them more or less attention accordingly. But we might not. Audiences (take it from someone who engaged them several times per week for almost forty years) are wonderfully fickle and even contrarian; you simply cannot guarantee that they will notice what you want them to notice, and they may do the opposite just out of spite. Their attention can wander. The guy beside them can sneeze at a critical moment. They can think the supporting actress is way prettier than the star and spend the evening watching her. Add to that the fact that all the actors in the scene are likely to be doing something, however trivial—the two lovers stage right trying to steal a kiss, the two kids stage left laughing at them or playing mumblety-peg or whatever, everyone engaged in a bit of stage business even if it is only striking a pose of mock horror—and the possibility of a certain percentage of the audience missing the point becomes something close to a statistical certainty.

Not so in film. Remember that last chapter about the camera doing our thinking? This is one place it really pays off. Rather than a scene that we receive in its totality, we have a controlled—and controlling—shot. We see only what the director and cameraman permit us to see. If it's a gunfight, say, and we cut from the hero's face to the villain's, then back, then back again, all in tight close-ups, we have no idea what the townspeople lining the boardwalk are up to. They're very likely biting their lips in anticipation and anxiety, but they could just as well be having a picnic or playing euchre or dancing a jig for all we know. The director knows exactly what we'll be seeing because it's all he permits us to see. Yes, we can miss it. Mr. Sneeze can be next to us again, or we can be canoodling (hey, I visited a *lot* of movies at the drive-in), in which case we'll miss the whole shot, but if we're looking at the screen, we don't have a lot of options about what to see—unless the director wants us to have options. Now, none of these close-ups of the antagonists' faces is a scene, nor is the combination of them one, unless it's unlike any celluloid gunfight I've ever seen. The fight, in fact, isn't the scene; rather, the scene is the whole process from the time that the first antagonist steps out into the street and the crowd begins either assembling or diving for cover until one party is horizontal and the townspeople move forward and the director yells "Cut!" In its entirety, it would run somewhere between ten and forty shots and thirty to seventy-five seconds. If directed by Sergio Leone, twelve minutes.

That scene of, say, eighteen shots spread over sixty-eight seconds is then linked with a scene or two before (one is guaranteed—the wife/girlfriend/best friend/sheriff tries to talk the hero out of walking out in the street) and another one or two after (including the return to wife/girlfriend/best friend/sheriff) to form a sequence, a series of linked scenes that form a coherent narrative package, almost a short story within the larger movie.

We'll come back to each of these elements presently, but for now, let's look at those shots in a classic gunfight. This is from Sergio Leone's 1968 masterpiece, *Once Upon a Time in the West*. I mention this opening elsewhere, but for now I want to focus just on the shoot-out at the dusty train depot. Our three desperados, Snaky (Jack Elam), Stony (Woody Strode), and Knuckles (Al Mulock)—great names, although they're not used in the film—have been waiting silently for someone to arrive on the train. We have no idea who that might be, but their interest provokes ours. We'll pick it up there, with these three taking up positions, Stony near the engine, Snaky about halfway back, Knuckles by the caboose. Whatever else this may be, it isn't planned as a fair fight.

1) Long shot of Stony (near) and others in background, framed by water tank and train engine (10:18)

2) Reverse-angle close-up of Stony, watchful

3) Close-up of Snaky, watchful, with Knuckles in the background

4) Medium shot of mail car door sliding open

5) Close-up of Stony's head jerking toward sound

6) Close-up of Stony's hand reaching for his sawed-off Winchester

7) Close-up of Snaky's hand reaching for his revolver

8) Close-up of Snaky realizing the sound was a false alarm

9) Medium shot of mail car guard tossing down a heavy package

10) Close-up of Snaky's hand relaxing away from his revolver

11) Close-up of Knuckles looking bemused: there's nothing here, so where is it?

12) Close-up of Snaky's head from behind, looking toward Stony

13) Close-up of Stony looking back at Snaky, smiling slightly

14) Close-up of Snaky smiling derisively, then looking suspicious

15) Close-up of Snaky's hand drumming a beat on his holster

16) Close-up of Snaky shaking his head slightly, as if he doesn't quite get what has happened, then flicking his head to summon Stony and then Knuckles

17) Long shot of the three gunmen from behind Knuckles as they move together near Snaky's position—SLOWLY (they do nothing fast)—still watchful but slightly confused. As the train pulls out, they turn to go. A harmonica begins a haunting melody.

18) Close-up of Snaky, with Stony and Knuckles (all facing camera) behind and moving train in background

19) Same shot as men turn away from camera and train pulls away to reveal another man, whom we will know as Harmonica. He is framed by Snaky on left and Stony on right. Snaky nods to Stony and it is on: this is the guy. The three turn to face the newcomer, their hands at the ready. He has slipped off the train on the far side.

20) Close-up of battered cowboy hat with a harmonica being played. Hat tilts up to reveal the weather-beaten face of Charles Bronson looking at his enemies out of the corner of his eyes.

21) Reverse shot from behind Harmonica across tracks toward the three gunmen. He's still playing the same eerie four-note theme.

22) Close-up of Snaky's crooked face

23) Close-up of Harmonica as he stops playing and asks, "Where's Frank?"

24) Medium shot of Stony (closer) and Snaky, who shakes his head and says, "Frank sent us"

25) Medium-long shot of Harmonica asking if they brought a horse for him

26) Close-up of Stony as he smiles evilly and turns his head toward Snaky

27) Medium shot of Snaky as he looks at the horses, then turns back and says, "Looks like we're shy one horse." Just in case there was any doubt as to intentions, his pistol is halfway out of holster, on the front of his hip.

28) Close-up of Harmonica scowling and shaking his head slightly as he says, "You brought two too many"

29) Close-up of Stony looking less assured, then Snaky sizing up the competition

30) Group shot of the four from behind the gunmen, each of whom moves his hand closer to his weapon

31) Medium shot of Harmonica, still holding his traveling bag, with no holster in sight

32) Brief shot of Snaky making his move, with sudden cut to

33) Harmonica, from behind, as the bag falls away from the revolver that he fires with deadly efficiency. The first two fall quickly, but we cut to

34) Medium shot of Stony getting off one good shot that finds Harmonica's shoulder

35) Medium shot of Harmonica spinning to the boardwalk

36) Medium shot of Stony as he falls backwards, dead

37) Close-up of windmill turning, ending in a pullback to medium shot; at twenty-six seconds, the longest shot in the scene

38) Close-up of Harmonica's eye, pull back to show head, then full body as he painfully rises and surveys the carnage

39) Long shot of three bodies on the uneven boards with horses tied up in background

40) Medium shot of Harmonica fashioning a sling from his duster coat, replaces his hat, and picks up his gun before rising and walking forward out of shot

41) Close-up of Harmonica's boots and bag; both show heavy wear. He slides revolver back into hiding place in bag, then picks up bag and walks away out of frame and

42) CUT

This may be the purest gunfight ever filmed. No moving curtains that may or may not have a rifle behind them, no teary bystanders, no spectators peering over—or under—the saloon doors; just men, space, and guns. And silence. A whole lot of silence. It's part of the Leone aesthetic. His laconic Westerners aren't merely stoic; they're quiet to the point of pathology. And his movies feature a lot of space to be silent. Compare this to the Bourne fight scene we discussed earlier. This one has about forty-five shots (I ran a few together) in 4:56 of film time. The camera lingers, dawdles, but always to a purpose. It seems to be waiting—we seem to be waiting—like the henchmen at the station, for something momentous to be said or done. High drama can't be rushed. It may seem as if the seconds per shot is not that long: 8.8 seconds per shot is fairly slow, especially when many of them are just a second or two. That leaves plenty of time to expand other shots. The shot where Harmonica first reveals his face, for instance, seems to take forever, although in reality it's only eleven seconds. Even so, when the other facial close-ups have been in the neighborhood of three or four seconds, eleven is a lot.

Never mind the details, though; just focus on how many shots it takes to get the job done. And when a film is done right, and this one is, every single one of them is critical. Each shot tells us something, adds some specific detail—an attitude, a state of nervousness (or calm), the geometry of the attack, the response to surprise, the passage of time. Even that spinning windmill at the end suggests the desolate loneliness of the spot: all that mayhem and no one to witness it.

Which leads to our second point here. This scene is part of something larger. It's not the first scene in the movie, but it is related to it—in fact, grows directly from it. So here's what the opening sequence looks like. I would call it three scenes, but others might say only two. Let's give them names for easy identification. First, the Takeover: the three desperados appear at this nearly deserted train station and take over, locking away the station agent and sending his native woman helper away. Second, the Waiting: the trio tries to fill the minutes before the train arrives without actually doing anything. Third, the Confrontation: the arrival of the train signals the gunfight to come, as we have just seen. Now, reasonable people can disagree on whether those first two scenes are actually one since they occur in the same space and comprise related actions. And it is possible to argue that the arrival of the train is its own scene, but that strikes me as a little less reasonable. My logic is that the period from the opening of the rickety door to the native woman running away is a single, completed action with beginning, middle, and end, while the bits of stage business the three gunslingers get up to during the passage of time until the train pulls in constitute another completed whole, again with beginning (satisfying themselves that they now own the station), middle (the stoic fidgeting), and end (the train). The arrival of the train, on the other hand, even though it is made up of more than one shot, is too fleeting to be a scene and is therefore the final segment of the Waiting. However we judge the matter, it is important to see that the scene we broke down in detail is part of a larger narrative arc, indeed is the ending to a sequence that begins with the Takeover.

So let's go back to those three elements. What's their deal, anyway?

- A shot conveys visual (and possibly auditory) information.

- A scene carries a piece of story and is built of those articles of visual information that are shots. The scene will be a completed action of no fixed duration.

- A sequence uses those larger pieces of story—scenes—and encompasses a story arc with, however brief, beginning, middle, and end.

Got that? You're now a film expert. Or on your way. Now, there are nuances that can be confusing.

How many shots in a scene, for instance? As many as it takes. The Leone example, for instance, has forty-five shots. The *Bourne* scene we looked at earlier, sixty-three in roughly half as much time. Others might have five. Or three. The only number not available is zero.

Can the number be one? Yes.

So a shot can be a scene? Yes again, but it's not terribly common.

I hate to ask, but how many scenes in a sequence? Same answer: as many as it takes, from one to infinity (and beyond). Or at least to quite a few.

Okay then, how long is a shot? A scene? A sequence? And how many sequences in a movie? Really? Must I say it again?

Shots

Let's start with the shot. Its main function, as we noted above, is to provide a piece of visual information on which the movie can build. Yes, auditory as well, but for now we'll pretend that all movies are silent and concentrate on the visual element. The shot can be as long or as short as the movie (or the director) demands. Traditionally, the upper limit for a single shot was about eleven minutes, which is how much could fit on a single reel of film. In the digital age, one supposes that the upper limit of a shot's duration is infinite. But naturally, filmmakers being who they are, someone already tried to make sequences in a single shot. Someone would try to transcend the limits of his medium. And just as naturally, that someone was Alfred Hitchcock, in his 1948 look at the Leopold and Loeb thrill killing,

Rope. The legend is that each reel (around sixteen minutes) comprises a single continuous shot, without edits. I'm not sure that's entirely true, but it appears to be true (in which case, the edits are really subtle).

Reel Fun

The traditional movie reel holds 1,000 feet of film. Sound movies play at 24 frames per second (silent were at 16–18 frames per second and, in the handheld camera days when cameramen cranked by hand, could vary considerably). Modern movies employ so-called split reels, which hold twice as much film, and a two-hour movie uses about five split reels, which is much handier than ten or eleven would be for changeover from one reel to the next.

You can watch for the signal (called the *cue mark*) to the projectionist to change reels whenever you're watching a nondigital movie: there will be a little symbol, usually in the upper right-hand corner, something like a bright dot or circle. Actually, there are two: one about 8 seconds from the end of the reel, called the *motor cue*, meaning to start your engine, and the second just one second from the end called the *changeover cue*, and its rule was absolute. The projectionist would know to start the second, or *incoming*, projector on the motor cue, which had, you guessed it, 8 seconds of countdown. On the changeover cue, he flipped two solenoids, little switches, one of which opens the incoming projector, the second shutting the *outgoing projector*. Eventually, all this got automated, but the terminology of measuring films by their reels remained.

But you have to be quick: each cue mark lasts only four frames, or .17 seconds. Of course, in the age of digital film, which we have now entered, all bets are off. No reels, no cue marks, just digital information on a disk or hard drive and a playlist to activate the showing. I miss the dot.

In fact, one of my favorite dissonant elements in the 1939 John Ford classic *Stagecoach* involves just such shots. In a film that owes so much to movement, Ford inserts these very clunky static shots of key characters—John Wayne's Ringo Kid, Claire Trevor's Dallas, the embezzling banker Gatewood, even the head of the purse-lipped League of Decency, and she's not getting on board—whose net effect is to stop the movie dead in its tracks each time one is inserted. It's one of the less-than-perfect elements of the movie.

Scene

So what can we say first, that a scene is not a shot? We could just say that. Except that it's not true. In some circumstances, a shot can be an entire scene, although that's quite rare. For that matter, a sequence can be a single shot, although that is extremely rare. In *Birdman* (2014), director Alejandro González Iñárritu makes the movie look as if most of it is one continuous take. That's not really possible, of course, but artful editing can hide a lot of cuts. But that's another, longer story. For now, we're talking scenes. Sometimes it isn't clear where one scene ends and another begins. This muddle is especially true when we're dealing with *intercut scenes*, that is, a period of screen time during which two complete scenes, usually taking place at the same time, are taken apart and layered in (or cut in) between one another.

In the climactic battle sequence of *Marvel's The Avengers* (2012), for instance, the film cuts back and forth between the bridge of the mother ship and the fighting down below. That fighting in turn comprises several scenes, although it may appear as one when we first watch it. Each of the superheroes has his or her own scene (or more than one); through most of the sequence, we follow, say, Iron Man for a bit, then cut to Black Widow, then to Thor or Hulk or Captain America as each one struggles with his or her bit of fighting the aliens. Occasionally we move back to the ship, where Nick Fury (Samuel L. Jackson) is trying to hold off his superiors, who want to end the emergency by launching a nuclear weapon and annihilating New York City. We experience this rapid intercutting as one long, slightly disjointed event, but in fact it is made up of several smaller scenes—Hulk and Loki, Captain America and the aliens, Black Widow hitching a ride on an alien vehicle, Hawkeye shooting everything in sight, Iron Man and the bomb, Nick Fury and the pinhead overlords, and so on—that only finally come together after Iron Man closes the cosmic hole and explodes the warhead in the alien world, then crashes back to Earth among his fellow warriors. And each of these scenes is in one way or another complete in itself: a single action by a character in a single place (or chain of places), after which he or she will go on to another action in another place. To show these scenes sequentially, of course, would create the illusion that they are happening sequentially rather than simul-taneously, so director Joss Whedon must resort to intercutting them to convey the proper sense of all this mayhem happening at once. Besides, it's a lot more thrilling this way. What matters here is that a scene is a complete action, however small that action might be. A shot, by contrast, may be a complete action but need not be—and in fact usually isn't. And while we've jumped the gun a bit, this leads us to the . . .

Sequence

You can see the pattern here, right? We're building up, which is exactly what movies do. Shots accrue to become scenes, and scenes add up to sequences. But it's not just random addition; the scenes need to cohere around something, usually a piece of story, and each needs to add something to that process of building up the story.

And how many scenes in a sequence?

Really? Again? Always with the counting!

A sequence can contain as few as one scene or as many as, who knows, maybe thirty? Oh, and they can run from a minute or so to maybe half an hour. On average, scene counts are probably in the mid to high single digits. Single-scene sequences are a hazard to continuity. At the very least, you wouldn't want many of those in a film. At the other extreme, the more scenes in a sequence, the more likely viewers are to lose the thread, as each small scene draws attention slightly away from the larger narrative arc.

You remember the confusion about these three elements I spoke of at the beginning of the chapter? Nowhere is it more in evidence than when we speak of chases. They're almost always called "scenes," but they're just as likely to be sequences: the chase scene in *Bullitt*, the chase scene in *The French Connection* (1971), the chase scene in *Butch Cassidy and the Sundance Kid* (1969). We can debate the first one. It's a fairly continuous piece of action, and while I think of it as a sequence, you might see the switches from car to car as shots rather than scenes, in which case for you, it really is a chase scene. On the last two, however, there can be no doubt. When we go not merely from car to El train but even inside the train to watch a bad guy kill an officer and shoot another man, back to Gene Hackman's Popeye Doyle in his car, and up to the train as it wrecks, that's definitely multiple scenes. As with *The Avengers*, there is a good deal of intercutting here, so it feels like a single experience.

The one I really want to talk about, though, is *Butch Cassidy*. This is one of the great chases of all time—no motors involved. It is also one of the longest: from the moment the whistle on the following one-car train screams and the door of the boxcar rams open to release the already mounted posse, until Butch and Sundance come to rest at Etta Place's house, twenty-six minutes elapse. From the true beginning, when they stop what will be their last train, it's thirty seconds short of thirty. Now *that's* a sequence. Think about putting that in the synopsis: by the way, we're going to have a half-hour chase sequence. On horseback. The money guys would just *love* that one. Are they mounted and riding the whole time? No, no one could take that much horsemanship. But during a lot of it. And more silence than you can believe. For a film so famous for its taglines—"Who are those guys?" "You keep thinkin', Butch. That's what you're good at." "I'll leave if he invites us to stay"—*Butch* has an amazing amount of screen time without dialogue. Needless to say, when two men are riding for their lives, they're not likely to spend a lot of energy on excess conversation. Moreover, neither of them completely trusts himself to keep his fear in check if they start talking. Periodically, however, they have to talk, if only to plan their next move. And it is a sequence full of movement. Hunted and hunters ride across the high prairie, up hills and down valleys, into towns and up onto buttes. The chase is interrupted by two brief stays in towns, once in Butch's favorite bordello, where they hope to give the posse false information. That fails, naturally, precipitating further flight. The second time is to try to give themselves up to a local sheriff so they can join the war against Spain. That strategy meets with similar success. The posse, headed by famous lawman Joe LeFors and featuring the native tracker calling himself "Lord Baltimore," is implacable, relentless, infallible, mechanical—and never seen as much more than dots on the horizon. It's not so much an entity in its own right as a representation of time catching up with our heroes. Their time, as Sheriff Bledsoe tells them when they come to him for help, is gone and not coming back. That's the message of those indefatigable hoofbeats tracking them down. We share Butch and Sundance's point of view, and since they don't ever meet up with the posse, neither do we.

Now, here's what's remarkable about the sequence: we don't get tired of it. I've seen two-minute scenes that drag. There are other scenes and sequences in this very movie that we have every right to question, but there's not an extraneous frame in these twenty-six minutes. Everything advances the cause, whether filling in personal history (as with the way the prostitutes treat Butch) or building suspense or revealing anxieties without words (as when Sundance shoots the rattlesnake, mistaking it for a person who has snuck up on them) or developing character. It's a thing of beauty, every last second.

The other beautiful thing is how much access we have these days to movies and how many tools we have to break them down. Once upon a time, we could only watch movies fleetingly on a big screen at a movie house or drive-in or else on a small screen at home (earlier, of course, not even that second option was possible). If you wanted to break down a scene with forty-five shots into its constituent elements, no problem: you only had to buy forty-five tickets and record each shot in order. Now? We can take movies home or have them delivered or stream them on various devices. We can move backward and forward and sometimes even hear from the filmmakers themselves about their intentions and techniques. Almost everyone can do things—easily—that once upon a time could only be done in a film studies class and even then only with considerable difficulty.

And one of the huge benefits of this ease of access is that we can learn so much more about these three structural components of film. Let's reconsider for a moment that huge *Bourne* fight scene—which is, after all, just a scene. It sits fairly late in a sequence and occupies just 2:17 out of 12:04. The sequence begins with Bourne and Marie at the door of his apartment building, which of course he does not remember. They are let in by his landlady, who does remember, and go up to his flat, where he spends considerable time trying to recall something about his life there, while she goes to freshen up. He then discovers that one of his other identities is "dead" and lying in the morgue and figures out that his phone and apartment are almost certainly bugged. This is roughly the point at which Castel makes his Errol Flynn entrance, which we've already discussed. Having dispatched the assassin, however, neither Bourne nor the sequence is finished. He must drag Marie, who is in shock and incoherent, down the spiral stairway and past the landlady, whom Castel has shot in the forehead, then out past the gathering crowd, among whom one middle-aged man eyes them with suspicion. The camera then cuts to the neutral tones of another building and we cut to a new sequence. There you go: shot, scene, sequence.

But don't take my word for it. Rather, take a movie you like and know well, find a key sequence and break it down into scenes, then at least one scene into shots. Dig into it. See how it works. Wear out the pause/play and rewind functions as you make your way toward total understanding of that sequence. Which one? I don't care. Try Harry's encounter with Voldemort in the first Harry Potter film. Heck, take pretty much any encounter with Voldemort in any Harry Potter film. Not a fan of wizards? Use *The Hunger Games*. Use *Casino Royale* or *Skyfall* or any other James Bond film. Anything you don't mind looking at over and over again. It really doesn't matter which film; they're all built with the same pieces.

Once you've mastered that sequence, you'll never look at films quite the same way again. You'll still think they're amazing, but you'll also think, And I know how they do it. That's what you're after, right?

4

Silence Is Golden

The first great innovation in motion pictures was, predictably, motion. Kinda had that one figured, didn't you? The second was sound. Or, specifically, synchronized sound, which made the talkies viable. The gap between the two was about thirty years. It was a great step forward, unless you were a musician. Prior to sync-sound, every movie house needed at least a piano player or two, and the big-city theaters had orchestras. Movies arrived with scores, which the musicians had to keep tuned to the action on the screen. The major novelist and minor composer Anthony Burgess told the story of his father being a piano player at the local movie house and, later, the local pub, which explains his own interest in music and his late novel, *The Piano Players*, about that very brief cultural phenomenon. When sound hit film, musicians on both sides of the Atlantic got their very own Depression a few years ahead of everyone else. Up until that fateful moment (not the first but the most famous) when Al Jolson opened his mouth and belted out a tune as Jackie Rabinowitz in *The Jazz Singer* (1927), silent movies had been a blessing to the music community.

To the rest of us, too. The great thing about the absence of sound from early cinema was that filmmakers had to learn how to tell their stories without dialogue. They learned what I've been telling you thus far, that film is first and foremost a visual medium, that the only thing you can really trust is the image. That it's real only if we see it. Had sound been available from the beginning, all sorts of important lessons about storytelling in the new medium might have been lost in the mass of words. Certainly the evidence of more recent movies is that dialogue is sometimes the enemy, not the ally, of film narrative. But sound wasn't available, and directors and cinematographers learned to use images to the maximum, and we all learned from them, and the course of film history was set. Then sound came in and silent movies went away and that's that, right?

Not a chance.

From the moment the Lumière brothers put those first flickering images on a screen, much of the best filmmaking has been silent. Even when sound was present.

You want examples? Okay, here you go.

I came across this first one while looking up a far more notorious scene. When Tony Richardson wants to establish the world of *Tom Jones* (1963) and the character of his hero, he shuts down the language function of his film. Oh, a few words are said, but they're in the way of being background noises; Richardson makes a point of not letting us focus on them *as dialogue*, keeping them relegated to the general din of the gathering. Instead, he opts for a lengthy hunting sequence from the arrival of the various local gentry to the moment when Tom rescues the girl of his dreams. We get shots of everything we need to know—the drunken pre-hunt carousing of the country rowdies, the brutality of whips and spurs, the sheer recklessness of the hunt as horses fall and riders lose their mounts in their crazed efforts to run down the deer, the dogs falling on the deer, Sophie Western's horse panicking in the face of the bloody carcass, and Tom's heroic chasing and subduing of the terrified creature, saving Sophie from certain harm. That he pays no heed to his own peril is confirmed by the broken arm, the pain of which causes him to faint, but only after he has established that the young lady is all right. The amount of detail is stunning, from Squire Western flipping up the skirts of a local wench (who takes no offense) to the individual riding styles to the myriad minor activities that cram the screen to the flight of the stag and the mad scramble of hounds and horses and riders. There is simply more visual data than any eye can process in a single viewing. Which is part of the point.

Meanwhile, we become part of the chase. The camera swoops high and low, now running at eye level with the horses, now observing the action from ground level, now careering from an anachronistic helicopter's-eye view, sometimes in parallel with the chase, sometimes cutting across the lines, capturing the jittery, madcap hunt in all its frenzy and brutality. At the end, we may feel as breathless as the horses and riders. The movie is in many ways clunky and old-fashioned, particularly in terms of acting style, so much of its moment that it may at times be hard to watch in ours, but the direction of this one sequence—a sort of silent movie within a talkie—is timeless.

Before going forward, we should think a bit about classic silents. The thing about silent movies (and here I'll limit our discussion to comedy, although a similar observation can be made for dramas) is that the gags are different.

Quiet?

Yeah, sure. Be that way. No, the real difference in silent gags isn't that they are silent, wise guy, but in how they must be presented since they are silent. The first three sight gags (can there be any other sort?) in the Harold Lloyd classic *Safety Last!* (1923) illustrate the point. At the very start, the Boy (Lloyd) seems to be in prison and awaiting execution. He's visited through the bars by his mother and his girl with what seems to be a noose in the background. Then the perspective changes as the women walk around the bars, and the "noose" turns out to be a message loop on a railroad gantry, not a gallows at all. Then, as they are saying their goodbyes, a black woman comes in with a baby in a carrier that is a little too similar in size and shape to Harold's valise, and sits the baby between the young man and his case. Harold, hurrying to catch the train, grabs the wrong handle, and the mother, panicked, grabs his valise and chases him down to make the swap. In the confusion, the train begins to pull away and a horse-drawn wagon comes between the Boy and his conveyance. Harold, blithely waving to the women, grabs on to the back of the wagon, which begins taking him away at an angle from the departing train. Harold realizes his mistake just in time and jumps down to race after his departing ride, barely making it. Gag one, the noose, is only funny because we can't hear the conversation between the Boy and the women; if we could, the mystery would be lost. Gag two works because of the exaggerated motions of the silent movie form—the Boy is so intent on his farewells that he can't notice the changed surroundings, specifically the baby crate. And the action of swapping suitcase for baby is sped up because no words are heard. Dialogue sometimes has a way of slowing action. Gag three, in its turn, succeeds not because he can't hear the clip-clop of hooves beside the departing train but because we can't; we attribute our sound deprivation to him. And again, he is so involved in his farewells and the swap that he can't be bothered to look up. These antics demonstrate how the rest of the movie will work. When Harold is besieged at his dry goods counter during a sale, the action is more frenetic because there is no stopping for dialogue; everyone can be talking at once without fear of cacophony, since none of the voices are audible. At one point he is being pulled apart by two women, until he manages to wriggle out of his jacket. And when he realizes the impossibility of handing a package to an elderly woman because of the unruly crowd, he calls out (we see via the title card) "Who dropped that fifty dollar bill," sending every woman to the floor in search of the mythic currency—or every woman except his target, who presumably is deaf. Throughout the movie things take place that are funnier because we can't hear any dialogue or ambient sound, and often they transpire because of that very lack of sound.

And the soundless system worked. Consider this: when the arguably greatest silent film director made one of his most sublime films without audible dialogue, he didn't have to. The year was 1934, and Charlie Chaplin wanted to make a great movie of the times—*Modern Times* (1936). It was a perfect moment for the Little Tramp, who had always experienced personal hard times; now, with the Great Depression still great, he had a reason for the going to be tough. Moreover, he had found a radiant, charismatic young costar who was his match in the delightful Paulette Goddard. Chaplin's Tramp is a curious mixture of clumsiness and lithe athleticism; Goddard's "gamine" similarly mixes sinuous grace and headlong desperation. Naturally, the two of them find more chances to get into trouble than any ten people could manage under normal circumstances.

When we think of the Little Tramp, the scenes that compel

our imaginations are those of physical comedy, of the desperate chase in *The Gold Rush* (1925), for instance, in which the outsize roommate (his foils always loom over him in stature and weight), driven by hunger to hallucination, sees Charlie as an entrée and Charlie literally has to race for his life. Such moments abound in *Modern Times*, as when the Tramp, showing off for his new girlfriend by bringing her into the department store on his first and only night as watchman, figure-skates blindfolded on a mezzanine, not realizing that the balustrade has been broken and removed. With each loop he skates, he comes perilously close to the precipice, at times even swinging his foot over the void as he executes a step-over turn. Charlie is always courting disaster, especially when trying to impress the girl; in this case she is impressed and also terrified, not knowing how to stop him without initiating catastrophe.

Here's a basic truth about the cinema: **We never say that we're going to hear a movie.** I doubt that anyone has ever said that. We watch one. Always.

The finest silent film of the 1960s is one in which the characters seemingly can't stop talking: *Butch Cassidy and the Sundance Kid* (1969). To say that Butch (Paul Newman) himself is loquacious is to damn with faint praise. True, Sundance (Robert Redford) is the silent type, in part the better to play off Butch. Of course, both actors are playing off their more or less standard screen personas, which is to say, largely off their real-life personalities. There are actually two sequences that qualify in my book as high-quality silent moviemaking. The first is the chase we looked at in discussing scenes and sequences. In nearly half an hour of flight, our two men exchange very little, very sporadic dialogue, most of which consists of the line, "Who are those guys?"

The second example comes a bit earlier in the film, when Butch is trying out this modern invention, the bicycle. On the morning after Sundance has finally returned to Etta Place's (Katharine Ross) farm, Butch comes riding around and around the farmhouse making creepy-comic, stage villain noises that are barely audible on, as he calls it, "the future." This particular model has two wheels and pedals. Etta hops on the handlebars (which, to be fair, do look rather like a perch, if not a seat) and they ride around her spread. After a bit of riding, Etta hops off and climbs into the mow of the barn, the better to witness Butch's antics. And he has plenty, circling the barn with his feet on the handlebars, then balancing with one foot on the saddle, then in full layout on the saddle, and finally pedaling while seated backward. This last maneuver leads to disaster as he crashes through the fence that pens in the resident bull. The two then have to retreat at considerable speed to avoid the bull's shortsighted ire. The only false note (okay, lots of them) is that the sequence isn't played entirely in silence but to the accompaniment of B. J. Thomas singing the Burt Bacharach/Hal David song, "Raindrops Keep Falling on My Head." Rarely has a musical interlude been so misguided, but that's for another discussion. For our purposes here, the bicycling is a textbook example of what can be achieved in silence. The riding establishes the easy relationship between Butch and Etta, as opposed to the edgier love affair she has with Sundance, his sense that the future is coming, her openness to experience, his grace and style and humor, and his inclination to court calamity. When, at the end of this four minutes or so, he asks whether she ever wonders what would have happened had she met him before Sundance, we understand their relationship so well that the question seems superfluous.

Intriguingly, Redford would go on to make a silent, or at least a virtually dialogue-free, movie late in his career. Of course, there are long stretches of such films as *Jeremiah Johnson*

(1972) or *The Natural* (1984) in which his characters don't have a lot to say for themselves. But in *All Is Lost* (2013), there are a couple of lines of dialogue—monologue, really—at the beginning, then no more talk. That makes sense, given that it is a castaway movie and there is a notable lack of auditors, but the same situation doesn't stop Tom Hanks in *Cast Away* from doing plenty of talking. This character, known as Our Man, says nothing except for those few sentences that conclude with the title words, and then the narrative flashes back to the events, small in themselves, that have brought him to this point of extremity. He is the only character, so no purpose in talking, which only gives away desperately needed energy. For the remainder of the film, we hear only his attempts at an SOS call on his radio and cries of "Help!" at a passing ship that nevertheless fails to see him. This kind of filmmaking is beyond daring; it challenges its audience to overcome their expectations and offers, as a reward, sheer brilliance.

When I began thinking about this book—and especially this chapter—I had one fixed certainty, one piece of knowledge on which the rest of the chapter could build: **Silent film is dead and not coming back.** A safer statement, it seemed, had never been uttered. But then, a funny thing happened on the way to the chapter: a French maniac brought out a movie that was not only silent but black-and-white. In late 2011 and early 2012, *The Artist* took the movie world by storm, winning critical praise, audience attention, and five Oscars. For the record, the maniac's name is Michel Hazanavicius, and another word for *maniac* is *genius*. If your mad scheme succeeds and you win, say, a best director Oscar, we apply the kinder word. On the other hand, if you sink a gazillion dollars into a movie that nobody wants to watch and sink the studio, as Michael Cimino did with *Heaven's Gate* (1980), then we're not so kind. But back to happier topics. *The Artist* also won Academy Awards for Best Picture, Best Original Score (Ludovic Bource), Best Costume Design (Mark Bridges), and Best Actor (Jean Dujardin). It was also nominated in the categories of Art Direction, Film Editing, Cinematography, Original Screenplay (Hazanavicius again), and Supporting Actress for the luminous Bérénice Bejo. Plenty of room to quibble in all that success—that Bejo should have won, that she should have been nominated in the Leading Actress category, that John Goodman, in his best role in years, maybe ever, deserved at least a nomination as Supporting Actor, that the best actor in the film was not Dujardin but Uggie the Jack Russell terrier (who is, admittedly, awfully good). For my money, the most astonishing achievement nearly a century after the birth of talkies is Hazanavicius's ability to craft a screenplay that does not rely on language. But I digress. Again. The main point here is that this film works on every level that we expect from the movies except for snappy dialogue. And really, hasn't that all been written already?

Okay, okay, it's not really a silent film. There are a couple of words of dialogue at the end, and we have abundant sound in the form of music and sound effects throughout the movie. But no film was ever silent; some merely lacked sync-sound and had to rely on theater orchestras or organists or pianists and sound effects men. The point is, the movie is intended as silent, observing the conventions and limitations of cinema without speech.

One of the truly brilliant moments in *The Artist* comes right after George, our silent movie idol, has been shown a clip of film with sync-sound. We don't hear it, although he does. He just doesn't believe it. The producer (Goodman) tells him it's the future, but he scoffs, not knowing that the future is about to run him over. Back in his dressing room, however, something strange occurs—strange for him and for us. He's at his dressing table removing his makeup when he sets down his water glass. He hears it. *We* hear it. Up till now, we've heard nothing from within George's world. All our sound has been on the outside, in the form of the score. It all makes sense if you think about it: George lives in a cinematic world before Jack Foley, the first and greatest sound effects man in movie history. Foley spent more than thirty years at Universal perfecting the techniques of reproducing, imitating, and synchronizing sounds for things like footsteps, breaking glass, Roman armor (with a set of keys for *Spartacus*, his last film), horse hooves, you name it. Those who follow in his steps are known as Foley artists. Now *there's* an impact on the movies. George, however, doesn't know Jack about Foley, so his experience has heretofore been silent. Now, though, his glass makes a clink (perfectly timed) when he sets it down. So do his shaving brush and comb, each distinct from the others. In fact, everything makes sound—the barking of Uggie the terrier, the toppling chair he knocks over in a panic, the ringing telephone, the laughing chorus girls as they pass (they multiply from one to three to many in a Fellini-worthy moment)—absolutely everything. Except him. His voice doesn't sound as a whisper or a shout; his footsteps when he runs outside in panic do not register. Finally, he sees a crow's feather falling to the pavement, where it lands with a resounding boom, waking him up. In this nightmare scene, as it turns out to be, one thing is clear: George is not cut out for the world of sound.

In truth, I already should have known, and maybe did, that silent movies have never died. Mostly, they simply exist in bits around the edges and in corners of talkies. You doubt? Watch *Schindler's List*. Watch *The King's Speech*. Watch *Easy Rider*. What the heck, go down-market and watch the stalking scene in virtually any horror film. Silent filmmaking exists in every genre, in almost every movie ever made. Just a couple of years before *The Artist* appeared, Pixar gave moviegoers a silent gift: the opening sequence of *Up*. In a handful of minutes, with only Michael Giacchino's simple, beautiful, Oscar-nominated score as sound, the opening montage captures the entirety of Carl's and Ellie's lives together from first encounter through wedding and family hopes through infertility and childlessness, through aging and illness and, finally, Ellie's death and Carl's subsequent desolation. The sequence is one of the most elegant, charming, and heartbreaking pieces of footage ever animated. Most important, it provides the necessary backstory for why Carl is a sedentary grump, which he must be for the story line to work even though Ellie, naturally enough, never appears in the plot. As the British newspaper the *Daily Express* said, if the film had ended right there, it would still have warranted five stars.

That's why—and how—silence matters in movies. We will never go back to silent movies, of course, any more than we will return to black-and-white or hand-cranked cinematography. But there will always be a place for good storytelling accomplished with pictures only for the simplest of all reasons: it works.

Come to think of it, *Heaven's Gate* might have benefited from silence.

5

In Between the
Dark and the Light

How about a theory? This one's not mine, but I like it a lot even if it's not strictly accurate: there are two genuinely American film genres, the Western and film noir. The Western we're mostly dealing with elsewhere, although it comes into play here as well. Here, however, is exactly the place to consider the latter, especially the second word. *Noir*, for those of you who, like me, wasted your time studying Spanish in high school, is French for "black" or "dark." One might be tempted to think that black film would be hard to see, and indeed it is, but it's also not uniformly devoid of light. During the 1930s and '40s, a style of filmmaking sprang up that shot movies with dark themes on dark film stock with minimal light sources. Many scenes took place at night and in dark alleys, and about half the movies starred Humphrey Bogart. The rest had George Raft. These films were generally about crime and detection, focusing on the murkier depths of society. "Heroes," to the extent that they existed at all, were ambiguous figures at best, and audiences often couldn't be sure that the good guys were all that good.

These films were rarely taken very seriously by the Hollywood establishment. They were seen as strictly commercial enterprises, vehicles for stars, nothing very special. Nor did American audiences see these dark movies as anything like high art. Entertaining, yes. Popular, certainly. Artistic? Not so much. As so often happens, we needed the French to help us see ourselves. The New Wave directors and critics embraced the genre, especially critic Nino Frank, who named the form in 1946, François Truffaut, Jean-Pierre Melville, and Louis Malle. And, as so often happens subsequently, we follow their lead and figure out that we really have something after all. Happened with Poe. Faulkner. Jerry Lewis? Well, no system's perfect. But film noir for sure.

And what's the most important element of a noir movie? Light. Yeah, yeah, the light that's not there. But absence implies a presence, as darkness implies light. Above all others, this genre is about the absence of light. No one, viewers included, can see clearly.

Let's consider an example. THE example. *The Maltese Falcon* (1941) is the noirest of the noir, the übernoir, if I can mix language families here. It's darker, murkier, more morally ambiguous than almost any movie you'll meet in a day's walk. When Sam Spade's partner, Miles Archer, is murdered, it's at night. He has taken the assignment because of the undeniable beauty of "Miss Wonderly," whom we will later know as Brigid O'Shaughnessy, hoping for a chance to bed her and never guessing that the attraction he feels will be his undoing. Spade is called out to the scene of the crime in the middle of the night, where he meets up with the police and an encompassing darkness, with Miles at the bottom of a hill, which only deepens the gloom around the body. Later, when Spade finds the ship *La Paloma* torched and, shortly thereafter, the dying ship's captain smuggles the eponymous statuette to Spade's office, both events are shrouded in black. Indeed, when Captain Jacoby staggers into the office, he seems to carry the darkness in with him. And, of course, during the very long session involving Spade and all the suspects, they are waiting through the night for a time when daylight returns and his secretary can retrieve the black bird from the bus terminal locker where Spade has stashed it and bring it to them. Once Spade has it in his hands, the most noticeable thing about the scene is the shadow of man and bird behind him on the wall. Indeed, shadows are nearly everywhere in the film, precluded only by periods of darkness too complete to throw them. And most of the principals, excepting Mary Astor's Brigid, display a penchant for garments of black or navy, which come to the same thing in a black-and-white film. What's interesting about the movie is that, for the black/white dichotomy of tones, the ethical tone is more black/gray. Sure, sure, there are plenty of out-and-out villains here: the femme most fatale Brigid, Sydney Greenstreet's Kasper Gutman and his henchman, Wilmer, and Peter Lorre's effeminate Joel Cairo (showing that this was a less enlightened time). But even the good people aren't all that good. Miles gets killed for following his libido rather than his common sense. His widow, Iva (Gladys George), has had an affair with Spade that is over in his mind but not in hers and now believes, quite mistakenly, that he may have killed Archer to have a clearer path to her. Spade himself plays fast and loose with the truth, including his reputation for being morally challenged, and he is willing to bully, cajole, and possibly commit violence to meet his ends. Only his secretary, Effie, comes off as an upstanding citizen. What a crowd.

If my claim that *The Maltese Falcon* is one of the darkest pictures ever made is not true, it is only because of Carol Reed's *The Third Man* (1949). A great film with outstanding people engaged in some very nasty goings-on, the film features a war-ravaged Vienna along with Orson Welles and Joseph Cotten as childhood buddies who come close to being reunited. That is to say, Cotten's Holly Martins, a writer of pulp Western novels, keeps looking for Welles's Harry Lime, who is supposed to be dead, although the stories about his death keep getting in each other's way. Lime has been involved in the black market, running a ring that steals penicillin (making it perhaps the first film to use the new wonder drug as a key plot element) from military posts and selling it wherever it can fetch the best price. When the two do finally meet up, Harry alternately threatens Holly and tries to buy him off with an offer of a job. He also tells Holly how lightly he views the deaths of the people, chiefly servicemen, who died because of the fake penicillin his agents swapped for the real drug. He is willing to kill anyone who gets in his way, a point driven home when one of Holly's sources dies violently before he can pass along his information. Before he is killed, Harry will try to shoot his way out of a desperate situation, even seeing shooting his old friend as a welcome possibility.

And the color scheme for this jolly tale of smuggling and murder? Black. Not black and white. Black. I'm pretty sure that Vienna has daytime, but you'd be hard-pressed to prove it by this film. It probably has more nighttime minutes of screen time as a proportion of the whole than any film that doesn't feature vampires. At one point, Harry has hidden—at night, of course—in a darkened doorway, with only the sheen of his polished black shoes—and his lover's cat—visible. It is remarkable that one city can have so many darkened corners, doorways, and alcoves. And then there's the sewer system in which the final chase takes place. Darkness, blind turns, shadows, dim light seeping in occasionally, dark motives, dark clothing, dark outcome. Now *that's* noir. It seems that director Carol Reed decided to take the idea of film noir and push it as far as it can possibly be pushed. And then pushed one step more. The movie has powerhouse actors, a terrific story, and a screenplay by English novelist Graham Greene (who a short time later penned the novella based on the film), but its real achievement is the brilliant direction and cinematography making use of such a restricted color palette.

What's its opposite, a standard-bearer for what we might call *film blanc*? Maybe *Lawrence of Arabia*. Oh, sure, we could go with one of Sergio Leone's sun-drenched, eyeball-blistering spaghetti Westerns, *The Good, the Bad, and the Ugly* (1966), say, or *Once Upon a Time in the West*, but even there a certain darkness seeps in at the corners. Let's stick with David Lean's 1962 epic. I'm tempted to say "masterpiece," except that he had four or five of them—*Brief Encounter* (1945), *Great Expectations* (1946), *The Bridge on the River Kwai* (1957), *Doctor Zhivago* (1965), *A Passage to India* (1984, his last), take your pick(s). What a film *Lawrence* is! The half-dismissive term *biopic* has no place in this story of a real man-cum-legend. It has the best of everything, from a screenplay by playwright Robert Bolt, author of *A Man for All Seasons*, to music by Maurice Jarre, to cinematography by Freddie Young, to great performances by Peter O'Toole, Omar Sharif, Anthony Quinn, Alec Guinness (for the first of many times in flowing robes), José Ferrer, Claude Rains, Anthony Quayle—not so much an all-star cast (O'Toole and Sharif would become stars on the basis of the film) as an all-actor cast.

Time and again we are treated to shots of humans as tiny dark spots on vast, brilliant landscapes, emphasizing both their puniness and their difference from the inhospitable environment. When Lawrence risks his life to rescue one of his comrades who has fallen on "the anvil of God," we are given shots of a perfectly level horizon cutting between the gleaming white sand below and the empty blue sky above. Where they meet, there is very little to distinguish between them.

Later, when Sherif Ali has burned Lawrence's Western clothing and "awarded" him the robes of a sherif, Lawrence, alone, performs a sort of private dance, trying them out, running in them, holding up the polished dagger to see his reflection, and, in the most compelling moment, bowing to his own shadow, which he has watched to see how he moves in his new duds.

Figure 3. *It doesn't get any brighter.* Lawrence of
Arabia. *Courtesy of Columbia Pictures*

Later, after the first train has been dynamited in the desert, Lawrence walks along the top of the captured train to the applause of the Arab fighters below. We see not him but them. And his robed shadow, walking ahead of them. In a film chock-full of stunning camera shots, this could be the most brilliant—Lawrence as a sort of ghost, a figure unseen yet

Figure 4. Sunlight and shadow in Lawrence of
Arabia. *Courtesy of Columbia Pictures*

dominating the landscape. Come, it says, and make whatever
metaphor you need out of me.

In a film with so many brilliant images, this one stands out
for the way it takes blazing light and turns it into the darkest of
images. We associate darkness with night and fog and rain and
gloom; Lean reminds us that we can also arrive at darkness via
the desert sun.

In truth, if we want to study the uses of darkness and light
in film, we could do far worse than to stick with the works
of David Lean. His early *Great Expectations* captures all the
darkness and foreboding of Dickens's original, the scariness
of the fens in the opening sequence supplanted only by the
crumbling mansion of the mad Miss Havisham living among
the moldering ruins of her long-ago wedding feast. His late
Doctor Zhivago, with its endless expanses of snow, and still later
A Passage to India, with its miles and miles of sun-bleached
plains and barren hills, could each give *Lawrence* a run for its
eye-burning money. Yet what is important with Lean is that his
use of dark and light, sun and shadow, day and night, is never
programmatic. Rather, he matches lighting to the demands of

the films' actions, which marks both his pragmatism and his greatness.

So then, *Lawrence* is one of the brightest films going, *Falcon* one of the darkest. There's a lot of room in between, and most of the really interesting action happens where the two extremes meet. Surprises are forever emerging from the shadows or stepping into darkened rooms from brilliant sunshine. Even with all the innovations of color and 3-D, moviemaking still comes down to playing off the light against the dark.

A (Well) Matched Pair

It is curious how actors' lives sometimes intersect. Peter O'Toole and Omar Sharif were almost perfect contemporaries, born four months apart in 1932 and dying a mere nineteen months apart (O'Toole in December 2013 and Sharif in July 2015). It is unlikely that either would have achieved the same level of fame and respect had they not appeared together in their first big Hollywood film. The sparks between them were unmistakable, and according to O'Toole, they had a marvelous, rowdy time making the film. Afterward, of course, they became huge stars, between them largely owning the sixties. Yet neither of them ever won an Oscar, despite Sharif's two nominations and O'Toole's eight—a record for someone who never won. That two such prodigious talents never hoisted the statuette (although O'Toole was given an honorary Oscar in 2007 for lifetime achievement) is a reminder of the outsize role luck and timing play in award season.

Consider this little gem from Peter Jackson's *The Lord of the Rings: The Two Towers* (2002). The whole of the Battle for Helm's Deep takes place at night. In fact, the sequence took four months to shoot, working exclusively at night, so these actors and crew got the full effect of darkness. As morning approaches and things look utterly desperate, Aragorn (Viggo Mortensen) and the Rohirrim ride out to meet the dreadful army of Uruk-hai and orcs, hoping that this surprising change of plan will allow their women and children to escape farther into the mountains. Just then, Gandalf the White (Ian McKellen) appears over the crest of the hill bringing the rising sun; nay, he is the rising sun, so forceful is his raiment of light. Sorry, one gets carried away writing about things Tolkienish. But you get the idea: this is the ultimate heroic reveal. This is the bugle call of the cavalry charge in *Stagecoach*; it's Superman reversing time to save the dead Lois Lane; it's every miraculous rescue from certain destruction since the movies began. It doesn't hurt, of course, that Gandalf is accompanied by a huge army of his own, led by Éomer (Karl Urban). The point is, any normal filmmaker would be embarrassed by this brazen use of light to bathe a character who is already all in white as a way of bringing us out of the darkness of that enormous, all-night battle. Happily, Jackson is not easily shamed, and we are rewarded with a breathtaking light show.

This example, as you will have noted, occurs in a film that otherwise stresses the contrast between dark and light, good and evil, purity and sinfulness. The Uruk-hai are creations of a mind of pure evil, Sauron, and another mind corrupted by the allure of power, Saruman. This is pretty standard fare. Batman's world is far darker than that of his alter ego, Bruce Wayne. In fact, it is often stated in the films that Bruce must embrace the darkness (and he has plenty of psychic darkness in his background) in order to meet the criminal element on its own terms. And he pays a great price for that dark turn.

It is not inevitably the case that all films employing contrasts between dark and light will have such thematic emphases, even if a great many do, but if you are making such a movie and don't make use of the visual equivalents, just what *are* you thinking?

6

Image Is Everything

IT'S ALL WELL AND GOOD to talk about these building blocks—shots, scenes, sequences—that constitute the framework on which we hang a movie. Very important, those. Couldn't make or understand films without them. They're what we view when we watch one; they're how we process information. They're just not what we see. And they're not what we remember. For that, we need to think in slightly different units. The things that really register with us, that stay with us long after we leave the movie, are images. Some we never forget.

Examples? How long do you have?

Okay, here are three, taken at something less than random: a cowboy carrying a saddle and twirling a Winchester by its oversize lever, a naked woman cringing and screaming in the shower, and a gigantic furnace consuming a child's sled. If you ever saw these three films, you already know that the names are John Wayne (as the Ringo Kid), Janet Leigh (as Marion Crane), and Rosebud (as itself), in *Stagecoach* (1939), *Psycho* (1960), and *Citizen Kane* (1941). Great movies, all three. They're tremendously well directed and acted and shot. Different genres, to be sure—a Western, a thriller, and a character study—with different aims, but the thing they have in common is that they leave us with unforgettable images, and not just the three I've singled out.

Here's one viewers can't shake, no matter how hard they try: it's an eye, perfectly still. Actually, there are two eyes, staring up from under a bowler hat as if they're maybe seeing as much of the brim as of the camera into which they are ostensibly gazing. But the one—his right—commands the attention; it's mascaraed and fitted with false lashes long enough to do a B-movie starlet proud. And this is on a guy. In 1971, when the movie came out, that wasn't normal. In truth, I don't know when in human history having long, false lashes on just one eye would be the norm. Turns out, it's okay: he's not normal, either. Not by a long chalk. At the moment, as it happens, he's drugged. That would explain the stillness. How Malcolm McDowell could keep his eye so still is a question for the ages, but it is a remarkable shot. For this is, of course, the opening image of *A Clockwork Orange*, Stanley Kubrick's adaptation of the Anthony Burgess novel from nine years before. What we discover from that image, what we know just eight or nine seconds into the movie, is that this is creepy and unsettling.

When the camera pulls back to reveal first Alex, the owner of the disturbing eye, and then his "droogs," as he calls his gang members, it is no less creepy. They're dressed all in white, aside from the bowlers, complete with codpieces, which remind us, along with the rather baroque insults Alex delivers, that there is for all its modernity a highly Elizabethan aspect to the novel

*Figure 5. A very alarming start: Malcolm McDowell
as Alex.* Clockwork Orange, *Warner Bros.*

(and therefore the film). Since Burgess was, in his student days, an Elizabethan scholar who would go on to write biographical novels about Shakespeare and Christopher Marlowe, this interest of his is hardly surprising. Whether Kubrick was respecting that element of his source fiction or merely got lucky, I cannot say, but it definitely works.

Images can work on multiple levels simply as images. Remember those scenes in *Lawrence of Arabia* when Sherif Ali outfits Lawrence in blazing white robes and again when we see him striding along the top of the train after the Arabs dynamite the tracks? What do they tell us about the man and his current environment? In the first, Peter O'Toole mugs not for the camera but for himself; his chief concern is with how he appears in this new uniform. On one hand, the scene gives us an image: Lawrence transformed. That one is pretty straightforward. At the same time, we see not only that image but another: Lawrence captivated by this new image of himself. That meaning is cemented by his use of the brilliantly polished knife blade as a mirror. We can be excused for understanding that scene in terms of excessive self-regard, a failing of which Lawrence is certainly guilty. Even so, if we stop there we miss a key aspect of that concern with his image. What matters, aside from personal gratification, is how he will appear to others, both those he leads and those he opposes, or with whom he must contend. While no words are spoken, Lawrence knows that he can't appear ridiculous or inept in his new threads. For someone who has been careless about his British Army uniform, he cares almost too much about his appearance in the desert robes. The payoff for this scene, then, comes later, with his striding over the top of the train—or rather, his shadow striding over the shadow of the train, for that is what the camera captures. Lawrence has been desperate not merely to be accepted but to become one of *them*. And here he does, gliding across the train roof to the cheers and shouts of his victorious followers: shadows have no race.

Here's one you've seen somewhere. A big movie star is on the decline, a young one on the rise. At some point, we will be shown posters of each of them; in fact, the story will be told through those posters, one of them becoming more prominent (bigger billboards, greater frequency). But there's another shot we're certain to see: the former star's poster in the street, in the gutter, trampled underfoot. I witnessed it most recently in *The Artist*, the retro-silent movie about the movies. George Valentin (Jean Dujardin) has had the misfortune to have his self-produced, self-directed, self-funded new silent film open on the same evening as Peppy Miller's new talkie, *Beauty Spot* (a particularly tough blow, since George gave her the beauty spot that becomes her trademark). George's image gets a double slam here. First, he arrives home to find the final goodbye note, informing him he has two weeks to clear out, from his wife—

on the back of one of his publicity stills. Then, after Peppy (Bérénice Bejo) comes out to try to make amends for some inadvertently rude comments from the night before and to say she likes his film, we cut to the exterior of the two theaters and to feet walking. All over his rain-soaked poster. Yes, we've seen it a thousand times. And yes, it still works. A filmmaker has to be careful about how he uses it, but the image even at this late date retains its visual power. That is why, of course, images become clichés: because they do hold the power to convey a meaning. And because they become clichés, they have to be reinvented from time to time.

The Artist is filled with marvelous images, as befits a black-and-white silent film, but another that stands out is George's battle with his own shadow. Immediately before he burns his cache of his movies—and accidentally his apartment, when all that acetate stock flares out of control—the last movie he has been watching ends, leaving him with a blank screen. When he stands in front of it and sees his shadow, he berates it for his own shortcomings, and it exits the screen in more of a slow burn than a huff, leaving George in the odd position of casting no shadow. We can do much with that image. He's already dead inside; he has allowed himself to become hollow or invisible; he is estranged from his own true self, or his true self from his image; this is an apt metaphor for his current status in Hollywood, among other possibilities. Do with it what you will, the image cries out to us for interpretation, for understanding it in the larger context, which is what the best images do.

The time has come, alas, to define perhaps the squishiest word in literary or cinematic criticism: *image*. So what's wrong with *image*? Only that it can mean almost anything, which is to say that it means almost nothing. The more or less standard definition comes from around 1948, compliments of British poet C. Day-Lewis (father of actor Daniel, of whom you may have heard): an image is a picture in words. Most of us can live with that most of the time. In practice, however, an image can be anything from a picture of a thing to something more like an idea, very nearly a theme, so amorphous may it be, all the way to symbol or metaphor, whose company images often keep, although no self-respecting image should actually go so far as to be a symbol, at least not without announcing its intentions. Worse still, in film, that "picture in words" bit has no meaning, since movies are made up of what? Pictures. So it's a picture made of pictures. How not helpful is that? After all, every single frame of a movie is an image, right? That's 120 minutes times 60 seconds times 24 frames: 172,800 images, although, admittedly, there are quite a lot of duplicates in there. The brain spins. So if *image* is going to mean anything for our purposes, we need to shift the definition a bit. Let's say that, rather than a picture made of pictures, an image is a picture that imprints itself firmly in the mind. And what makes that picture take hold? Typically, some piece of information beyond itself, not merely the visuals themselves but a suggestion or hint or allegation. Of course, the image must be striking in itself; without that, it isn't likely to take hold. But if it is really going to stick, it needs to carry some secondary meaning beyond its mere stickiness. In our Lawrence example, the vivid picture is of him holding up that polished dagger. The extended meaning—his fascination with his own image, the image he has been cultivating and which is now completed by his new threads—gives that picture significance and weight with viewers. How much weight we choose to give it, and of what sort—is this an instance of narcissism or of wonder at his transformation or of some newfound power—will be for each viewer to decide. But I would guess that, if we stop and think about it, nearly everyone would recognize that moment as containing some meaning beyond the mere visual data.

Images can be static or moving. Since these are *motion* pictures, the latter is often the case. Lawrence's shadow striding along the top of the train's shadow would be an instance of the latter. Indeed, static images, or at least those that are consciously static, can come across as hokey or forced. For example, John Ford's use in *Stagecoach* of the one-shot of various characters, the Ringo Kid, Gatewood, the pinch-faced League of Decency lady, strikes us as contrived, the more so with each repetition of the device, a serious misstep in a movie that does so much right. On the other hand, that frozen moment at the end of *Butch Cassidy and the Sundance Kid* when they dive out into sepia forever amid a hail of bullets strikes us as completely natural and organic, however sad. More common than either of these techniques is the still picture amid ongoing action, when a character stops for a moment or the camera cuts to something unmoving amid the bustle. Reaction shots would be one such example, when the camera cuts to a character to show how he or she takes in whatever action or message has just been conveyed. *The Thin Man* movies of the thirties can almost be described as one long reaction shot; either Nick (William Powell) or Nora (Myrna Loy) Charles, our hard-drinking, fast-talking wealthy sleuths, is forever striking a pose in reaction to whatever quip or insult the other has just delivered. Characters needn't mug for the camera quite as much as Nick and Nora do for something to be a reaction shot; often, the characters are acting for the benefit of one another, while Powell and Loy are acting for the cameras. Does that distinction make sense? Nor are they the only people in the movie whose reactions are caught on film. At the end of each movie, Nick (the professional detective) convenes a gathering of all the suspects, police, and interested parties. Nick's technique in these inquisitions is to assert some fact about the murders and then, seemingly (although not really) at random, call out the name of a suspect. Their reactions, surprise, shock, real or feigned outrage, often deliver more information than any statement they might make.

Who Shot the Image?

So how does *image* differ from our earlier term, *shot*? Does it differ at all? Ah, this is where things get tricky. By definition, cinematic images grow out of shots; indeed, every one of those 172,800 frames has the potential to grow up to be an image. Not all of them do. The vast majority of shots whiz by the vast majority of eyeballs as mere conveyors of information. Nothing wrong with that. In fact, we would be exhausted if every shot were an arresting image. It's the "arresting" part that distinguishes the two, something that makes us pause, makes us remember, makes us invest that particular shot with greater meaning than the majority of its brethren.

I recently heard director Ang Lee speaking about movies in 3-D ultimately supplanting 2-D films, something he once doubted but now takes as a given. The occasion was an interview about his 2012 adaptation of Yann Martel's *Life of Pi*. The film makes considerable use of not only the third dimension but also computer-generated imagery (CGI), which is the only safe way to put a human in a lifeboat with a tiger. I hope he is incorrect, since I am one of those people who are treated badly by the 3-D experience, and in fact I opted for *Pi* in the traditional two dimensions. What matters most, however, isn't the number of dimensions but the clout of the images. On that basis, *Life of Pi* is a powerhouse. Repeatedly, Lee gives us images of Pi's isolation: the lifeboat itself, of course; the raft he builds to keep himself away from the tiger, named Richard Parker; the island he finds devoid of animal life except for the meerkats who climb to safety each night when the island becomes carnivorous; even the spectacular display of glowing jellyfish, who serve chiefly to emphasize Pi's aloneness. Other directors have tried the lifeboat before as emblems of isolation and puniness; often, however, as with Hitchcock's *Lifeboat* (1944), the boat serves as the container of a small community rather than as a vessel of solitude. And because Pi (Suraj Sharma) spends nearly the entire movie in the lifeboat, it becomes an ever-starker signifier of his solitude, his vulnerability, and his fragile hold on life. Everything is, by powers of magnitude, bigger, stronger, more dangerous than he is.

Up till now, we have been discussing images in isolation, but of course they never really exist in isolation. Rather, they combine with other images to form a dialogue. This happens in all literature, as when the writer in Hemingway's "The Snows of Kilimanjaro," dying from an infection in his leg on the plains below the mountain, imagines a plane carrying him to the snowy summit. The contrast between the heat of the lowlands and the corruption of his blood on the one hand and the purity and cold and whiteness of the mountaintop on the other gives the two images combined a power neither could have on its own. Contrastive images work very nicely on celluloid (or digits—we really must invent new terms), too. An example everyone remembers, even if they haven't seen the movie, is from *Titanic* (1997). Consider its two most famous shots, first, Jack Dawson (Leonardo DiCaprio) holding Rose DeWitt (Kate Winslet) in the prow of the great ship, and second, Jack supporting Rose on a piece of flotsam only big enough for one, assuring her that she will die an old lady, warm in bed. Or if you prefer, the shot when she discovers that he has succumbed to the cold. Together those two images mark the alpha and omega of their relationship, the first signifying that Rose can trust Jack—and with more than merely her security in a scary-but-exhilarating spot, the second that her trust in him has been borne out by the self-sacrifice on her behalf. They are the more piquant because each contains the other. In that first shot, so full of life and promise, a sense of doom hangs over it because we bring it with us: saddled with the history of the voyage, we know this story can't end well, however much we may wish otherwise. The second recalls the first: Jack's confidence, his support of her, his complete investment in her well-being. Of course Jack would die to let her live; we've known it all along. Neither image, compelling as both are on their own, is as powerful without the other.

Another way images can and often do combine, though, is through accretion. Similar images are added to one another until they form a pattern. In a sense, it is a single image type that finds expression in numerous instances, rather like the "conceit" of seventeenth-century poetry. There, a single dominating image would organize and shape the meaning of a poem. John Donne, for instance, in "A Valediction: Forbidding Mourning," uses the conceit of a compass—the kind for drawing circles, not for finding true north—to reassure his love of his return. You, he says, need not sorrow over my departure because you are the fixed foot of a compass of which I am the free foot, so no matter how far out I range, you will always be the center of my transit, and I will be inevitably drawn back to you. A cynic might notice that this is both a lovely promise and a permission given by oneself to permit one to rove widely, but we'll let that pass for now. The *conceit*, or controlling figure, comes and goes in poetry, which like most other human endeavors is a fashion industry.

That mastering image or metaphor can also be employed in film, but with necessary differences. A poem may last a few lines or a few pages; a Hollywood movie for two hours or more. You can only hit the viewer with it so often before bruising begins. So how do these recurring images build up to something like a conceit or maybe a trope? Let's take an example from a movie everyone knows, or thinks he knows. I'll bet five whole cents there's something you've never observed about *Casablanca* (1942): the closed-door trope. Don't panic at a new word: a trope is a figurative element, usually linguistic, although not in this case—a metaphor, a simile, an image—that is repeated through some portion of the text of a work or across multiple works. In our instance, you will note, the figure, or image, is visual rather than language-based. That makes sense, since the visual image, as we have discussed, *is* the language of film. Nevertheless, the repetition functions in the same manner as a trope does in a short story or novel: to emphasize. That is, as the image is repeated, it drums something into the audience—readers, or in this case, viewers—that will enhance an effect, underscore a theme, highlight some important element. What that effect is, we'll come back to shortly. For now, just consider the variety of ways characters are impeded, excluded, caught, trapped:

- the paddy wagon used in initial roundup of suspects;

- while watching the Lisbon plane land, the hopefuls are framed by arches, and behind those, closed doors;

- the door to Rick's American Café, which is open or closed, locked or unlocked, to various people at various times throughout the film;

- the door to the gambling room, which is used several times, especially to keep out the official from Deutsche Bank;

- the door to Rick's office—he invites Victor Laszlo and, somewhat later, Captain Renault in, although Ilsa gains admittance without Rick's knowledge or approval, just as she works her way, against his will, back into his heart;

- in the room, a safe Rick opens in front of Renault;

- the cash cage in the gambling room;

- in his desperate attempt to escape the gendarmes, Ugarte (Peter Lorre) pulls the gambling door shut, and as they burst out of the room, he shoots two of them;

- Rick hides the letters of transit in the upright piano, the lid of which is another door;

- earlier than her appearance in his room, Ilsa comes into the darkened bar and closes the door behind her;

- Rick admits and bars people as he pleases;

- when Rick and Victor Laszlo speak in his office, the door is closed; he denies the letters of transit to Laszlo but agrees to use them to take Ilsa away;

- a Chinese screen in the bar that hides the entrance to the kitchen; it's nearly always visible;

- Rick opens the door to his room slightly and peers out to see Carl, the maître d', and Laszlo, fresh from a narrow escape at a meeting of the Resistance;

- in the final sequence, just before they head for the airport, he admits Renault, then Ilsa and Victor, to the café; the fog is another sort of door;

- Renault's office also has a famous door, behind which he grants exit visas in exchange for monetary or sexual bribes.

You may at this point object that any movie about bars and illegal gambling will inevitably involve a certain number of doors. Okay, then explain this:

- In Paris, the views are longer; even inside a hotel room, the window is open to the empty sky, the crowd on the dance floor seems to recede into the distance; Rick and Ilsa are at a sidewalk café when they hear of the Germans' approach; when the announcement is made that the Germans will enter the city forthwith, the lovers are in a café in which there are windows, which admit light and air. In the entire sequence, there is not a single door.

The entire flashback sequence, until the train-in-the-rain-with-heartbreak final scene, is wide open and sunny. In Casablanca, even when it's sunny, it's dark. Doors and windows, even the air itself, seem to be closed, determined to keep the inhabitants in and the light and air out.

Do you have to see all those doors opening and closing in order to enjoy the film? You've seen it, right? But not seen anything special about the doors? Well, there you go. And here we get to the difference between viewing and reading a movie. When you watch the film, you see Rick keeping someone out of a room and you intuit that he's hiding something or protecting something, or you watch as he closes a door to tell another character a detail not divulged to anyone else—often because we're told as much visually and/or verbally—and on you go. We know from our vast experience in reading stories and watching films and television programs that doors hide things. The hiding can be comic, suspenseful, or tragic, and the same door can, in different situations, fulfill different functions. But when we go from merely watching the action to *reading* it, we actively engage the material to better understand it. We know, if we consider the matter, that the door that opens just slightly will mean something different in, say, *Psycho* and an episode of *Scooby-Doo*. Yes, there's a surprise coming, but the nature of it will be very different. After all, comedy and tragedy are merely two sides of the same mask. Reading this movie, or any movie, like reading a book, is largely a matter of taking the time to notice what's going on: what sorts of devices are being used, what elements of visual or auditory language are being employed and in what ways, what items get repeated, how shots are framed, and so on. I would argue that reading movies proves to be the harder task since they roll relentlessly forward, twenty-four frames to the second, with no pauses for reflection. If you stop to analyze what just happened, you miss what's happening now. To seriously read a film, then, requires multiple viewings. The first one takes care of the plot and gets the surprises out of the way; each subsequent one reveals more details that we might have missed previously. And we miss a lot. At least I do. I hope I'm not insulting you by generalizing from my experience.

At the end of the film, Rick closes one metaphorical door, sending Ilsa on her way with Laszlo, and opens another, with Renault. In truth, he has been playing with those imaginary doors for some time, admitting Laszlo, Ilsa, and Renault into different rooms, in which they are given different explanations. He tells Ilsa that she can stay with him and he will let Laszlo fly to freedom, while telling Laszlo that he will take Ilsa away to safety, and then telling Renault that he can arrest the two fugitives, thereby scoring points with his Nazi masters. Only when they are all at the runway does he throw open the doors and permit them all to read the same text, sending Ilsa and Laszlo off to continue their work while, after shooting Major Strasser, walking into his own uncertain future in league with Renault. Could the movie get there without all those opening and closing doors, all those gatekeepers and traps and cages? Yes, probably. But it wouldn't resonate the way it does, wouldn't build up the same constellation of meaning, wouldn't be *Casablanca*.

Your *Casablanca* Ain't Like Mine

So you never noticed the doors and barriers in *Casablanca*? Big deal. In a very informal survey of friends and colleagues, including someone who teaches the film, no one else did, either. Oh, some of them knew they were there, but no one had really considered their function. But almost everyone who is a serious consumer of cinema (a couple weren't) had noticed other elements that I hadn't. The point isn't that you must see what I see but that we all notice different elements of the film. And a lot of that noticing comes not so much from the film itself as from what we bring to it. What I'm offering you here, merely as an example, is a fairly idiosyncratic reading of the film. I'm the guy, after all, who in his senior seminar on Charles Dickens wrote a paper on escape themes in *Our Mutual Friend*, who when teaching James Joyce's *Dubliners* tries to point out to students all the instances of railings, barriers, turnstiles, and other impediments as emblems of the personal and social frustrations in the stories. So that's my bias going in. You have them, too, I'm sure. Feel free to use them. Trust your instincts, which are right more often than not.

Casablanca isn't the only movie you can do this with, of course. Not every film will reward the search for aggregated imagery, but many will. I suspect that it would be a fairly easy matter to write a paper on the use of shadows in *Lawrence of Arabia*, maybe even of shadows of Lawrence himself. Or, since I also mentioned it earlier, reflections and other images of the self in *The Artist*. It's a movie about image, after all, about the way the world sees actors and indeed, how they see themselves. There are some key shots of actual mirrors, as well as a highly polished bar in which George sees himself while drowning his sorrows, and in which characters from his current movie, a flop, come to visit him like Scrooge's ghosts. And don't get me started on images of flight, escape, and adventure in *Up* or we'll be here all night, and I'm sure neither of us wants that.

7

Near and Far

FAVORITE WESTERN MOVIE SHOT: a speck starts to materialize on the horizon. Over some period of time it begins to grow larger, first into a larger speck, then a dot, then a shadow, then a figure, then a figure with clearly articulated limbs, then ... oh, you get the idea. It's been with us more or less since the beginning of film, and we've seen almost every hero and a significant number of the villains appear that way. In fact, it eventually became a cliché. And then Sergio Leone got hold of it in his "spaghetti" Westerns and did what should be done with clichés: he drove it straight into the ground, killing part of it while making something new and strange from what was left. Everything and everyone in a Leone film seems to show up that way, Clint Eastwood, of course, but also Lee Van Cleef,

Henry Fonda (in flashback, no less, thereby maximizing the cliché quotient), Charles Bronson, various trains, horses, mules, and probably coyotes, although none spring to mind at the moment.

But here's the thing: there's nothing new, original, or particularly special about Leone's use of distance. It's been there since the start. Part of the magic of film lies in perspective. From the wide-open spaces of Monument Valley to the inside of a phone booth, distance really matters. Not only that, but "far" can be as close as just out of focus in a two-shot. Whether it's the claustrophobic enclosures favored by Hitchcock or those dusty vistas of Leone, directors speak the language of space. Not only that, but proximity or its opposite can suggest all sorts of emotional and psychological states, from anxiety to alienation to closeness to aggression. These people know what they're doing. We need to think about how we react to characters and events based on their distance from the camera.

Since I've brought up Hitch, let's start with him. He knows that there are many situations that creep us out and that two of the most important are dizzying heights and tight spaces. So his two favorite things to do with a hero or heroine are to 1) dangle them from a place where they can easily fall to their deaths—making sure we get a really good view of the distance of the fall and/or the landing spot way, way, way down there— and 2) put them in an enclosure. Sometimes, he manages to do both. The critical moments of *Vertigo*, for instance, involve a small space in a very high place—a steeple, in other words— and an acrophobic Jimmy Stewart. He's so unsettled by the height of the place that he can't think clearly. I'm in complete sympathy, and I'm not alone. Usually, however, he can manage only one of those at a time, and one is plenty. We see Jimmy Stewart hanging from rooftops and stairways and anything the Master can imagine not just in this movie but also in *The Man Who Knew Too Much*, where he's hanging on not just for dear

*Figure 6. Too close for comfort: Cary Grant, Eva Marie
Saint, and part of a president. Licensed By: Warner
Bros. Entertainment. All Rights Reserved.*

life but for his son's life. He has Cary Grant walking all over,
and nearly falling off of, the rooftops of the French Riviera in
To Catch a Thief. And most famously, he plasters Grant to the
face of Mount Rushmore with Eva Marie Saint hanging even
more precariously below him. Since we have just watched the
evil Martin Landau fall into what seems a bottomless void, we
understand perfectly the danger they're in.

Yes, Hitchcock extracts them in the slickest possible way,
but the important part, in terms of what works for us, is the
setup, the peril. Throughout the movie, perspective has been
critical. Grant's Roger Thornhill is mistaken by gangsters in a
restaurant for a secret agent whom they are intent on taking
out. Roger spends the rest of the movie determinedly not
being taken out. Yet until the very end, he cannot see either the
source of the danger or the rationale, however muddled. When
he's drunkenly careening down the mountain road or diving
for his life into the corn to avoid the strafing crop duster, he
can only see the immediate peril. It's a matter of perspective:

only someone outside the Thornhill bubble could see what his larger problem is. He is too busy inside that bubble trying not to be dead. Only when he meets up with the Professor, played by Leo G. Carroll, who was the intended target all along, does Roger begin to understand the larger scene.

Perspective predates film by a few thousand years. There are things in *The Iliad* that Achilles cannot understand or behave properly about; he absents himself from the war when his "war prize," which is to say his concubine or girlfriend or intended bride, is taken from him by Agamemnon. And Jonathan Swift gives us lesson after lesson on perspective in *Gulliver's Travels*. First, Gulliver takes the tiny Lilliputians (something around a tenth of human scale) to be perfectly formed only because the disparity between their size and his makes him unable to see their imperfections, although their diminutive stature and realms make their disputes seem ludicrous. When he moves on to Brobdingnag, he is disgusted by the grossness of the inhabitants, who are ten or twelve times his size. Among other things, their pores are like craters and the breasts of the women—well, let's just leave it there. In Poe, a tiny creature seen through a telescope takes on an extraordinarily ferocious appearance, and many other characters are either too close or too distant, physically or psychologically or both, from the thing they're observing to see it for what it is.

But the thing literature can never give us is the very thing film cannot avoid. The movies let us actually see distances for what they are. We know if something is pressing up against the hero or a million miles away.

Peter Jackson's *Lord of the Rings* trilogy makes use, many times over, of every possible shot, from the extreme close-up to the extreme long shot. Think of the attack on Helm's Deep—that horde of monstrous beings, orcs and Uruk-hai and who knows what unthinkable critters, seemingly unending, the humans trapped inside the old citadel. Then we see the humans, puny, penned in, crowded all on top of one another. It sort of looks like a choice of death by onslaught or death by suffocation. Some choice. At the same time, what we think we're seeing, certain death, isn't nearly as certain as it seems. There may be a way out. Of course, this whole sequence also plays on lots of other tricks of the trade—light and dark (mostly dark), shifting POV, swift cuts, close-ups of sweating or anguished or determined faces, pretty much the lot. Still, in many ways, the mix of long and short shots—showing us things near and far—is what makes the sequence powerful. Finally, it's a long shot, the radiant Gandalf the White backlit on the crest of the ridge, that signals the rescue of the Rohirrim, who ride out of their enclosure and into the wide-open spaces of battle. Indeed, that split of near and far is in some ways the thing most characteristic of the entire trilogy. And as we might expect, it's always about perspective. Most characters lack it, too caught up in their own small concerns to notice the great events happening around them, or too selfish to recognize the greater good. Sometimes, those are the same thing. The Hobbits are famously shortsighted, believing their Shire is all the world they need care about. Various human figures, and even the leader of the elves, cannot see beyond their own narrow interests. The Ring that causes all the fuss exacerbates those selfish tendencies, as we see most starkly in the obsessed Gollum, deformed physically and morally by his long possession of the accursed band. Those figures who, like Gandalf or Aragorn or Legolas, can take a longer view are truly magical.

———

Here's a conundrum regarding near and far for you budding directors out there: try for both at once. How can you get claustrophobia worked into a vast emptiness? Oh, yes, it can be done. Has been, in fact. Take a really big empty—a desert, say. Now put something small and cramped in there. A stagecoach, maybe? Six people inside, another three up on top? Nine souls (ten counting the impending and, later, realized baby) bouncing and jouncing against each other in tight quarters was never a pleasant ride if you were only going to the next village ten miles away. Crossing hundreds of miles of hot sand is something worthy of Jean-Paul Sartre. I'm sure he'd have used that as his version of Hell in *No Exit* had he only been American. John Ford was American, but he's less interested in Hell than in hellions, which he envisioned as riding ponies and wearing feathers. In movie after movie until, in 1956, he offered *The Searchers* as a sort of *apologia pro vita sua*, a defense (and amends in this case) of his life to that point. We're not there yet, however. We're still in *Stagecoach*. It must have been a cinematographer's fondest dream. Or the thing that woke him in a cold sweat. Sweeping vistas *and* tight shots. Interiors with the exterior just out the window. Face after face after face inside, a faceless swarm off in the distance. In other words, contrast, which brings all things into sharper relief and makes them more vivid. We'll talk later about how those shots inside the coach are arranged, but for now the important thing is the sheer amount of time spent in there. That claustrophobic envelope of the stagecoach, of course, is present long before the Indian attack, and to a great degree is the point of the movie: very different people from diverse backgrounds (as diverse as they got in nonintegrated 1939 America), each with a particular motivation for being there—some to get to the next place, some to escape the last, one or two simply on the move—are thrown together and must make the best, or at least whatever they can, of the situation. Those conditions obtain, along with the heat and discomfort, whether Geronimo is on the prowl or not. As it happens, he is.

So that explains the tight interiors somewhat. What about the really, really long shots, both before and during the chase? Perhaps more important, what about the contrast? Those huge vistas emphasize the relative smallness of the travelers and, by extension, ourselves. Think of turning the cameras around and shooting from the endpoint on the horizon toward the stage-coach; it becomes a moving dot on the horizon, little more. But Ford doesn't shoot the movie that way. This is a POV film, in which nearly everything is seen from the point of view of the stagecoach. When we see exteriors of it, which we frequently do, they're not from the perspective of any other participant in the action but from a sort of phantom twin, another, invisible stagecoach right beside the one we care about. So our lessons about scale are chiefly taught by looking at other things and other beings. We see this most clearly when the camera reveals an Apache or three off in the distance watching, planning, trailing: Look! Way up there! They're tiny! Except that they're not. They're just really far away.

And the contrast? What does that tell us? First of all, that these travelers are tiny figures in a huge world. Sure, we already know that, and maybe they do, too. No one in the desert Southwest can miss that point. But beyond that, their concerns are equally minuscule. What do their individual motivations matter next to the geopolitical realities that none of them can entirely get their heads around? Sure, being with your husband for the birth of your first child matters. So, I suppose, does embezzling fifty thousand dollars and trying to get away with it, or leaving town at the behest of the ladies' vice patrol. But not in the way that getting your head handed to you by indigenous insurgents matters. Not the way that breakdowns between one people one nation, and another matter. In a sense, the film is telling us these small concerns that drive each of the passengers and crew are not only tiny in comparison, but they may actively blind them to the larger reality. There's something really momentous happening, but they either can't see it or can't grasp it because they're too locked into their private realities. Now, some people, English professors, for instance, might at this juncture point out that the year of the film is 1939, and that while the coming war has not arrived in America, it is out there, and that if we haven't noticed, it's because of the smallness of our own thoughts, aspirations, and fears. It is not the case that there may be a war; there is a war, and it has begun already, but we haven't been paying attention. Yes, that is precisely what some people might tell you. Happily, I'm not one of those people, but you might meet one someday.

So, the interior of a stagecoach and the very big empty. John Ford is the master of both. Not only that, but Ford controls the emptiness. Limits it. One of the many reasons he returned to Monument Valley in southern Utah and northern Arizona time and again is that it provided those limits. The monuments, those wonderful red-rock outcroppings, frame the action by providing borders. Yes, of course they were also grand places for Apaches to be hiding or riding down from or whatever, but they also had the effect of cutting down the *endlessness* of the desert wilderness. The human eye distrusts truly empty vistas. We feel lost and more than a little unsettled if there is no frame of reference, something David Lean exploits in *Lawrence of Arabia*. Is that horizon two miles away or two hundred? We don't know, and we don't like not knowing. Lean, we do know, was seeking that sense that the desert is endless and the task might prove impossible. By contrast, Ford offers us an emptiness that is almost manageable. If we can't see to the end of it, we can at least see to the next object, and that's a little comforting. No viewer is ever likely to mistake Monument Valley for home, but we take small comforts where we can find them in a harsh viewing landscape.

Ford didn't do things so differently from other directors of the genre, especially since so many others learned from him. Of course, by convention, they didn't shoot in Monument Valley, but they shot the same way. George Stevens found a way around that limitation in 1953: he set *Shane* in the shadow of Wyoming's Grand Tetons. We get splendid vistas, very long shots, plenty of room for a horseman to mosey, but the action of the film, from farming to gunfighting, is shot in comparative close-up. It proved to be such a good idea that Clint Eastwood did much the same thing in *Pale Rider* (1985). Nothing like framing human action with distant magnificence to convey the sense that these people are puny, their concerns insignificant in the grand order.

Once in a great while, if you're very lucky, you can achieve both shots in one, a sort of near-far shot. In *Jeremiah Johnson* (1972), Robert Redford's title mountain man comes across a homestead that has been raided by hostile natives. All the males have been killed save one young boy, who, in the way of these things, will become a sort of son for Jeremiah. But before that, the victims must be buried. Jeremiah sees to that, accompanied by the boy's mother, known only as Crazy Woman. When the final makeshift cross has been hammered into the ground, Crazy Woman insists that they sing "Shall We Gather at the River." Director Sydney Pollack gives us this wonderful two-shot of them singing together, first in a medium-close shot, then pulling back. And back. And back. And back, zooming out until we have something like a God's-eye view down this notch in the mountain toward two tiny pinpoints that are different in color from the nature that surrounds them. "Ah," the shot says, "see how small the tribulations and even the lives of these puny mortals are compared with the majesty that encompasses them?" Perspective all but negates suffering on a merely human scale. Even so, it fascinates us: the dots that were human forms still command our attention even when nearly lost in the landscape.

There is one other category of shot we have not discussed: the medium shot. It is what it sounds like, a shot where you can see the character's nose but are not looking up it. The medium shot is what comprises most moviemaking—people at a party, children in a schoolroom, four friends hanging out on a small hillside. We can see all of them, and none too well. Or we can see the single person and her immediate surroundings, her room, say. The medium shot is where we live; it's sort of the shot you get with a 55-millimeter lens on a single-lens reflex camera, with which you can focus on things from just beyond arm's reach to across the room or so. You can shoot a house in town from the street and get the whole thing. The medium shot approximates how we see the world, assuming we see it on a screen twenty feet high. People don't win cinematography Oscars with medium shots, but perhaps they should: we viewers need them. Medium shots on average provide more information than any others. Close-ups are too full of their immediate subjects to include much else; long shots have lots of space but often little pertinent visual data. Not only that, but medium shots let us recover. This has nothing to do with action, of course; you can have just as much mayhem and frenzy in one type of shot as another. No, here we're just talking visual information. Both close-ups and long shots are tiring, the former causing us to guess about what's going on around that face, around that hand, around that dwindling number on the timer, while the latter makes us kind of squint to make out details. If someone were to shoot a film with nothing but long shots and really tight close-ups—and I have no doubt that somebody will, even possibly that somebody already has—the audience would be a wreck by the end. By contrast, the medium shot gives a break not so much to our eyes, which are experiencing everything at something like three or four or eleven or twelve times life size, but to our minds, which can process information best in the ratio with which we are most familiar. We need that break from extremes.

Of course, the extremes are only sometimes *that* extreme. We normally get only a few extreme long shots or extreme close-ups in even the most agitated movie. Oh, if someone's spending the movie in a coffin, say, or a telephone booth, then we're going to get a lot more extreme shots than the average. But on average, there won't be all that many. And like a lot of things, it's a sliding scale. Shots can be medium-long or medium-close, and then how medium is medium? These categories are never as fixed as they seem when we list them. One close-up may take a baby step back from the close-up before it, and then the next one another baby step, and so on. As with so many other things about the cinema, it's a process.

Here's what a medium shot—and the right perspective—can do. No one has ever done more with perspective, especially the perspective of vast spaces, than George Miller in his *Mad Max* films. He looks up from below, down from above, far from behind a nearby head, up appallingly close, and sometimes just far, far, far. The perspective, like the landscape and a fair number of the people, is inhuman. You could write a treatise on the use of long shots just in *Fury Road* alone. But that's not where he ends things.

For that, he wants an intensely human moment. So he goes back to the inhuman beginning. Dave has been thinking about all this, as he tells Lexi:

"Hey, I took another look at the ending of *Fury Road*. It's really awesome."

"You bought a copy?"

"The day it came out, yeah."

"Awesome, you say."

"Yeah, terrific. You know how, when the film starts, Immortan Joe's up there above all his people from way up high—looking down on them, granting just enough water to keep them thirsty, reminding them who's boss? Now, that wack truck, you know, with those two Cadillacs on top of each other, has come back, but different. Max and Furiosa are bringing his body back to prove that he has been defeated. Everybody's really happy. Well, almost. His one son or whatever knows he's toast but can't get away. Anyway, as Furiosa and Joe's breeder "wives" are being raised above the crowd in a shot from way below, we shift to a sort of medium shot, maybe between medium and close-up, of her face. She's all battered and bloodied, right, and she turns to find that Max has just, like, snuck away from the platform. She searches the crowd below for a moment and he's just sliding off into the crowd. We see him in a medium shot from above with several other people around him, but it's not as far away as she would be. Then that's followed by a close-up of her from below. Back to the same shot of him, he nods; then back to the same shot of her, and she nods; back to him as he turns to go. It's really great."

"What makes it great?" asks Lexi.

"Well, this is not Max's scene. He's gonna always be the outsider, but that's okay with her in charge. It's like they both know it and agree on it. Then they head in their separate directions, up and into the middle of things for her, out and away for him. I don't think it's what they really want, but it's what they've got to do. And that's okay. You know, like things will work out better this way.

"But here's what's weird. Neither one of them appears the way the other sees them. It's kind of the right way. I mean, he would see her from below, and she would see him from above. I get that. But he wouldn't even be that big from where she is on that elevator thing. And there's no way he could see her in close-up."

"So what do you think is going on there?"

"Well, it's not about what they need to see, is it? It's about what we need. This is where the movie ends. We can't exactly see her as a dot on the screen. And anyway, the shots are about them as people. They're damaged but not beaten. They're not symbols or anything. Just people."

Dave's right, of course. Those shots tell us what the characters are thinking. And who they are. There is nothing more important that characters can be than people. And there are no words that can surpass those two nods in eloquence.

8

Art Without Color

ONE OF THE WORST MOVIE EXPERIENCES I have ever had—and I have seen *Wild in the Streets*—was watching *The Maltese Falcon* in color. What's that? You didn't know it was in color? It wasn't. Instead, it was *colorized*. Horrible term, horrible idea. Here's what happened. In 1986, media mogul Ted Turner, following along from his conquest of cable television, purchased the film studio MGM/UA, giving him access to the libraries of Metro-Goldwyn-Mayer, some of United Artists, much of RKO Pictures, and the pre–1950 Warner Bros. That sounds as if he owned all of black-and-white movie history, but there were a few other studios in the old days. Still, enough. And he had determined that most modern people (meaning, one assumes, him) would not watch movies in something as stale and stuffy as monochrome.

Part of my problem, I'm sure, was that this *Maltese Falcon* was not a maiden voyage. I had seen the film a number of times, loved it, knew most of the lines, and here's what I found: it isn't the same movie. Yes, the same stuff happens, but it doesn't *look* the same, and with movies, looking matters. First of all, the colors chosen are unlikely to be right; in some cases they're positively garish. Skin tones are all wrong. The colors of Brigid O'Shaughnessy's dress when she makes the curtains flutter at Spade's apartment are dubious at best. Worst of all, the shadows, conceived in monochrome, simply look faked in color. If you can't have an honest black, what good is film? Nothing is right with that colorization. Simply put, *The Maltese Falcon* was conceived for black-and-white shooting, from set design to costumes to blocking to lighting. If you make a change as momentous as adding color (as opposed to shooting in it), the whole visual component goes haywire. Happily, the barbarians have mostly given up on such ventures; happier still, we can still see it in glorious grayscale, as nature intended.

Once upon a time, filmmakers did not have color film at their disposal. They gave us white hats and black hats, but also a whole lot more. Then Dorothy moved from gray Kansas to Technicolor Oz, and before long only *artistes* shot in black and white. And viewers forgot how to watch monochromatic movies and *somebody* got the bright idea to colorize the old ones. What a terrible fate for great movies—or even only fair ones. As you might imagine, this did not go down well with film lovers, and especially film lovers who happened to be critics. Gene Siskel and Roger Ebert gave this move two thumbs down, devoting a special episode of the *Siskel & Ebert & the Movies* to what they called "Hollywood's New Vandalism." Ebert asked what was so terrible about black-and-white movies in the first place, adding, "By filming in black and white, movies can sometimes be more dreamlike and elegant and stylized and mysterious. They can add a whole dimension to reality, whereas color sometimes just supplies additional unnecessary information." He knew full well, of course, that many black-and-white movies were so filmed because there was no other option, but that doesn't stop his—nor should it our—appreciation.

Actually, it isn't quite true that color was not available. It was color film that didn't exist. The impulse toward color was present early on in film history. In fact, right at the beginning, and long before color film existed. Some films by the pioneers of the industry, such as Georges Méliès's *A Trip to the Moon* (1902) and *The Kingdom of the Fairies* (1903), were selectively colorized. That is to say some elements of the movies were hand-tinted. Studios, most notably Elisabeth Thuillier's coloring studio and, later, Pathécolor, sprang up in Paris (along with the Handschiegl process at Famous Players-Lasky studios in America) to accommodate the desire for at least parts of films to have color. Thuillier employed some two hundred artists, each responsible for a single color to be painted on individual frames one by one. She is said to have produced some sixty copies of *A Trip to the Moon*, of which only one is known to survive. Because it is in the public domain, we can easily view it online, and we notice instantly that something less than the whole frame is filled with color. When the scientists (looking a lot more like medieval wizards) gather in the opening scene, for instance, only the principals have colored robes; the others are gray imitations. This was typical of early colorized films, where the labor-intensive nature of the process meant that color was used as a condiment, not the meat and potatoes of the flick. Such use made the selected items really pop off the screen compared to their dim surroundings. This was also a process in which the moviemakers had a direct hand, unlike later colorization, so the aesthetics, whatever we may think of them, are in concert with the directors' visions. And of course when color film technology became available and affordable, filmmakers leapt at the chance to use it. Sometimes. Cost and artistic judgments led to sparing use of color during the early decades of its existence, and only in the mid to late 1960s did color movies become the only sort made.

If you want to talk more about the colorizing debacle, stop over sometime and I can bore you silly. For now, however, let's focus on happier subjects. Like why black-and-white movies are so great. Because they are, you know. Great.

Here's a statement you may not like, but that's never stopped me before: the single most damaging change to the art of cinema was the death of black-and-white film. Yes, I said it. And why not? It's true. Of all the changes that movies have undergone during their first century, the one that has done the most damage is the end of movies in two colors. This is not the same as the introduction of color film or the rise of really excellent color techniques or anything else. This is about the end of serious moviemaking in monochromatic splendor.

To be clear, I am not a cinematic Luddite. I love nearly all the innovations that have come out of Hollywood over the years. The exceptions being IMAX, which tends to make me ill, and 3-D, which tends to result in dopiness as well as exacerbating my fear of heights (must *every* 3-D movie involve some dizzying precipice?). But I love color movies. Period. Would I want the yellow brick road to be gray or the ruby slippers to be black? Of course not. Besides, that's how I saw them on television when I was growing up, and they required just a little too much imagination. Color is a blast. Walt Disney could never have been Uncle Walt without color. *The Red Balloon*

(1956) just wouldn't be the same if all balloons were different shades of the same dull color; nor could the balloon have
contrasted so spectacularly with the rest of the drab city. And
the Carnaby Street mod element of *Blow-Up* (1966) would
be completely lost in black and white, even with all the geo-
metric patterns in the clothing. Sometimes you must have the
color. See also, *Fantasia*. Nope, taken any way you want, color
movies are great.

So what's the problem?

Us. At some point, we seem to have decided that black-
and-white film is un-American. To be fair, it did seem that
way. The only movies that came our way *sans colour* were
brooding Swedish masterpieces or grainy and jumpy French
things (but not *The French Connection*). And when Woody Allen
tries to be brooding and Swedish, he only reminds us that he's
Brooklyn and Jewish, not Scandinavian and Lutheran—and
we beg him to get back to colorized hilarity. What's the latest black-and-white American film that most of us will have
seen? Maybe a better way to ask that is: when did b&w cease
as a part of regular studio production? I nominate 1960, give
or take a year: that's the year of *Psycho*, followed the next year
by *The Absent-Minded Professor*. Oh, there were a few sporadic
contributions after that, even some from major studios, but for
the most part black-and-white movies have been relegated to
independent filmmakers and foreigners for the last half century. And that, friends, is a darned shame.

Now, don't start whining. I've heard it all before. Movies
without color are old-fashioned. Less realistic. Hard to see.
Dark. Boring. Yeah, yeah, yeah. Tell it to the Marines. In fact,
Pride of the Marines (1945) was shot in black and white. So was
The Pride of the Yankees (1942). So there.

You say there are lots of things that black-and-white film
can't do. That's true, but there are more that it can. Inky shadows are inkier. Contrasts are greater. But so is the possibility

of subtle gradations. Let's go back to the *Psycho* example. The decision to use black and white was not based on aesthetics. Rather, it was born of desperation. Hitchcock's previous two projects had died before being realized, so even coming off the hit *North by Northwest,* he was on the outs with the studio. Then, too, the studio had already rejected the idea of acquiring the rights to Robert Bloch's novel of the same title. So Hitch had himself an uphill fight. Even his offer to finance the film himself *and* shoot in black and white *and* use his television series studio and crew was turned down. Finally, as a last-ditch effort, he offered to refuse his standard quarter-million-dollar director's fee in lieu of a 60 percent stake in the negative. In other words, he had everything riding on this particular dice roll. In addition, he was filming a story—laden with sex, graphic violence, and one very disturbed psyche—that would make the censors at the Production Code office blanch. The chances of having this film not be released were great, the financial pressures enormous. So he shot quickly and in monochrome.

Best thing that ever happened to a movie. Maybe second, after Howard Hawks discovering nineteen-year-old Lauren Bacall for *To Have and Have Not* (1944). That, however, is a very different story, although also in black and white.

So what does a one-color palette do for the movie? Just about everything. For one thing, as Ebert suggests, it takes us out of the world of excessive verisimilitude. That will prove a relief when the mayhem gets going. Black and white provides just enough distance from the world as we experience it that, although we have no difficulty identifying Janet Leigh's Marion Crane or Anthony Perkins's Norman Bates as humans living in something like ordinary reality (except for the homicidal maniac bit), we can stand back just the tiniest step from their reality. That distance will wage battle with Hitchcock's techniques (subjective camera, steady close-ups) that draw us in tighter, to create an uneasy tension in viewers. Then, too, the darkness of many scenes and the grisly taxidermy seem more foreboding, even ghastly, because of the black and white. She is forced to seek a room at the Bates Motel, for instance, by the darkest, rainiest night in the history of dark, rainy nights. Add to that the reduced visual information the eye receives in black and white—little pieces of data that might announce themselves more clearly were they presented in color—and we know less than we might, although later we will come to understand that we *had* seen this or that item or person, although it didn't register at the time. The shadows are murkier, the lake where he buries the car inkier, the darkness more all-encompassing in grays and blacks. Come to think of it, even the daytime is pretty dark at the Bates Motel. All this fits nicely with the ethical murkiness of the tale. Marion Crane is no mere innocent victim of mistaken identity. Oh, she's a victim all right. Just not innocent. The first two things we see her do are finish off an assignation with her lover, then go back and embezzle forty thousand dollars, enough for a very nice house in 1960. Her moral issues, of course, have nothing to do with Norman's villainy, but they do taint the sympathy we can have toward her just a little. Those issues all come together in her folding the stolen funds into a newspaper in her room's wastebasket. Norman, whose real interest isn't money in any case, fails to notice the paper's contents in his rush to clear the room of incriminating evidence and buries it with Marion in the trunk of the car. In the final twist of the knife, when the car is dredged up from the tarn, the last thing we see is the newspaper: the answer to the mystery is revealed, as it were, in black and white.

So black and white can be useful for distancing us from psychopaths. Does it have other uses? How about nuclear annihilation? Four years after *Psycho*, Stanley Kubrick released the black comedy *Dr. Strangelove* (1964). The story encompassed in the film is dirt-simple: a paranoid, renegade American general launches a nuclear strike on the Soviet Union, which leads to deliberations by various parties, all of whom are more than a little mad. There's an inept, indecisive president, the title character, a partially paralyzed expert in nuclear war who seems to be inherited from the Nazis, a British RAF officer (these three all played by Peter Sellers), a jingoistic general (George C. Scott) who is terrified of letting the Russians know our plans, even when those plans will destroy us all, the paranoid general (Sterling Hayden), and the most motley bombardier crew imaginable, with Slim Pickens as the wild cowboy who ultimately rides the bomb to perdition. The film begins with this terrible scenario of a mistaken or unauthorized nuclear strike and ends with picture after picture of mushroom clouds to the strains of "We'll Meet Again." The movie is one of the funniest and scariest ever made precisely because it was so entirely possible. Other books and movies—*Fail-Safe, Red Alert* (on which this movie is partly based)—were coming out in this same historical period about the very real possibility of what we called "mutual assured destruction" happening at any moment. As a child growing up ten or twelve miles from Strategic Air Command headquarters at Ohio's Wright-Patterson Air Force Base and practicing air raid and duck-and-cover drills at school, I can promise you it wasn't all that comic. Now, satire or not, do you really want to see that in color? "Some sunny day," indeed.

Black and white is also excellent for fantasy. Think dream sequence. Think things that can never happen. Now, this is not mine. This is from Werner Herzog, so pay attention:

> *Arguably, or for me, the greatest single sequence in all of film history [is] Fred Astaire dancing with his own shadows, and all of a sudden he stops and the shadows become independent and dance without him and he has to catch up with*

*them. It's so quintessential movie. It can't get more beau-
tiful. It's actually from* Swing Time *[1936]. And when
you look at the cave and certain panels, there's evidence of
some fires on the ground. They're not for cooking. They
were used for illumination. You have to step in front of these
fires to look at the images, and when you move, you must
see your own shadow. And immediately, Fred Astaire comes
to mind—who did something 32,000 years later which is
essentially what we can imagine for early Paleolithic people.*

Herzog is speaking about Astaire in the context of his own
documentary about the Lascaux cave paintings in France, and
the scene he describes is truly remarkable: Astaire, in bowler
hat and blackface as a tribute to Bill "Bojangles" Robinson and
Astaire's own former dance teacher John W. Bubbles, dances
to the up-tempo "Bojangles in Harlem" with his own shadow,
times three. Through the magic of film and the brilliant choreography of Hermes Pan—one of the great names in the
history of film, or of anything, for that matter—the shadows
take on a synchronized life of their own, so that when Astaire
pauses, they continue making the human and the simulacra
fall out of sync; the human dancer then races madly to catch
up with his shadows again, but they're never entirely in sync
again, although they're close enough that it seems a sort of race
or contest where no one loses. Certainly not the audience. At
the end of the routine, the shadows become disgusted with
Astaire's antics and walk off the screen, but he keeps going.
When someone says, "They don't make movies like that any-
more," this is exactly what they mean.

Were this an Ingmar Bergman film, the scene would be a
commentary on alienation and dislocation of sensibility. But
it is not. Because it is a George Stevens film, the scene is joy-
ous, celebratory, frenetic, and a little goofy. It's less a statement
about life than one about art: you can't have this experience

anywhere but at the movies. What isn't said but that I would assert is that you can't have that experience anywhere but at the movies in black and white.

I said earlier that black and white had mostly vanished from the scene in the contemporary era. But it isn't as if no one has been making monochrome movies since 1960. Indeed, some of our most significant films have exploited the device. In the list of greatest black-and-white movies compiled by the Internet Movie Database, for instance, the first three entries are completely predictable: *Citizen Kane*, William Wyler's *The Best Years of Our Lives*, and Jean Renoir's *La Grande Illusion*. The most recent of those, Wyler's film, was 1946 (Renoir's appeared in 1937). Then the list jumps forward forty-seven years to 1993 with *Schindler's List*. Director Steven Spielberg labored under none of the financial or technical exigencies that affected the other directors, certainly not the ones that would have inhibited Orson Welles had he wished to shoot *Kane* in color, so shooting *Schindler* in black and white was clearly a choice. In this case, the use of monochrome (shot on sepia stock) not only imparts an old-time movie look, it also creates the atmosphere of a documentary. One has only to think about that footage of the liberated camps that has made so many of us queasy down the decades to see that connection. Then, too, detractors and supporters alike admit that black and white has a distancing effect—we live in a world full of color, however drab our lives may seem to us at any given moment, so stripping away the colors automatically makes a film feel a little less real. In this case, that distance is a great relief; the movie is so unsettling that any small respite from the horrors of Nazi rule is welcome. Finally, there is the fact that this is not a black-and-white film. There is a scene in which Jews are being herded down the street, among them a small girl wearing a vivid red coat. Every other thing in the scene is monochrome, so the coat really stands out. In rounding her up, the movie asserts, the Nazis have obliterated the last remaining color from the world. And when Oskar Schindler comes across her murdered body a bit later, you don't need advanced degrees to understand the meaning of the red coat by which we recognize her. Spielberg has said, "For me, the symbol of life is color. That's why a film about the Holocaust has to be in black-and-white." Except that it isn't. Not all. Besides the red coat, the opening scene of an ordinary Shabbat meal affords some color before fading out, as the life of European Jewry was about to do. At the end, when Oskar Schindler organizes another Shabbat meal, the warmth of the candles again slips into the film's palette.

There are, naturally, other reasons for a filmmaker to select black and white. *Pleasantville* (1998) plays with the very idea of monochromatic versus color media as its central premise. Twins David (Tobey Maguire) and Jennifer (Reese Witherspoon), who live in the colorful age of MTV, find themselves whisked into the black-and-white world of a 1950s sitcom that gives the movie its title. Well, what other color scheme could such a movie employ?

When we discuss the use of black and white, we tend to think of the classics and especially of certain genres: silent comedies such as Chaplin's *The Gold Rush*, Keaton's *The General* (1926) or *Steamboat Bill, Jr.* (1928), or Harold Lloyd's *Safety Last*, noir mysteries on the order of *Little Caesar* or *The Public Enemy* (both 1931), *Scarface* (the original, 1932), *The Maltese Falcon*, or *The Third Man*. But of course all genres were filmed in monochrome before the advent of color, and many were afterward. The year that gave us full-color spectaculars in *The Wizard of Oz* and *Gone with the Wind*, arguably the greatest year in motion picture history, 1939, also gave us black and white in the adaptation of Kipling's poem "Gunga-Din," Garbo going comic in *Ninotchka*, everybody's favorite bell ringer in *The Hunchback of Notre Dame*, Laurence Olivier in *Wuthering*

Heights, and arguably the first truly great Western, *Stagecoach*. And that barely touches the surface. Some of those films, like *Ninotchka*, hardly needed color, others seemed unworthy to studio heads of the expense, and some were done quickly and didn't allow for the time. Watching them, we discover things we didn't know. For instance, while I have nothing against Monument Valley in color, and I definitely want it in color if I visit in person, and John Ford certainly made good use of it in color in later films like *The Searchers*, as a cinematic proposition, it views much better in black and white. I think that has to do with what monochrome presentation does for stark landscapes. They take on an almost nightmarish unreality. The same can be said for John Huston's *The Treasure of the Sierra Madre* (1948), whose landscape looks like nowhere you've ever been and especially like nowhere you wish to live.

Happily, the form has never left us entirely. Contemporary filmmakers occasionally turn out work in black and white for a host of artistic reasons. They may be striving for starkness, as in Alexander Payne's *Nebraska* (2013), starring Bruce Dern as a cantankerous old man, or Frank Miller and Robert Rodriguez's *Sin City* (2005), an adaptation of Miller's graphic novel, although to be fair, some elements of the latter film are in color. Still, the effect is chiefly monochromatic, which also has the advantage of distancing the audience from the action, which is stylized and brutal. The attempt at providing distance can also be seen in such films as Oliver Stone's *Natural Born Killers* (1994) and Tony Kaye's *American History X* (1998), where the story is sufficiently vicious that a less mimetic, more stylized approach can make it slightly more palatable. Sometimes, however, as with *Schindler's List*, nothing can make a movie's subject matter palatable. Only less sickening.

Filmmakers may be attempting to match period styles, as with George Clooney's film about Edward R. Murrow, *Good Night, and Good Luck* (2005), or Mary Harron's film about an erotica model and actress, *The Notorious Bettie Page* (2006). Tim Burton's *Ed Wood* (1994), about the cult film director, both invokes the era and the format in which Wood's sensational (and generally quite awful) movies were themselves shot. This impulse ties the movie to *Pleasantville*: there are times when one wants to shoot a film in the format of its historical moment because that's how the films or television shows would have appeared. The champion of the mode would have to be Michel Hazanavicius's *The Artist* (2011); the choice clearly makes sense in this instance. Perhaps Richard Attenborough's *Chaplin* (1992) would have fared better had the director made the same choice, although color film is not the movie's only misstep.

And sometimes, black and white is just about mood and tone. That tone doesn't have to be somber or horrifying; it can be wistful, elegiac, even comic. It can be anything you want it to be. I made fun, some little time ago, of *Stardust Memories*, the Woody-Allen-impersonates-Ingmar-Bergman film of artistic angst. It's not really that bad, only not him at his Woodiest. On the other hand, it is the second b&w film in as many years, following the huge achievement of *Annie Hall* and the subsequent success of *Interiors* (1978). The first was *Manhattan* (1979). It was magnificent. If the entire history of cinema in black and white existed so that we could have *Schindler's List* and *Manhattan*, they would be reason enough.

9

What Happens During Popcorn Time

YOU KNOW THIS ONE. The house lights go down and we see our hero, or the back of him: worn leather jacket, well-worn fedora, something dangling from his hip that we can't quite make out. When we finally see his face, which takes a couple of minutes, he's a ruggedly handsome sort who in a different age would have been played by Stewart Granger. Was, in fact, only with different names. He's making his way toward a mysterious spot with two sidekicks who chiefly look as if they want to kick him in the side. In fact, before he reaches the magical spot, the lesser figure draws his gun only to be undone by the flick of a bullwhip. Soon our hero arrives at his target, making his way through a cave with his remaining untrustworthy assistant, and this place is a deathtrap. Every step can loose a new version of death on the unwary or unlucky: spears out of walls, poison darts, weights from ceilings, stones that give way and—who knows? As reminders, the walls bear as decorations the skeletons of previous adventurers who weren't wary or knowledgeable or lucky enough. But he makes his way past every trap and deadfall to the golden idol that is his target. Of course, it too sits on a booby-trapped pedestal, but he bears the solution, a bag of sand weighing exactly the right amount, which he masterfully transfers to the spot being vacated by the idol, as his greedy right-hand man drools over the treasure. And then the fun really begins.

The transfer, you will recall, doesn't quite take; the pedestal sinks into its stand; walls shift and debris falls, and something really bad is coming. He runs like mad, avoiding all the afore-mentioned traps, nearly makes it, nearly gets killed, in desper-ation tosses the idol to the assistant, who leaves him high and dry. Through luck and pluck and cool thinking during sheer panic, our hero saves himself from the immediate peril and races through the cave only to find that the perfidious sidekick has not been so lucky. He's been well ventilated by one of the deadly walls. Our hero collects the idol and then finds out what all the fuss has been about.

A wall opens and reveals the biggest honkin' boulder you ever saw, which begins chasing our hero, who once again runs like mad, beating the stone that would seal the exit and his fate, and then he lurches out into daylight and tumbles down the steep exit ramp. At the feet of his nemesis, no less.

Who is not alone. Pointed at our hero are some of the thousands of poisoned darts and arrows that the nemesis has at his disposal thanks to more local tribesmen than any bad guy could require. Having been informed that there is nothing he can find that the baddie cannot take away, our hero makes a dash for freedom, replete with a hail of venomous but ill-aimed barbs, a race through the jungle, a fedora that seems to be (and really was in filming) stapled to his head, a fortuitously placed vine for swinging—and why can we never find such a vine when *we* need one?—and a waiting floatplane. Just as he is being lifted to safety, he finds that he, the man evidently with no fear, is sharing the cockpit with the one creature of which he is terrified: a snake. By my stopwatch, it takes twelve minutes and thirty-seven seconds. We don't even see the idol until the six-minute mark.

All of this happens, by the way, while viewers are still settling into their seats and surveying the spoils of their raid on the concession stand. Clearly, someone—director, screenwriter, everyone involved—wants to make sure we pay more attention to their film than to our snacks. Wants to make sure to win the battle of Popcorn Time.

Such is our very first introduction to Indiana Jones in his first feature, *Raiders of the Lost Ark* (1981). He's had more action than many characters have in a whole movie, maybe in five movies, and we're a dozen minutes in. No wonder we're breathless: cave, spears, traps, pedestal, idol, giant bowling ball, more spears, closing wall, bullwhip, dead assistant, idol again, nemesis, poison arrows, race, jungle, vine, plane, snake, hat. It's excessive. It's over the top. In fact, merely over the top doesn't begin to touch it. Insanely over the top. In other words, it's perfect.

There's just one thing. What does all this busyness tell us about the plot?

Nothing.

Everything.

You choose.

At this point in the film, we know nothing about the plot, which will be introduced when our intrepid adventurer returns to campus and becomes a comparatively ordinary professor of archaeology. The G-men show up with tales of Nazis and the Lost Ark of the Covenant, and before long we've got mayhem and burning saloons and dotted lines on maps and snakes and commandeered trucks and the whole crazy story that is *Raiders*. Here, however, we have just a mini-movie that could be titled *Meet Indiana Jones*.

So does that make it useless, a mere bauble added to the front of the film? Not a bit. In fact, almost the opposite: nearly everything we really need to make sense of what follows is here. If we distill down that list I tossed about earlier to its important features, here's what we have: a rough-and-ready adventurer and knowledgeable archaeologist, danger at every turn, hair's-breadth escapes, powerful nemesis, action aplenty, emblems of adventure (jacket, fedora, whip). Pretty much everything that follows will partake of one of those elements. Not a bad introduction, and it's so frenetic that we don't even notice we're getting something useful.

In the old days, the plot tie-in was often more direct. Orson Welles's *Citizen Kane* (1941) begins with the dying Charles Foster Kane dropping a snow globe and croaking out the single word "Rosebud." This cryptic utterance becomes the putative reason for the subsequent biography of the great man, as a reporter is dispatched to ferret out the object or creature to which Kane might have been referring. We do get an answer in the film's final frame, unlike the hapless newsman, but it turns out to be a classic instance of what another great director, Alfred Hitchcock, would call a "McGuffin," an object that drives the story but turns out to carry a lot less importance than it initially promised. Rosebud is a tiny element in the story and, while illuminating in its way, far less so than the larger story of the rise and fall of a newspaper tycoon. Still, that tiny piece of information conveys a great deal more. We learn, among other things, that the dying man who voiced the name was very important indeed—not just a big enough entity to have private nurses but to cause newspapermen to pursue a cryptic utterance. That, for us, is the greater mystery:

why should we care not about the word but about the speaker? Why was he such a big deal? And off we go in search of the answer to that one.

But there's so much more to the opening of that movie than just a snow globe. Here's how it begins: night, a darkened mansion—nay, palace, cathedral, choose your own term for architecture on an out-of-control scale—with a single light on. The place is all gothic gloom and foreboding. Our POV is from street level, outside the chain-link fence with the no-trespassing sign, outside the wrought iron gate, so we're looking up very high at that lone source of light. Welles shows us several angles—from the menagerie, reflected in the lagoon, from the ruined golf course, always with the solitary lighted window. We're drawn into the window only to have the light go out. When it seems to come on again, it takes a moment to realize that we're now inside the room and that the light is the rising sun. Except that in that moment, it also seems to snow, as we're drawn into the globe, seeing first only snowflakes, then pulling back to reveal that they're inside the ornament, although for an instant or two there also appear to be flakes in the air around the hand that holds it. Then we see a man's aged lips and mustache as he croaks out, "Rosebud." Then to the hand, which drops the globe, which in its turn rolls down the two steps of the elevated bed and smashes on the stone floor. Only when the nurse steps into the room to look for the cause of the sound do we get something on a human scale. Up till now, everything has been in extreme close-up or extreme long shot. Now we have entered the realm of the medium shot, and the film proper can begin, launching us into the journalist's inquiry into the great man's life, complete with flashbacks to his childhood and every stage of existence thereafter. In essence, Welles has given us what in an opera would be called an overture: a short piece that serves as a sort of warm-up for the larger piece that will follow.

Like *Citizen Kane*, *Lawrence of Arabia* begins with the great man's death (sort of seems like a trend, doesn't it?), then leads us back by a series of questions to his life, in this case, the part of the life that matters to world history. We begin not with the beginning but the end, the motorcycle ride that T. E. Lawrence, ever restive and thrill-seeking, takes on narrow, winding country lanes to his demise. As with *Kane*, we then meet a journalist whose interrogations open up a flashback that takes us back to the beginning, to the events, or in some cases nonevents, that led to Lawrence's posting to the Arabian Peninsula. En route, we encounter the ennui and racism among the officer corps, the cynicism of diplomats and generals, and the complete lack of vision or original thinking that makes Lawrence both singular and dangerous. We see him playing his favorite trick, letting a match burn down to his fingers, snuffing itself out against his skin, amazing or appalling onlookers. When asked what the trick is to keep it from hurting, he assures them that it "hurts like hell. The trick," he says, "is not minding that it hurts." This tiny piece of a huge film tells us volumes about his tendencies toward masochism, exhibitionism, self-destructive actions, phenomenal self-control, and complete lack of irony or self-doubt. He may well be a megalomaniac, but he's *our* megalomaniac. That may also be a constituent element of the hero, for hero he certainly is. In this opening sequence, we also meet the major British forces: Donald Wolfit as General Murray and Claude Rains as the cynical and suitably oily Mr. Dryden. The two represent the military and diplomatic worlds, neither of which has any great love for or belief in the Arabs they govern.

It's about fourteen minutes in when Peter O'Toole's Lawrence blows out the match in Dryden's office and we switch to the spectacular desert sunrise. And that's after the four full minutes of "Overture," Maurice Jarre's wonderful theme played against a screen blank but for a shimmering, indistinguishable image. To be sure, fourteen minutes is a rather more leisurely pace than the average, but this is no average film; *Lawrence of Arabia* is moviemaking on an epic scale, so things can take longer. In that time, however, we learn a very great deal:

- There is a war on, specifically, what we Americans now call World War I;

- Lawrence is a special man;

- Special men are not inevitably cut out for life in the military, or at least not in a military garrison;

- British authorities have an extremely low estimation of the Arabs;

- British authorities are bigoted, cynical, rule-bound dolts;

- The Arabs might be useful in combating the Turks, if only (in British thinking) they were useful for anything;

- If an enterprise is doomed to failure, one might as well send a man whose failure is neither unexpected nor particularly to be mourned;

- Lawrence will not fail.

That last point is a bit tricky. How do we know that he will not fail? What's the movie called again? In the language of film, the forces arrayed against him during this introduction all but assure that Our Hero must succeed. Only rarely, as in Roland Joffé's *The Mission* (1986), with Jeremy Irons in the O'Toole idealistic-hero part, does the heartless establishment actually send the protagonist out to failure and doom. And that wasn't even the plan there.

But to return to our movie, almost everything we need is

present in that opening. The moment he blows out the match, then, we know we're leaving the mundane behind and should expect the wonderful, and we get it. The recipe is nearly complete. Just add Bedouins.

Elia Kazan's masterly *On the Waterfront* (1954) launches us into the problem immediately. Marlon Brando's Terry Malloy, holding something under his jacket where another man might reach for a revolver, approaches some very tough-looking men standing in front of a plate glass window. Words are exchanged, and he goes off to a tenement building, where he calls out to his friend Joey Doyle that he's found Joey's homing pigeon. They arrange to meet on the roof, Joey's window closes, and Terry releases the bird, which the camera follows upward until we see two more thugs on the roof. In moments we hear a scream and see a falling body, telling us that sometimes a pigeon can be as deadly as a pistol. Soon a crowd gathers, including Joey's sister, Edie, played by Eva Marie Saint in what is likely her finest role, Karl Malden as the crusading priest, Father Barry, and any number of members of the docklands community, all of whom express the opinion that Joey brought it on himself by cooperating with the police. When we next see Terry, tougher than he is bright, he is asking Lee J. Cobb's ironically named union boss, Johnny Friendly, why Joey had to die, when all Terry had been told was that Friendly's men wanted to talk to him. Friendly responds that maybe he didn't talk nice enough, which we understand as a thinly veiled admission that talk had never been the intention.

Setup, problem, main character, villain, future love interest, all introduced in a handful of minutes. It's a wonder of economy.

Here's the thing I've learned from reading novels that we can apply to film: every novel is a lesson in how to read that novel, and the lesson is strongest where it's most urgently needed, at the beginning. Same thing with films. Every movie is a little bit different from every other one, so we may need a little help. The help is there. Oh, it's not as if the director sits around with the cinematographer and the rest of the crew and says something like, "How can we help out those poor sods in the theater? They'll never figure this one out." Rather, it's an automatic thing—by the elements it uses from the beginning, the movie offers clues and cues as to how it can best be read by viewers.

And what does this long opening teach us about how to watch *Once Upon a Time in the West*, about which we spoke earlier? A great many things, among them:

1) Be patient. This will not move fast, or at least not fast when you want it to.

2) Ambient sounds matter. This movie is the Foley artist's playground; how great to be able to put in all those sounds! Windmill, door swinging in wind, chalk on blackboard, flies buzzing, boot steps, spurs, telegraph key, wind through machinery and walls, and of course harmonicas, although that may be voiced and not ambient—all these speak vastly more than dialogue.

3) Dialogue (1): there won't be much.

4) Dialogue (2): when it comes, it will be important, so don't miss it.

5) Harmonica's unearthly—and only—tune sounds suspiciously like something Ennio Morricone would come up with.

6) The unconscious subtext of virtually all Westerns that guns are sexual emblems is not unconscious here. Nor subtext. Not even a little.

7) The real inspiration for this film may have been not John Ford but rather Samuel Beckett. The rate of revelation—even the sum total of revelation—may not be all we hope for.

8) Faces are unforgettable. You can't take your eyes off them.

9) This fictional world is not populated by angels. Even Bronson's hat is at best a dingy gray-tan, certainly not a Tom Mix white.

10) There will be blood.

11) Charles Bronson's eyes are really frightening.

12) This film may not be for everyone.

How's that for a dirty dozen? We could add a baker's extra: We have no idea what the movie is about. Except personal antipathy. We haven't met Frank or learned why he would plan such a welcome for the new Man with No Name. We don't know his motivations. We only know that, when they meet, he and Frank aren't likely to adore each other. Haven't encountered the plot or even a whisper thereof. Haven't met the heroine. We'll get there—learn much, if not all, of what we need to know, see the problem, watch it all play out, get the inevitable showdown—but not now, and not right away.

The thing is, hardly anyone knew what they were seeing when the film came out. It not only wasn't like other Westerns; in many ways, it wasn't even like other Leone Westerns. This time, it was personal. Henry Fonda as a serious villain. Is that even legal? Like most geniuses, Leone spent too much of his career ahead of the curve. Most critics and viewers in the sixties simply thought he was making disposable entertainments on the cheap, working in Spain with Italian crews and only a handful of Hollywood actors, most of them either over the hill or still on the rise. And then there was that music. You can't hum a Morricone theme, can't really whistle it even if it's whistled on the soundtrack. Plus, the instrumentation is, well, peculiar, and voices do what voices are not normally asked to do. It's strange, disorienting, bombastic. In other words, perfect for Leone's movies. No, the great man may always have been serious, but it took a while for the rest of us to get serious about him. Not until *Once Upon a Time in America*, his gangster epic, did we really figure him out. But we should have. The first fifteen minutes of any of his movies teach us what we need to know.

I mentioned a little while back the wonder that is the opening silent sequence of the animated film *UP*. Wonderful in itself, it points to one sort of opening: the origin story. In the lovely, gentle, and ultimately heartbreaking series of vignettes that make up the sequence, we get the entire tale of Carl Fredricksen, from chubby, awkward child to grumpy old man who uses his surliness to hide his vulnerability. From that moment on, his character makes sense to us. On a wildly different action level, *The Avengers* does much the same thing. We get character backstory as our heroes are called to action and comply in various degrees of (un)willingness: Scarlett Johansson's Natasha Romanoff/Black Widow, although appearing to be in mortal peril, is on a job and in full control of the situation, so her only inconvenience is dispensing bad guys a bit sooner than planned, while Mark Ruffalo's Bruce Banner/The Hulk must be hunted to somewhere very close to the ends of the earth and returns only under the strongest protest.

In other movies, the script is flipped and the film is the backstory to the situation in the opening. The most noteworthy recent instance of this may well be *The Great Gatsby* (2013), with Nick Carraway (Tobey Maguire) in a sanitarium being treated for alcoholism several years after the events the movie will depict. Nearly everyone who has a fondness for Fitzgerald's novel—which is to say, nearly everyone—objected to that device as untrue to the novel, to the character of Nick, and indeed to the spirit of the movie to follow. It also led to the visual device of Fitzgerald's words floating up onto the screen in 3-D, which was not universally admired. It is safe to say that this was a bold experiment that failed, but the reasons for that failure may have nothing to do with the experiment itself but rather with the novel being adapted. In other words, had this been an original screenplay and not a version of one of America's most widely known and beloved novels, it would be fine, or at least acceptable. Lives destroyed by the excesses of the Jazz Age, and the only person left to tell the tale suffering through alcoholism and a breakdown? Sure, why not? Floating words? We'll get back to you on that. As it is, this opening steps on too many toes, offends too many sensibilities. But even so, it does something essential, something every opening must do: give us enough information to start the movie. It needs to do something: introduce the hero(es), provide background, provide setting or context, give us a taste of the movie to follow, and make us want to watch more. If *Gatsby*'s opening sequence fails—and I think it does—it is on that last point. Even there, the problem is extrinsic to the device, which works well enough on its own. Filmmaking is trial and error. Sometimes error wins out.

10

Whose Story Is It?
And What's His Story?

SURE, IT'S PRETTY EASY TO FIGURE OUT who the main character is. What we really want to know is, what does she want and, more important, what does she need? Every main character needs to go somewhere, to develop some attribute that's missing at the beginning of the film. They're like the Tin Man and the Cowardly Lion, and movies are quests to supply the missing parts. Brains? Heart? Maturity? Compassion? Those needs, those missing qualities, are at the heart of understanding movies.

One of those early tasks we confront when the movie begins is establishing who, exactly, we care about and if the caring is worth the bother. Most of the time, we have only to latch on to the first face we see. It may be a face we don't care to see, but that matters not. Stanley Kubrick's *A Clockwork Orange* begins, as we mentioned earlier, with a very alarming face. Yikes, we think, this guy is creepy! But creep or not, he's our boy. To the bombastic strains of Henry Purcell's "Music for the Funeral of Queen Mary–March," the camera initiates what seems like the world's slowest "pull back to reveal"—a move archieved through either pulling away from a close-up to a longer shot via either pulling focus or moving the camera back on a dolly. We find that our creepy lad has three equally disturbing, equally stoned pals sitting next to him. They're drinking milk of some sort (we discover that it is spiked with man-made drugs) in a "milk bar" that is the opposite of wholesome, replete with tables in the form of nude female figures, and where the almost universal white color strikes us as more than a little ominous. Then the voice-over starts, and our protagonist identifies himself as Alex, and he makes it clear that he is the star of his own show. But let's be clear on this point: protagonist, not hero. Alex is actually something called an "antihero," a sort of villainous main character who can command our interest but would never be our choice for next-door neighbor. Not every movie has a hero; almost every one has a protagonist. We sometimes use the terms as if they are interchangeable, but some important distinctions are lost in the process. Here is where the confusion comes in. Heroes are a very special class of character, usually main characters (except in certain kinds of comic or ironic works), upright, virtuous, self-sacrificing, stronger than average, more efficient than average. Think John Wayne in, oh, just about anything.

Usually, the question of whose story it is turns out to be a no-brainer. Look at the title, figure out the protagonist. If we see the title *Schindler's List* and there's a guy named Schindler, we're going to bet the ranch on that horse. Same with *Citizen Kane*, *Lawrence of Arabia*, *The Thomas Crown Affair* (1968), *Life of*

Pi (although that one is made easier by only having one available human). Oh, we can get fooled with *Who Framed Roger Rabbit* (1988) or *The Wizard of Oz*, but that doesn't change the general trend. With a film like *Her* (2013), there's a bit of misdirection, since following the customary model we might well expect the eponymous female to be the figure we care about most. But that female, Samantha, is the disembodied voice of an operating system, and even if she does sound suspiciously like Scarlett Johansson, it's hard for someone who looks like a cell phone to carry a movie. Instead, the movie belongs to Joaquin Phoenix's Theodore, a man who at the beginning is not so much stuck in a rut as cemented into it. And in truth, we might have noted the clue embedded in the pronominal title: one can't really be a third person (Her) unless someone else occupies the first-person position, or put another way, being the voice in the phone suggests someone else must wield the phone. Come to think of it, the same phenomenon is true with *Girl with a Pearl Earring* (2003), so it may just be a Scarlett Johansson thing.

So far, swell. But what's his *story*? That's the thing that matters. Once we know the man, we can figure out the movie. Or maybe, once we know the movie, we can understand the man. Or woman. And don't be misled by the billing. The name above the marquee may be the star attraction, indeed may even be the main character if by that we mean the driving force of the film, but that doesn't guarantee that his or her story is the one that drives *us*. This situation isn't all that common, but it happens. As an example, take *The French Lieutenant's Woman* (1981). Both the title and the credits (as well as the movie posters, although those are largely lost to the majority of contemporary viewers) suggest that Meryl Streep's Anna/Sarah is the driving force of the movie, and indeed her mystery and exotic appeal of the forbidden, both in the framing tale of the actors portraying the characters from the novel and in that interior movie they are shooting, is certainly the irritant that drives Mike/Charles (Jeremy Irons) forward. But here's where it gets tricky. In that Victorian story, it is indeed Charles who drives the action forward—needing answers, feeling repulsed yet strangely attracted by the tale of this "fallen" woman, pursuing her at the cost of his engagement and his reputation, making decision upon decision that drives the plot. On the other hand, between the two "actors" in the outer story, it is Anna who must make the fateful and indeed painful decision.

This one's not at all common, but the character driving the narrative train, the one whose story really matters in the end, isn't the one portrayed by the name above the title on the marquee. This is comparatively rare. Such an instance occurs in *The Grand Budapest Hotel* (2014). Ralph Fiennes and F. Murray Abraham receive uppermost billing as M. Gustave and the elderly Mr. Moustafa, yet it is Moustafa's younger self, Zero (Tony Revolori), who drives the action. It is not so much Gustave's often preposterous actions but Zero's reaction to them, such as his ability to carry out orders or fail to do so in significant ways, that pushes the movie forward. The real question the film asks, sometimes overwhelmed by the silliness and violence of the plot, is how the utterly inexperienced Zero can become the worldly Mr. Moustafa. We should note that this situation is quite rare. Usually, name placement on the marquee is a clue we trust utterly as we carry it with us into the theater.

A somewhat more common sort of movie is one where the title misleads us as to whose story is primary. Two related films demonstrate this. We've mentioned *Annie Hall* (1977) before, and if you've watched it you know that, from the first moment, the movie belongs not to Annie but to her erstwhile lover, Alvy Singer. And if you know Woody Allen's oeuvre, you will have suspected going in that the title is a red herring; the movie, whatever it is, pretty much always belongs to him. Thirty-two years on, director Marc Webb gave us *(500) Days of Summer*, Summer in this case possessing the surname Finn, played by Zooey Deschanel. Yet the focus of the film is not Summer but Tom Hansen (Joseph Gordon-Levitt), an architect by training currently trapped in the job of greeting-card writer. As with Annie and Alvy, the film takes its narrative cues from the man's memories of the relationship. This subjective attachment to Alvy and Tom has its complement in Annie and Summer being the ones to declare that their relationship is not working for them. There are many other similarities between the films, not least because *(500) Days* is a very knowing film in terms of movie history, especially the history of romantic comedies. For our purposes, however, we're interested in the way that each subverts the expectations set up by its eponymous title.

Sometimes there can be competing character interests, and one must inevitably win out. Here's a tale of two movies. With two stars. Together in both. Once upon a time—in the West, no less, but not *that* time—there was a buddy film. Actually, a buddy-caper film. With six-shooters. And these buddies get equal billing: *Butch Cassidy and the Sundance Kid* (1969). The thing is, though, there's hardly ever equal story-ing, whatever the title asserts. So whose story is this? Screenwriter William Goldman leaves no doubt: this one belongs to Butch. Right from the beginning we see him (Paul Newman) casing a bank and flummoxed by all the security measures that the new bank—in a town where he had robbed the old one—has installed. We instantly see that he sees the truth: there will be no robbing the new bank. He asks a security guard what happened to the old bank, which he calls "beautiful." "People kept robbing it," the guard says, to which Butch replies, "Small price to pay for beauty." Right there is the movie in a nutshell. The old bank robber has outlived his time; his only choices will be to go straight or find another line of criminality. The whole film is about these choices, and the decisions he makes about how the gang will proceed, as well as what calamities befall the gang because of those decisions. Four years later, the two were again paired in *The Sting*, and this time the roles were reversed. Redford's character, Johnny Hooker, a small-time grifter, pulls a con that gets his partner killed, as a result of which remorse and revenge vie for the upper hand in his thoughts. He drags Henry Gondorff (Newman), a more experienced con man, out of a booze-riddled torpor to help him get the vengeance he seeks against someone vastly more powerful. While it may be Henry's expertise that pulls the forces together to complete the Big Con, as they call it, there is never any doubt but that Johnny is the driving force behind this sting. Two movies, same actors, equal billing, but divergent levels of importance for the characters, if not for the actors.

Which brings up a point worth mentioning: it's no easier to play a second banana. Or third, fourth, or twenty-seventh. What matters is that each actor understands his character's role within the drama as much as he does his (or her, of course) motivation, backstory, drives, and desires. Otherwise, he will keep wanting more than the screenplay gives him. I once heard bassist Phil Lesh, I believe it was, say that his band the Grateful Dead was able to stay together for so many years when other rock bands had long since imploded because each member was able to harbor the illusion that he was the leader. That may work in hippie jam bands but not in the world of major motion pictures. Or minor ones, for that matter.

Here's proof that size isn't a requirement to fill up the frame. One of the leading ladies nominated in the Best Actress category for the 2013 Academy Awards made her film debut when she was six years old. Quvenzhané Wallis not only features in almost every scene but narrates much of the *Beasts of the Southern Wild*. She rivets our attention in ways that must be the envy of seasoned actors; the camera loves her, while she seemingly doesn't know it exists. The late Roger Ebert called her "a force of nature," a phrase that is hard to improve upon. All this, of course, has to do with the tiny actress; yes, it is surprising that she can take over the movie from her first frames, but only because of her size and age. What is not surprising is that she is given the chance to do so. From the very beginning, this movie belonged to that character, Hushpuppy. She is in not only most scenes but most shots in those scenes, and she narrates, something that not many film characters do. We know from our literature classes that minor characters can narrate stories about more important ones—think *The Great Gatsby* or *Moby-Dick*—but we nevertheless expect narrators to be central figures in the dramas they tell to us, at least until proven otherwise. The movie is really about what Hushpuppy learns that can enable her to survive this new world of melting polar ice caps and released prehistoric beasts and, most important, dying fathers. When Wink (Dwight Henry, a somewhat older film newcomer) dies, she will have to make her way in the world alone, and that story is more compelling and frightening than any natural disaster in the movie.

Up till now we've been talking about fairly conventional movies in which there is a clear lead, or maybe a pair of them contesting for lead status. There is, however, another class of film to consider: the ensemble movie. We're not talking here about *Murder on the Orient Express* (1974) or *Death on the Nile* (1978), where a clear hero (Agatha Christie's detective Hercule Poirot in both cases) comes up against a veritable mob scene of suspects. Rather, the true ensemble film includes a large cast with varying stories and problems and no clear-cut protagonist. Most of them seem to have been directed by Robert Altman, although I'm sure there are others who have worked in the genre as well. In *M*A*S*H* (1970), for instance, the tandem of Hawkeye Pierce (Donald Sutherland) and Trapper John McIntyre (Elliott Gould) is nowhere near as dominant as those two characters would become in the television series that followed. True, they are significant figures in this mobile surgical hospital in the Korean War, but their stories are not particularly more compelling than those of other characters. Indeed, an argument could be made that the driving personal story comes from the villain, that the central issue is Major Frank Burns's problem and how to solve it. For those who know only the TV series, the film's Frank Burns (Robert Duvall) is a much nastier piece of work, not merely disagreeable and rule-bound, but aggressively so, to the point that he threatens to ruin the workings of the unit—and people's lives. He psychologically destroys a young orderly (Bud Cort) over not knowing something (the appearance and location of a heart needle) that he had never been trained to know. From that point on, open warfare breaks out between the movie's heroes and Burns, along with the equally gung-ho Major "Hot Lips" Houlihan (Sally Kellerman). The cruelties Hawkeye and Trapper John and company inflict are out of all proportion to the damage caused by Burns and Houlihan. In truth, the movie is several separate movies, each focusing on a different aspect of the community serving together in the hellhole of an army field hospital, and different characters drive different story lines.

This ensemble approach would become a standard element in many of Altman's films, especially in *Nashville* (1975); his fashion house satire, *Prêt-à-Porter* (1994, also released as *Ready to Wear*); the manor house send-up *Gosford Park* (2001); and his last film, *A Prairie Home Companion* (2006). In each, we follow several possible lead, or at least interesting, characters but none clearly stamped as "protagonist" material. Each has problems, backstory, drives, desires, motivations, strengths, and weaknesses. These films often frustrate moviegoers accustomed to clearly demarcated main characters, yet they can be interesting and rewarding precisely because we find ourselves slightly unsettled through not knowing where to hang our hats.

Ensemble movies are the far end of a spectrum from, say, *The Wizard of Oz*, which could be retitled *All About Dorothy*. And yet, they may teach us something about more conventional approaches to character. In an Altman film, every character has his or her reason for being. They may or may not strike us as good reasons; the characters may be silly, shallow, self-consumed, driven entirely by the wrong motivations, but they have them. And so it is with most movies, assuming they're any good. Let's take the "all about Dorothy" example. It's true that Dorothy's needs drive the film: she simply must get to the Emerald City so that she can find her way back home. And yet, hers is not the only story that matters. Every character has a story. Even the bad ones. And every one of those stories means something important. Maybe especially those of the baddies. We know, for instance, what the Cowardly Lion, the Tin Woodsman, and the Scarecrow need because they tell us. Several times. So far, so good, right? But others also have needs, whether they involve being freed from the tyranny of the Wicked Witches or dealing with sibling rivalry and envy among witches or finding a way to survive in this strange land as a slightly misguided balloon- ist from Kansas. The Wicked Witch of the East is almost the only character whose backstory doesn't make an appearance, but since she appears only as a pair of ruby-slipper-clad feet sticking out from under Dorothy's farmhouse when it lands, she can be excused for this shortcoming. What matters here is that all characters have motivation, if the movie is any good, although we do not always hear what those motivations are. When screenwriters sit down to work, they need to figure out why each character does what he or she does, and simply falling back on "He's evil" or "He's bent on world domination" won't cut it. Unless he's a Bond villain. We tend not to accept characters who seem to act at random or without any clear reasons. Come to think of it, we're not crazy about such people in real life.

Sometimes, in order to be a better reader, it helps to think like a writer, so let's look at what screenwriters need to consider about the people they create. Say we're going to write a movie. We need to populate the thing, characters generally being recommended as inhabitants of stories. What do we need? More important, what do *they* need? Characters generally require several qualities to succeed, among them consistency, complexity, context, motivation, conflict, change, and the capacity to surprise. Those sound contradictory, I know, but hang in there. Let's consider them separately. First, consistency. It really helps if the people we know act like the people we know; if they don't like broccoli on Monday, they're probably still not liking it on Thursday, and if that's not true, we expect a good reason (such as "I tried it, and it was good"). Same with movie characters. If someone starts out timid and rabbity, it's probably best if they don't turn into Conan the Barbarian— unless the timidity is a disguise, in which case they can be as barbarous as they please. This works out well for plots. A hero type is going to do heroic things, even if they turn out to be to his own detriment or that of his friends or loved ones. Someone who is basically honest will probably stay generally honest throughout, absent a very good reason. Naturally, we're familiar with the trope of growth by trial, wherein the wallflower becomes the princess or the timid dormouse the warrior, but that is truly growth and not erratic behavior. Even there, the basics of character typically remain intact. Even within types there are subtypes. Take the irascible old coot. Show us one in the first reel, and we expect irascibility and cootishness from then on. Now, his grumpiness can be endearing and slightly brittle, as in the case of Carl Fredricksen in Disney's *Up*, or nasty and bigoted as with Clint Eastwood's *Gran Torino* (2008). It doesn't really matter, although we should not confuse them and have an animated Ed Asner suddenly start behaving like Eastwood's Korean War veteran Walt Kowalski. Or vice versa. For good and sound reasons, Carl must be Carl and Walt, Walt.

So far, so good, but there is such a thing as too far. The American philosopher Ralph Waldo Emerson said in his essay "Self-Reliance" that "[a] foolish consistency is the hobgoblin of little minds." He said a good deal more than that, but that line applies to our current consideration, since it is also the hobgoblin of limited plots. If characters are so consistent that no change is possible, then we can predict their every move, which is not good. We want, at least with our major characters, the ability to grow and change. In large measure, the ability to overcome consistency with the capacity for change is because of complexity, which is to say that they have multiple sides to their personality. Every fiction (or drama or screen-) writing guide enjoins students to give their characters complexity. From this simple instruction, much terrible writing ensues. At its worst, the idea creates horrible villains—think Darth Vader on steroids—who have a soft spot for puppies. Laugh if you will, but I've seen the results. They're not pretty. You'll sometimes feel this as you watch a not-so-good movie, especially of the made-for-television sort (I can give you the name of a cable channel or two if you wish). There is a sort of mechanical adherence to form in the creation of character; you can also see the instruction, "Stage 3, Minute 12: insert divergent quality here." So the characters limp through whatever flimsy drama that has been concocted for them with a mismatched collection of parts that is supposed to stand in for genuine complexity. Happily, in most movies the complexity feels more organic. Which is good. If Walt Kowalski or Carl Fredricksen is completely contained by the label "grumpy old man," there's nowhere for him to go. Stuff will happen to him, but it mostly can't happen because of him. And we really need for him to create some of the mayhem that he encounters.

Consistency and complexity are set in motion to a large degree by the next two items, context and motivation. By context, we mean their external situation: life experiences, relationships, job history, everything in life that can matter. Motivation, as we've already seen, is that intricate set of factors that boils down to a single question: what does the character need? That need can be overt and acknowledged: Darth Vader needs to dominate the universe (or serve his emperor, who does); or it can be hidden from the character: Carl Fredricksen needs to care about someone beyond himself and to have an adventure. Carl doesn't know that these are his needs; Lord Vader does.

In turn, context and motivation lead to conflict, and it is through conflict that we discover what characters are really made of. Conflict can be external—think the cobra and the mongoose—or internal—the struggle of the honest man who suddenly needs to either lie to protect someone else or tell the truth and allow that someone to be destroyed. When Alan Ladd's Shane, for instance, has to take down and strap on the gun belt he had formerly given up for a life of simple labor, he has multiple conflicts. The first is with himself: can he avoid the way of the gun, and if not, what does it mean? The second is with his surroundings: he didn't make the situation in which he finds himself, with a cattle baron at war with dirt farmers, nor did he make Stonewall Torey foolishly attempt to stand up to Jack Palance's murderous gunslinger, Wilson. Finally, his conflict is with Wilson and his henchmen. So, one internal and two external conflicts all in one arc of action. Not bad.

Conflict, in turn, leads to change. We don't, naturally, require all characters to change. With rare exceptions, blocking characters (both villains and mere nuisances who block the protagonists' paths) don't need to change, and only muck things up if they do. Sometimes, as with Darth Vader, a deathbed conversion is not a problem. And even most helping characters don't exhibit a lot of growth; their main function is to help someone else grow, as with, say, Michael Caine's Alfred the butler in *Batman Begins* (2005). With main characters, we want to see growth and change, or else the failure to seize the opportunity for some. In other words, a character can fail to improve, and that is also a form of development. To go back to our previous example, Shane discovers that circumstances won't permit him to stay in the valley; like the bad guys, he's a bringer of death unsuited to this new world of life the sodbusters are creating. That's not a personal failing, only an acknowledgment of the external realities. By contrast, Butch Cassidy sees the world change around him and, unable to change in ways that will work for him, talks Sundance and Etta Place into changing worlds instead. By and large, however, characters react to their changing realities and their conflicts by growing beyond the persons they were at the outset. In *The Artist*, George Valentin is tormented by the coming of talkies, yet he manages at the end to overcome his self-pity and, with the love of a good woman, adapt to the new world. It is a close-run thing, and he nearly succumbs to an accident that looks a great deal like de facto suicide before being rescued and ultimately saving himself. We have all grown up with this pattern, watching hero's journey stories in Disney films from *Bambi* and *Pinocchio* to *Finding Nemo* and *Toy Story* and forward to *Frozen* and, without doubt, whatever comes next. We learn about heroes and helping characters and blocking characters from our earliest film experiences. Without even trying, we develop our critical faculties, learning to expect growth from the protagonist and assistance or resistance from those around him or her.

That ability to change, in turn, means that characters have the capacity to surprise. Now, surprise can come in all sorts of forms in the movies. A homicidal attacker jumping out of the shadows no doubt delivers plenty of surprise, even shock, but that's not what we have in mind here. Rather, we're interested in the kinds of surprises that grow out of character complexity. You will have noticed, assuming you've been sentient for more than five minutes, that our friends and family are just full of surprises. Who knew that eighty-year-old Aunt Martha would say *that*? Or that little Roscoe was actually listening when his dad talked to himself and so knew how to fix the drain? Nearly all the time they are perfectly themselves, by which we mean that they stay consistent to our picture of them. And suddenly, they do . . . whatever. Upon reflection, however, we see that those surprises don't come from Mars but are themselves consistent with some nondominant but still present aspect of their character. Aunt Martha has always been something of a freethinker, and Roscoe sometimes stops playing with Legos long enough to eavesdrop on the world around him. Plus, there's the Lego thing, which suggests a certain handiness—we just hadn't thought of him that way before. When the final twist comes at the end of *Body Heat* and Ned realizes that Matty Walker is still alive, it comes as a surprise, yet he knows exactly how to find the answer, which grows out of traits he has seen in her throughout their relationship: deception, self-advancement, callousness toward others, and long-term planning. When, at the start of the potentially fatal knife fight with the gigantic Harvey Logan, Butch Cassidy kicks him in the crotch (a creative first for what would soon become a sorry cliché, which then refused to die), we're surprised but not alienated. Of course Butch would take unfair advantage: he has little regard for rules but a strong desire to live. He then delivers his second surprise, namely to adopt the idea (robbing trains instead of banks) that Harvey had insisted on and that Butch had been seemingly willing to risk death to oppose. This one is also in character, since Butch is pragmatic and, to a point, adaptable. Surprises, like most other things involving characterization, grow out of well-known traits; since major characters are complex, they allow for plenty of room to do the unexpected, and their ability to astonish is predictable rather than random.

Why does all this matter? Because movies contain characters, grow out of characters, live and die on characters. Because, as one standard formulation has it, plot is character in action. No, not character inaction. Just the opposite. From time to time you will see this idea, especially if you go near a creative writing class or a snarky book or movie review. It may be phrased differently, as, for example, "Characters' actions drive plot, while character is revealed through plot." That one is a little sticky on the tongue. It also is a little prescriptive in how it yokes these elements together. I prefer something slightly more general: **Plot and character cannot exist without one another.** A given plot will never come together without a particular set of character qualities. Swap one character for another, or give one of them different traits (for example, making the selfish one generous), and try as you might, you can't make the plot believably go to the same destination. Consider the modern superhero flick. We tend to think of those movies as guys in spandex, but the basics of screenwriting apply no less there than in *The Magnificent Ambersons* (1942). In *Superman* (1978), what happens on-screen can only happen because Christopher Reeve's Superman/Clark Kent, Margot Kidder's Lois Lane, and Gene Hackman's Lex Luthor possess precisely their particular constellations of qualities and behave in the ways that they do. That Lois is pushy and inquisitive to X degree and not, say, W or Y leads to certain outcomes while excluding others. That Superman has a need to conceal but also a countering need to reveal aspects of himself will drive the action forward. And so, too, with Hackman's Lex. We could extend this further and examine other characters, but our time here is limited. Or take the first *Batman* (1989). That particular plot works out because Michael Keaton's Bruce Wayne/Batman and Jack Nicholson's Joker are the ways they are, driven by the things they desire, fear, loathe, admire.

Characters make the plot world go round. That's true whether we're talking movies or novels or short stories or plays.

If you really want to see the interaction of character and plot, look no further than the comic book movie. The good ones. Why this genre? For starters, there's plenty of action to keep you interested and the plot is pretty easy to discern: some villain has set wheels in motion that promise disaster, and the hero or heroine or heroes, since they often come in sets, must avert said catastrophe. And second, the motivations and drives of superheroes are pretty near the surface. Whether it's revenge or parental approval or the spandex equivalent of 'roid rage, we don't have to hunt too far for what drives him/her/them. After all, in terms of character depth and development, *The Avengers* isn't *Annie Hall*. And once we understand those motivations, it is pretty easy to see how they play out in the plot. Iron Man's intelligence and technical knowledge serve him well, but his cockiness and lack of foresight occasionally bring difficulties. In the *X-Men* series, Wolverine's anger issues are not mere character flaws; they also lead to events or outcomes that drive the plot. Superman's need to protect those around him from the consequences of knowing his secret sometimes puts them in greater peril. As for Batman . . . which one? The several embodiments of the Dark Knight in the various franchises don't act in uniform ways, obviously, and their needs and drives may be a little different, just as the vision behind the movies is different—and not a little. So we have to decide whether we're talking about Michael Keaton's Batman or Christian Bale's or Val Kilmer's or George Clooney's. And how do Keaton's Batman's issues affect his plot versus those of Bale's Batman? How do those mixes of tenderness, toughness, obsessiveness, humility, arrogance, and anger play out in the movies? That might just be a homework assignment for Dave. Or you.

Interlude

30-60-30—Hike!

OKAY, THEN, YOU'RE SITTING in a movie theater, no watch. What time is it? No, you may not ask your neighbor. And pulling out your cell phone is rude, so we know you won't do that. What, you never got the knack of telling time by the movie? Then it's high time you learned.

Movies have a structure so tight you can set your watch by it, and moviemakers—and savvy viewers—do. How do I know? I check my watch. Not only must things happen for a reason; they must also happen on time.

That three-act structure, as it is known in the trade, is 30-60-30. This is the most basic item in the screenwriter's toolkit: 30-60-30. What's that mean? Those numbers represent minutes and they are the most important numbers in the movie business. Except the box-office totals. To which they are related, if only slightly. A movie consists of three acts of different lengths, the second act being roughly twice as long as the first and third. Didn't know that? I'll bet you did. You've experienced it all your life, even if you didn't know you had. Here it is in a nutshell: The first thirty minutes, which nearly everyone calls Act I, introduce us to characters and the basic situation. At roughly the half-hour mark, something momentous happens to spin the film off into its next phase. This event is known as the *first plot point*; it will have a corresponding *second plot point* at the ninety-minute mark. Before we get there, however, we have an hour-long Act II, in which the personalities and relationships and problems are developed to something like a fever pitch, a state of high agitation in which we feel, Something's got to happen. Which it does. This event, the second plot point, spins the plot out of further buildup and toward resolution in Act III. Now, what we hope for is that the events and developments grow out of one another, rather than being imposed by screenwriter fiat. The former feels organic and right, the latter contrived and lame. But even lame screenwriters have learned lesson one of the art of the script—30-60-30—and they will move heaven and earth to get there. The three-act structure also holds for shorter movies, as in old comedies that typically run only ninety minutes: three acts with approximate symmetry of 1X-2X-1X, the middle being about twice as long as the first and third acts.

You want to see how this works, right? Let's take an example everybody knows by heart—or as close as we're likely to get to universal knowledge. Right after he got back from a long time ago in a galaxy far, far away, Harrison Ford jumped into the more recent past of the 1930s as Indiana Jones in *Raid-*

ers of the Lost Ark. The film took a slightly degraded form, or more properly, two of them—the action-adventure movie and the Saturday afternoon serial adventure—and became the standard-bearer of the genre. We've already talked about the opening, but that's not the movie. Just the appetizer. When the G-men come to talk to Professor Jones about finding his old professor Abner Ravenwood, who is rumored to have the headpiece of the Staff of Ra, which leads Jones to conclude that they're after the Lost Ark of the Covenant before Hitler's men can lay their hands on it, that's when the movie gets going. That conversation sets the wheels in motion for Indy's travels, taking him first to Nepal, where Abner's daughter and Indy's former lover Marion (Karen Allen) runs a bar at or just beyond the edge of the world. Even that remoteness, however, isn't enough to forestall Nazis. Marion, her father now dead, unleashes her bitterness at how he treated her during their affair and rebuffs Indy's offer to buy the headpiece. Just after he leaves, the chief Nazi villain, Arnold Toht (Ronald Lacey), shows up with some serious henchmen to take by force what she won't sell. Indy returns to save her, but the rescue doesn't extend to the bar, which is burned down in the ensuing melee. With the bar gone, Marion demanding compensation and not trusting Indy out of her sight, and Nazis in pursuit, and Indy himself dealing with past guilt and the current crisis, the pair are forced to solve this mystery together, headed for Egypt. That moment, when the two not entirely friendly former lovers realize they're in a lot of trouble and stuck with each other, is our plot point, the moment the action turns from opening gambits to full-speed-ahead plot development and complication. The time: 33:39. The movie's plot development is slowed a bit from the lengthy opening sequence, but that is very much in the ballpark. So, too, with the second plot point, just a few seconds shy of 1:37. This one occurs when the Nazis have boarded Katanga's smuggling ship and seized not only the Ark but Marion as well. The prize is gone and Marion is in enemy hands (not merely the Germans but his personal nemesis, René Belloq). After all, when that happens, what can a guy do but hitch a ride across the Mediterranean on the conning tower of an enemy submarine? From that point on, everything goes like clockwork, for the movie, if not always for the characters. And for the audience? It's a headlong rush toward a thrilling conclusion. And there you have it: somewhere around a half hour in and then on or near a half hour from the end something momentous occurs, and that momentous event spins the film toward what it needs next, either further plot development or conclusion. The elements vary depending on the kind of movie, naturally, but the basic structure remains constant.

There's nothing divinely ordained or constitutionally mandated about these time marks. As with most elements of any grammar, they grew more or less organically. Through practice, filmmakers found a sweet spot for these major developments. The first describes a boundary between the time when audiences are not yet ready for a major reveal and the moment when they become restive and want to move forward. The second identifies a similar boundary where all the plot pieces are finally in place and viewers are anxious for events to begin the final cascade. If you try to make that turn too soon, it will feel forced or rely on incomplete information. Wait too long and the movie drags. That's why filmmakers care about the 30-60-30 three-act structure and why every Screenwriting 101 course teaches it. But you're not a screenwriter, are you? You're a reader of movies, and this is Screenreading 101. So what's in it for you? Just this: if you want to understand how movies work on you, you need to know what the people who make them know. As a viewer, you have probably never noticed anything so overt as "so this is the plot point," or "okay, here we go." But you've felt it. There's a little moment of fulfillment that happens with a well-designed and well-placed plot point, just an instant of gratification where we say something like, "Ah." If the casual viewer thinks about it—because of the way it occurs, not because we're talking about it here—then it fails. If she merely feels slightly satisfied, even if she doesn't notice, that's success.

What's that, you say? *Raiders* is just one movie. True enough. To be valid, an experiment should be repeatable. So how about *Harry Potter and the Sorcerer's Stone* (2001)? The first half hour of the film is given over to backstory (the wizards saving the infant Harry and handing him over to his aunt and uncle), to the wizarding world being rather different from our own (Diagon Alley, Gringotts Bank), and to Harry's being special (everyone seems to know about "the Boy Who Lived"). The big event that forms the first plot point, the moment that sets wheels in motion, takes place when Harry runs through the pillar at Platform 9¾ and finds the Hogwarts Express waiting (right at 34:00). Now those are some wheels. Harry doesn't know what he's in for, but he can tell just by the platform and the locomotive that it sure beats living under his uncle Vernon's stairs. And the second one? How about when Harry snags the key to the door from among all those other flying keys, gives it to Ron and Hermione, and then flies through it as they shut it against all those attacking keys, exactly on two hours in a movie that runs 2:32 (reminding us that what matters isn't the sixty minutes in between but the thirty minutes from the credit roll). This example reminds us that a good plot point isn't only about an event and a plot arc; it's also about character. Harry's eyes light up—and no child actor's eyes have ever lit up any better than Daniel Radcliffe's—as he sees the fulfillment of his dreams.

One more? Sure. In *No Country for Old Men* (2007), the first plot point arrives around minute twenty-six, when Llewelyn Moss (Josh Brolin), running for his life after swiping the two million dollars left behind when he stumbles on a drug deal gone wrong (that left no survivors), having barely escaped from the Mexicans and their killer dog, is dressing his wounds as he tells Carla Jean (Kelly Macdonald) to hide out at her mother's while he tries to figure out how to proceed. When the other side has killer dogs, you know it's time to hit the road. Their previous life, such as it has been, is over. The midpoint mini-climax comes right at the hour mark when Moss and Chigurh (Javier Bardem) have their shoot-out. All signs have led to this, and we might expect the confrontation to be the big finale, but in this case things are just getting rolling. Both men limp away wounded, leaving an innocent victim and massive property damage in their wake, each of them knowing it can't end here, that one or the other—even both—is going to have to die. The second plot point, the one that turns everything toward home, is the call Moss makes to Carson Wells's hotel room. Chigurh, having just murdered Wells—who, in fairness, has been hunting Chigurh down—answers instead and tells Moss that the only way he can save Carla Jean is to bring Chigurh the money. That's a beautiful hinge point, partly because it pairs so nicely with the earlier decision to flee from the peril but even more so because it offers the character a set of choices. The simple, if suicidal, one is to do as he's instructed. Moss is too much a survivor, or at least a believer in his ability to survive, to take that one. Another choice is to call Carla Jean and warn her to run as far and as fast as possible while at the same time running in the opposite direction. Instead of either of those, he chooses to not merely defy Chigurh but to threaten him and then to make plans to meet up with Carla Jean in El Paso. What remains for the audience is to watch catastrophe unfold. The three-act structure is a beautiful thing to behold, even when the contents of the movie aren't exactly lovely.

So there you go: time by the movie clock. And why should you care? Because you already do. All those movies you've watched have worked their rhythms on you. And it's not just these three movies; it's, well, pretty much all of them. *The 40-Year-Old Virgin* and *Goodfellas* and *Star Wars* and *Jaws* and *When Harry Met Sally*. I recently saw a news article about Timothy Busfield (*Field of Dreams*, television's *Thirtysome-thing*) visiting a creative writing class in a school not far from his Michigan home. His main point: movies are built around a three-act structure. It's a sure bet those kids will never forget that lesson, and neither should we. If the next time you went to the multiplex the film went forty-five or fifty minutes before hitting its first plot point, you would feel decidedly restless and uneasy—hey, let's get this show on the road! There may be nothing inevitable about the timing of the plot points, but we have learned and internalized it to the extent that we rely on it and are nearly always rewarded by it. It's a good deal all the way around. Don't take my word for it, though. The next movie you watch—I recommend home viewing so that you don't annoy your neighbors unduly (it's okay to annoy family in the pursuit of art or research; I do it all the time)—put the watch on the movie and see when important things happen and what effects they have on the plot. You'll feel like a film whiz and never see movies the same way again.

11

How Many Heads— and Where Are They?

At the end of *The King's Speech* (2010), during the eponymous radio broadcast, the camera cuts repeatedly from the king fighting his way past his stammer and into history to various of his subjects. Mostly, there are groups of subjects in all sorts of places—several soldiers overseas, African villagers, folks in English shops, but always multiples—hovering around their radios, but in one instance, there's a two-shot. The king's brother David, late the king and emperor Edward VIII, now the Duke of Windsor, is sitting with his wife, the American divorcée formerly known as Wallis Simpson. They are huddled together on a sofa in an outsize, seemingly hollow room with an even bigger, equally empty world beyond them through the bay windows. Rarely have two people seemed so few or so small or so isolated. It's a great shot. *This*, it says, is what the duke brought on himself. *This* is how removed he is from the life of the country. For those of us of a certain age or with knowledge of the time, the shot encapsulates a great deal about how little the government trusted his instincts or judgment and how much it wanted him safely out of the way. Not a word is spoken within the shot; the words all come from elsewhere, about other events, via the wireless. So how do we know all this? Visual language: two people crowded together in a space that requires no crowding, because of which we know so much that goes unsaid. Now that, friends, is filmmaking.

We know what's important by who is in a shot and where they stand—or sit or lie or dangle or otherwise occupy space—in relation to one another. Are they together or alone? Upstaging one another? Sharing focus? Shifting focus? In other words, how many heads are present, and where are they?

For filmmakers, of course, these choices are vitally important: the director and cinematographer are packaging information not merely through story but through the arrangement of each individual shot. That arrangement—the mise-en-scène, or "place in the scene," to employ an inadequate if accurate translation of the French—comprises more than simply the people involved. Yes, of course, people and the space(s) they occupy, but also objects, shadows, beams of light, right down to the last cobweb and bread crumb. Everything in that shot conveys meaning. Consider: a platter with an array of untouched cookies, that same platter with a few cookies remaining, and that selfsame item with no cookies, only a couple of bare serving papers with crumbs. Each of those tells us something different in terms of time, action, even emotional temperature. If the full platter appears in the shot right after the guests have slammed the door on the way out, we know that the dessert course did not even begin well. If we cut into the scene and see the half-full platter, we know that the participants have been at this for a while. And if the cupboard, as it were, is bare? Depends on the surrounding context: the message will differ depending on whether the diners are still seated around the coffee table or there's evidence of a dustup in which cookies may have been used as weapons. For the moment, however, we want to focus on that special class of selection within the broader scene-setting that has to do with the placement of people within shots. Those decisions about which characters to include in a shot can underline or intensify the action or the meaning of said shot, or subvert the more overt message, or further develop the theme of the film. So we should know about what's going on in those decisions.

Why? We're not making movies, right? Because we're engaged in that other imaginative act: reading them. In our Screen-reading 101 class, we're seeking to become more sophisticated consumers of cinematic art, and part of that improvement lies in understanding how those visual details convey meaning. As I've said elsewhere, there's nothing magical about these examples. Every single film you watch is an occasion to notice how it captures persons within scenes. Obviously, sometimes there won't be a lot to choose. If the movie is *Cast Away* with Tom Hanks or *The Martian* (2015) with Matt Damon or any of the latter-day castaway tales, the preponderance of shots will be singles; it's a basic truth of the human-alone-against-the-universe movie that you can't introduce a second human into the shot. More commonly, someone sneaking around to investigate something—think Humphrey Bogart as Sam Spade or Philip Marlowe, or pretty much any horror film heroine about to open the forbidden door—the single shot is a given, for much the same reasons. Most of the time, however, multiple persons are present in a scene and the makeup of any individual shot comes down to choice. By studying how those choices turn out, we can become stronger readers of cinematic texts.

Examples? Thought you'd never ask.

For starters, let's consider the single. We might expect the term to be *one-shot*, which would dovetail nicely with *two-shot* and *three-shot*, which do in fact name the number of persons in the frame. *One-shot*, while it is sometimes used, more commonly refers to a scene shot in a single long take, so for the sake of clarity (when I can remember to do so), the shot of one person in a frame will be called a "single." We can find examples everywhere, but let's take two newer films that show what singles can mean. It is hard to imagine two more different movies in terms of subject, tone, mood, really anything, than the inventive *Her* and the military biopic *American Sniper*. But you will rarely see more singles than in these films. Each hero has strong reasons to be on his own. Theodore's (Joaquin Phoenix) only companion through most of *Her* is his phone's operating system voice, Samantha (Scarlett Johansson's disembodied voice), so there is no one to show, unless you count the phone itself. To be fair, it is often on display, sometimes in rather creepy ways. One or two of these shots would not tell us anything definitive, but when the number gets into the dozens and dozens, it speaks to the character's isolation. We know Theodore is a basket case even before Samantha leaves him to go off with other operating systems to "find" themselves. In fact, his only hope for redemption lies in his being abandoned by his cyber companion. By contrast, the isolation of Chris Kyle (Bradley Cooper) in *American Sniper* is a professional requirement: he is alone looking through the scope of his rifle, and he alone is responsible for the deaths he sees there. In ways no other soldier can experience, snipers are intimately involved in their kills even if the distances are extreme, and they are similarly alone with the consequences, as we saw in those earlier scenes we examined. We also talked earlier about the single shots used when Kyle records his first kills of the mother and child who are trying to throw a grenade at his comrades. What the shot conveys most strongly is the anguish and outright grief at having to make these lethal decisions; having any other character in the frame would lessen that emotional freight.

While we can find no solace in the ending of *American Sniper,* there is one comforting element to all that solitude and outright loneliness in *Her:* at the end of the movie, Theodore has shared his grief with Amy (Amy Adams) and in so doing has moved closer to her. The final shot is of the two of them on the top of their building, sitting beside each other, as she lays her head on his shoulder. A most welcome two-shot.

Moving from singles to two-shots, we find that their use isn't limited by the size of the space in which the two people appear. Here's a great use of space from a movie that makes great use of, well, everything. If you've never seen *Singin' in the Rain* (1952), you simply must. Everyone remembers Gene Kelly's performance of the title number, along with a couple of other set pieces, including Donald O'Connor's zany "Make 'em Laugh" series of pratfalls. But for me the scene that really makes the movie is both quieter and more colorful. Don Lockwood (Kelly) and Kathy Selden (Debbie Reynolds) have gotten off to a rocky start. That tends to happen when you drop unannounced into a young woman's car from the top of a passing trolley. Don has developed feelings for Kathy, who may have done the same but remains wary. She asks him to express his feelings, but the only way he can is through the world he knows best, on an unoccupied soundstage, where he sings to woo her and they perform a pas de deux. Or *trois,* if you count the ladder. It is almost a third character in the scene. Don sets the scene—a sunset backdrop, lights from a garden, a moonlight-spot on the "lady on her balcony" (Kathy on a large stepladder), a wind machine to provide the breeze, and Don singing "You Were Meant for Me." As the song begins, Kathy is high on the ladder, Don opposite on the floor below. The spatial relations are clear: he is in the role of supplicant asking for her love. He climbs up his side, she down hers, suggesting that both want something else. When he also returns to the ground, they both rotate left around the ladder until they are on the side opposite the one they began on. Kathy is intent on keeping that barrier between them, the camera on shooting them together. Yet she doesn't look *through* the ladder but around the corner as Don has done before she moves to his original side. Were she looking through the ladder, the message would be clear that she doesn't want him; rather, looking around the edge says that she's interested. And their hands are doing this fascinating dance: his are around the leg of the ladder as if pulling it to him, embracing it, while hers are on the side nearer her, ready to shove off, showing that she is still contemplating a getaway. But then a curious and very telling gesture betrays her change of heart: as he is singing "The angels must have sent you," her left (outside) hand slips almost imperceptibly around the edge of that leg. She isn't reaching out yet, but she is sending him a more positive message. He receives it and, as he continues, "And they meant you just for me," he crosses to her side, which this time she does not abandon, and he offers his hand, which she takes. Think about that series of tiny movements: offer, refusal; approach, withdrawal; pursuit, retreat; offer, partial acceptance; approach, welcome; plea, approval. It is the finest, most subtle piece of choreography in the movie.

And they haven't started to dance yet.

But when they do—oh my! From tentative steps and slight separations to the paired dance steps while clasping hands to the tap routine and ultimately to that ultimate expression of sexual desire in dance, the lift, the entire sequence keeps them always in the frame together and moves them toward certainty. When they break from the dance and return to the ladder, Don repeats the line that she was meant just for him, but this time he occupies the superior position on the ladder with her looking up adoringly from the ground. In just over four minutes of screen time, they are not in the same frame for about twenty seconds. When Kathy is first atop the ladder and Don has turned on all the movie magic, including "five hundred thousand watts of stardust," the camera cuts to a single of her asking him to say what he had promised. Then it cuts to him saying that he will try and then moving toward the ladder as he begins the song. We reestablish the two-shot just as he sings "You were meant for me," and we never abandon it again. That separation at her challenge and his response and the coming back together, culminating in the lift, tell us everything we need to know about this newly minted couple.

The screenwriter Ernest Lehman told the story about working to adapt *The King and I* for the screen (1956), and suggesting to composer Richard Rodgers that the movie audience needed to hear the King say to Anna that he wants to make love to her. Rodgers politely but firmly explained that Lehman didn't grasp the grammar of the musical, saying that "when people sing together, it means, 'I want to make love to you,' and when they dance together, that is making love." During the lift in our scene, Debbie Reynolds's Kathy looks utterly transported. As Kelly's Don sets her gently on the boards again, they each have a tiny look that seems to say, I guess there's no going back now. If you want to know what that look is about, ask Richard Rodgers.

Eat your heart out, George Balanchine.

Two-shots can separate as well as bring together, of course. Consider the breakfast table. Orson Welles did. One of the smaller gems that collectively make up the masterpiece that is *Citizen Kane* (1941) involves just such an item—or several of them. In the first, Charles Foster Kane and his wife (number one, as it will turn out) are at breakfast. She is already seated when he comes up to serve her and compliment her extravagantly. It is the end of a very long night, although they look quite fresh in their evening attire. And they sit very close to

one another, she on the not-very-long side of the table, he
at the left end. In the next shot, the table has grown slightly
and they sit at opposite ends. She's mildly critical, he smugly
self-satisfied; the topic is her uncle, the president. They're
also somewhat more appropriately dressed than in the first,
although even here, they are far beyond any attire in which
I have ever appeared at breakfast. Next scene—slightly more
distant, somewhat better dressed, somewhat older, somewhat
at loggerheads. In the final scene, they are fully mature and
quite elegant, as well as utterly immune to each other. Their
"conversation" consists of her reading, rather ostentatiously,
the *San Francisco Chronicle* while he sticks to his own paper, the
Inquirer. That gesture says more than all the conversations we
hear between them.

That sequence is a wonder of compression. The great Swedish director Ingmar Bergman created a television series called
Scenes from a Marriage (1973), which ran nearly five hours. The
Welles version, in which we learn everything we need to know
about this failed marriage, lasts slightly over two minutes. And
part of what makes it work is that only the first scene and the
sixth (and last) present us with two-shots, one of the two love-
birds quite close, the other of two people fully tired of each
other at opposite ends of a table fit for banquets, not breakfasts.
In between, it's all singles as we cut from one increasingly dis-
gruntled partner to the other. That strategy underscores the
lack of communication and empathy; we get the feeling that
they must be talking *at* rather than *with* one another.

Or try this one from *Body Heat*, possibly exhibit A in the
noir revival of the eighties. In particular, it's a rough remake
of several, but chiefly *Double Indemnity* (1944), for which I am
particularly grateful. I was born too late to share in the forties
fascination with Barbara Stanwyck as a femme fatale; give
me Kathleen Turner any day. Happily, in *Body Heat* that's just
whom director Lawrence Kasdan does give us. This is a movie

chock-full of two-shots, often masquerading as singles (the evidently logical contrasting term, one-shot, actually denoting something else, namely something shot in a single take)—the lovers are that close. The shot that commands our attention, however, is not one of those. Rather, it is of the widest separation. After Matty Walker (Turner) has lured the hapless Ned Racine (William Hurt) into a passionate affair and then into the murder of her husband, a rift grows between the two. Well, you can't just tell us there's a rift, can you? We must see it for ourselves. Kasdan sets up a shot that's nearly perfect: open French doors with the two lovers standing on either side of the frame. Might as well be Lake Michigan between them.

In an earlier display of mastery of mise-en-scène, Kasdan tells us who's really in charge and who doesn't fathom the truth. There's a shot in which Matty is serving Ned a drink. He is seated. She is standing, first with her back to him as she pours his drink, then hovering over him as she hands it to him. He, naturally enough, sees himself being served—a good deal if he can get it. We, on the other hand, see her staking out the higher ground, in this case, the higher portion of the frame. Matty, clearly, has the upper hand. The shot as she hands him the drink is a perfect encapsulation of their situation. Matty is in control, as she has been and will continue to be throughout; while she permits Ned to think he is the king of her heart, in actuality he is a mere pawn in a game much bigger than he can understand.

This brilliant shot reminds us of a basic fact about how people are arrayed in film space. It certainly matters how many heads appear and how near or far they are from each other, but it matters even more where they are relative to one another. Let's say that we have a two-shot; on its own, that doesn't tell us much. Is one or the other foregrounded? If so, which one is in focus, the front one or the back? In the case of Kasdan's scene, is one of them higher than the other? What action is going on while they are so arranged? If one is lower, is it because he is on a lower step but standing or, as in this case, because he is seated and she is standing? What meaning will that convey? We may not be able to say in all cases that the person holding the superior position is in a superior position generally—not least because screenwriters and directors understand irony as well as their literary brethren—but Matty clearly occupies the higher ground in her relationship with Ned, and shot after shot reinforces that advantage. If you're shooting that scene, it is something you must consider. As I say elsewhere, there are decisions to be made every second of the film.

One of the greatest uses of a two-shot, actually a scene full of them, occurs in *The Lion in Winter* (1968). Fifteen amazing minutes, two magnificent actors, every possible degree of separation in the shots of them. Henry II (Peter O'Toole) and Eleanor of Aquitaine (Katharine Hepburn) have what we might construe as a troubled marriage. At least where I come from, keeping your wife jailed and only letting her out at Christmas and Easter would be a sign of marital issues. The situation is that, like King Lear, Henry cannot decide which of his three children—sons, in this case—he wishes to succeed him. His main concern seems to be thwarting the wishes of Eleanor, who wants Richard (the future Lion-Hearted), while Henry seems to want the ill-equipped John. History tells us that both shall sit on the English throne, but the unfortunate parents don't know that. To be fair, as no one is in this family, Eleanor's goals seem to mirror Henry's, although she stands more firmly by Richard than Henry does John. And at the climax of the plot—the point from which there is no turning back—the two are alone, at least after the exit of Henry's mistress, Alais (Jane Merrow), with whom Eleanor has been speaking before Henry's entrance. Talk about awkward conversations! That awkwardness recurs again and again in this scene as the two principals come together, move apart, pull one another closer only to push away again, turn toward, turn away. There is even an enormous fireplace to emphasize the separation between them. Yet they are rarely not in the frame together. There is no way to do justice to all the possibilities of the two-shot that are realized in this scene in mere words; you simply must see it for yourself.

If you really want classic, consider what John Ford accomplishes through the arrangement of heads in *Stagecoach*. For instance, during the vote on whether to go forward in the absence of the cavalry, there's a group shot encompassing nearly all the travelers. Mrs. Mallory is seated at the dinner table, with Hatfield attending to her; Dallas, the town prostitute, is seated along the wall to the left, with the Ringo Kid just beyond her, then Buck, Peacock, and Gatewood in a line from him that curves around the end of the room; Curley stands at the table between the seated figures and Buck. Only Doc Boone is out of the frame, off to the right with his old army buddy and fellow drunk Billy. Subsequently, as they break into their factions (the "proper" group of Hatfield, Mrs. Mallory, and the banker Gatewood in one group; the prostitute Dallas, the drunken Doc Boone, and jailbird Ringo Kid in the other), shots break down into two- and three-shots. In fact, Mrs. Mallory and Hatfield move from the end of the table nearest Dallas to the opposite end, beside Gatewood. Their move leaves Dallas and Ringo alone. Interestingly, Peacock, the milquetoast whiskey drummer, belongs to neither group of passengers. The shots tell us everything we need to know about the social dynamics of this small society, even if Ford loses his nerve and has Dallas and Doc Boone comment on being snubbed. Given how well he marshals his forces, he needn't have bothered with words.

Later, once Mrs. Mallory goes into labor, there is a great three-shot of Ringo, Curley, and Hatfield in the hallway of the way station looking, well, expectantly toward the room where she is having her baby. The scene is played chiefly for comedy, but there is an edge of tenderness in the way these hard men eagerly await the birth that will make their trip that much more arduous.

Not every shot in the movie is brilliant. In particular, the single shot is not Ford's friend. His introductions tend to be static singles—more like photographs on movie (or wanted) posters than viable movie shots. When Gatewood receives the fifty thousand dollars with which he will soon abscond, for instance, we get an ominous single of him. The introductory single of the Ringo Kid when he stops the coach is the sort of dreamy, soft-focus shot best reserved for fan magazines. Those missteps (or one misstep repeated several times) aside, the shooting of this movie is generally masterful.

An instance of that mastery comes on day two of the trip. On the first day, Gatewood, the heavyset banker, was placed uncomfortably between Dallas and Lucy Mallory. Immediately before the Apache attack on day two, Peacock, the whiskey drummer, takes Gatewood's place between the two women. He is obviously less judgmental than the hypocritical Gatewood, and, as a family man, he loves babies. In a two-shot with Dallas, Peacock urges them all "to have a little Christian charity one for the other," as he leans in toward Dallas, who is holding Lucy's baby. I guess that makes it a three-shot, doesn't it? In any event, we see Dallas as solicitous toward the exhausted woman and the tiny infant, and we see in Peacock that people can behave decently toward one another. Alas, that tender moment is interrupted by an arrow.

During the subsequent chase, there's a great shot of the stagecoach in profile of All Those Who Matter: Buck driving, his hat brim flattened back by wind, Curley on the seat beside him turned backward and firing the coach shotgun, Ringo lying on top firing his Winchester, Dallas in one window shielding the baby, Lucy in the back window covering her ears and looking none too well, and Doc, who has moved in between them, seeming to enjoy the action very much. For most of the sequence, however, we get singles of those inside the coach—Lucy praying, Dallas protecting the newborn, Hatfield showing perhaps too much glee in dispatching Apaches, and so on. This makes sense; after all, while passengers and crew in such a crisis may all be pulling together, each one is enacting his or her private drama. Ford proves expert at conveying throughout the movie the contrasting nature of private and public experience, even when, as in this case, the "public" is very tiny.

And now, a riddle: when is a one-shot an eight-shot? When it's *Citizen Kane*. When his second wife leaves him during a big weekend he has organized in his mansion, Xanadu (yeah, Welles thought big in his satire), he goes ballistic and shreds her room. In truth, it's a little princessy for a woman of her years, but it is what it is. He demolishes everything—until he finds the snow globe we see him drop at the beginning of the film. Needless to say, the ferocity and volume of his tantrum draws a crowd, and he exits the corridor her room is on past a throng of staff and guests, sliding the globe into his jacket pocket as he goes. He walks stiff-legged beyond all of them and into a foyer with facing mirrors. As with everything else in his palace of vanities, they are oversize and extremely elaborate. As Kane walks between them, we see a full shot of him, head-to-toe with plenty of room above, then at least six reflections in what seems an infinite regress of images. And *then* comes the kicker: the real Kane walks into the frame in a medium-close shot, the top of his head and the knuckles of his semi-closed hand filling the frame top to bottom. What we thought we had been watching—Charles Foster Kane in decline—was merely yet another image of him, a trick of light and silvered glass. Once he has passed by, the mirrors show nothing but an empty tunnel. The film is jam-packed with images of isolation and solitude, from single figures in the vastness of the Great Hall to barriers between Kane and other mortals, but this one takes the cake. Here is a man cut off from the rest of humanity, stuck with himself, living in the shell of his shattered dreams. If there is a more profound image of loneliness in the history of film, I don't know what it is.

12

In the Frame

YOU KNOW THAT DUAL-MIRROR TRICK from *Citizen Kane* that we discussed a minute ago? There's more there than just reflections of reflections. Each one of those reflections has something else: an ornate frame. Every one of those mirrors has a frame; stands to reason, when the original two do. So while what we're aware of are repetitions of Charlie Kane, what we also see is frame after frame after, oh, you get it. This may be the culminating, but still only one, instance of frames within the movie. Here are a few others:

- We see the "key" to the whole thing, the sled, through the door of the industrial-strength furnace;

- Kane standing in front of an outsize campaign poster of himself;

- The skylight through which we enter the sad night-club where Kane's second wife, Susan Alexander, drinks and pretends to still be a saloon singer;

- A bored Susan sitting in front of a gigantic stone fireplace in an even more monstrous great room of Xanadu, Kane's castle and monument to himself, working on a jigsaw puzzle;

- Ceilings! The great innovation of the movie (although it was not really the first one), the presence of ceilings inside the frame serves to limit the view—and there-fore the aspirations—of the participants.

- Of that last one, when the enraged Kane trashes Susan's bedroom as she is leaving him, the low ceiling along with the fancifully childish décor emphasizes the doll-like, almost creepy quality of the setting.

These are only a few examples the film offers, but they are essential to the vibe and meaning of the film. They convey information in ways no one has to articulate. For instance, when Susan is assembling her jigsaw puzzle in that cavern-ous room with its great maw of a fireplace, we don't need to hear that it dwarfs her; we can see it. It is not a house but a mausoleum, and the fact that he cannot see that tells us much, if not quite all, we need to know about him. If you would understand the use of frames in film, you could do worse than *Citizen Kane*. And not much better.

Just don't stop there. See a movie, find examples. Any movie. A-n-y movie.

We won't look at just any movie, of course, but at some very fine ones. And before we do, there's an item that requires a bit of sorting. That term, *framing*, has a specific technical meaning in film work. Which in turn has to do with the inevitable frame that is always present: the screen itself. Or, if we were looking at it from the filmmaker's viewpoint, the individual frame of film that is the irreducible minimum of film composition. When light pours through that cell, its contents show up on the frame of our screen—same thing, different perspective. When movie specialists speak of framing a shot, they mean determining how a shot is composed. Many elements go into that act. What visual elements, precisely, are included or excluded? How near or far are they from the camera; that is, do they fill the frame or is there empty space around them? Are they entirely contained by the frame or is part of them lopped off? It makes a difference, for instance, whether we see an entire lamppost or only the post itself and not the light, so that the light seems to emanate from somewhere above the scene. That's framing, and we can't really understand movies without looking at it, which we've done elsewhere.

It is not, however, what we want to contemplate here. Rather, let's look at the frames within the frames. One of the really interesting aspects of movies is how the people in charge of the visuals—directors and cinematographers—use other frames inside the larger rectangle of the screen as a way of controlling the visual field. The next time you're in a movie theater, take a good look at the screen. That's a whole lot of real estate. And depending on not only the movie but the particular spot in the movie, the director will have specific reasons for wanting to direct our attention to one portion or another rather than to the entire screen. If, for instance, there is an establishing shot of the Grand Tetons, then odds are that we are supposed to take in the whole awesome spectacle at once. If, on the other hand, a lone rider begins crossing that vast space on horseback, our attention will soon be drawn to him by, say, zooming slowly in, which will progressively diminish the vista in favor of a closer view of the human figure. In this instance, the framing is accomplished by reducing the amount of territory that the camera takes in as its length and point of focus change. For contrast, imagine the camera taking in our initial vista from a point in front of a homesteader's cabin—same vast sweep. Another way of limiting the view could be for the camera to move—either by dollying through the door or simply by cutting and reestablishing a new shooting position—to the interior of the cabin. Now that vista is reduced to whatever remains visible through the artificial frame of the door. The distance to the mountains is the same as before, but most of the view is hidden by the cabin walls. Not only that, but how we think about the scene will be changed.

That's the technique we want to examine. Happily, there is no shortage of examples; virtually every movie, at some point or other, employs such interior frames to limit, control, emphasize, contrast, combine, separate, and otherwise manage visual elements.

In *The Artist*, for instance, there's a remarkable bit early in the film. The ingénue, Peppy Miller (Bérénice Bejo), has landed a part in a movie starring the cinematic giant George Valentin (Jean Dujardin). In fact, they have just shot their first scene together, one fraught with errors as each discovers that the other one is pretty interesting. When they cut for lunch, Peppy sneaks into George's empty dressing room, writes "Thank you" on his mirror, and stages an amusing and touching bit of business with his evening jacket, causing it to embrace her, only to be interrupted in mid-snuggle by the great man himself. In the ensuing moments, he invests her with her "signature" difference, a grease-penciled mole on her upper lip. Then they examine the mole in his dressing table mirror (missing, maybe too conveniently, the message). In doing so, they realize that their reflections seem to be attracted to one another, and as they straighten up to look at each other, we catch them from a different angle in another mirror, an oval hung on a side wall. The camera pulls back, and we see them being drawn together only to separate, startled, when George's chauffeur, Clifton, bursts into the doorway, having returned from his errand—buying jewelry to mollify George's wife. Now, that is awkward. As one might expect of a movie about the movie business, *The Artist* is shot through with devices that frame, encompass, and sometimes exclude characters or things. It could serve as an instructional text for aspiring filmmakers—and readers—wanting to know how frames work. There are posters and doors and car windows and the screen on which George watches his old movies when he nearly self-immolates and—oh, everything. It is worth watching for all sorts of reasons, but highly worthwhile for this aspect alone.

So then, frames are very important, but they present a problem when shooting a movie: **It's very hard to capture the round world in a rectangular frame.** There are various ways to try to negotiate that conflict, all of them imperfect. We'll dismiss shooting round movies for the moment and concentrate on what can be managed.

- One could, for instance, strive for the most inclusive frame possible, which may partly explain the move toward gigantic screens and formats in the sixties. But it turns out there's only so much visual information we can process at any given moment.

- It might be possible to shoot everything in long, long, long shots to pull in the whole world. That approach tends to lack the personal touch.

- Or, you could cut the world down to size, shoot through or within rooms, automobiles, windows, doors, car windows, windshields, bigger doors, mirror frames, French doors, telephone booths (how filmmakers, to say nothing of Superman, are going to miss those!), closets, and apertures of all sorts.

Of those several items, I vote for that last one. The solution, like the problem, is about more than geometry.

But since we're on geometry, at least in part, here are two gems from the master of images and illusions, Hitchcock. We can range widely over his work, of course, but we can also find what we need in a single film, just two minutes apart, if that film is *Notorious* (1946). Here's the setup: a U.S. intelligence agent, Devlin (Cary Grant), has, on orders, used a playgirl named Alicia Huberman (Ingrid Bergman), notorious both for her lifestyle and for her father, recently convicted as a Nazi spy, to infiltrate a German plot involving atomic bomb research in Brazil. In order to do this, she has to marry one of them, her former admirer Alex Sebastian (Claude Rains), who ultimately finds out that she is a spy and begins, with the help of his scary mother (Leopoldine Konstantin), a sort of *Mater* Hari, to slowly poison her. As Devlin attempts to rescue Alicia from Sebastian's mansion, he is confronted on the stairs by the suspicious husband but overcomes him with threats and bluff. Below, the three main Nazi conspirators emerge from the room where they have been meeting—onto a checkerboard floor, where they array themselves with nearly flawless posture (they are Nazis, after all, and this is one thing Hollywood knows about them). One, the leader, is exactly on a dark square, the one upstage nearly so, while the third and farthest back straddles two, as if trying to make up his mind about a move. Perfect, we think: in a film about using a woman as a pawn, the enemy is arrayed like pieces on a chessboard. In fact, they are more than "arrayed"; they array themselves. Each cut from the stairs back to the floor reveals that one more of them has moved into position, with, ultimately, the most advanced "piece" overtaking the stationary other two. None of these shots lasts more than a couple of seconds, and it is easy to miss, yet—and this is typical of Hitchcock—once we notice, the effect is unmistakable. The other frame is the final one. Devlin forces Sebastian to help get Alicia into the car, then dives in and locks Sebastian out, leaving him to an all-too-certain fate at the hands of his Nazi playmates. One of them summons him back inside, and he mounts the steps of his mansion like a condemned man, which he is, and then, as he crosses the threshold, the massive black door swings shut like the judgment of doom. The scene has already used the frames of the black-and-white squares encompassing the standing figures, as well as doorways to Alicia's room and out the front, but the final, fatal frame of the outsize doorway and the puny Sebastian captures his fate as well as any shot ever has—or could.

This next one is a bit of a special case, but it demonstrates the larger point even while being a one-off. Something you will never notice on a first viewing about Peter Webber's *Girl with a Pearl Earring* (2003) is that there is no framing at the home of the non-artist. The movie begins at the frameless family home of the protagonist, Griet (the very young Scarlett Johansson). The first shot contains a doorway—two, actually, although the second door is closed—but Griet isn't visible in the first until we gain a slight angle through it, and she's never properly framed, as if we can't bring her into focus. Her first framing is literally the moment she enters the Vermeer house; she stops in a doorway. From there, it's Katy-bar-the-door, as it were.

- When she first goes to clean the artist's studio, she pauses in the doorway at the end of the hall, flanked by her two adversaries, Vermeer's wife, Catharina, and his awful daughter, Cornelia. Doors, by the way, work very well in this film: since seventeenth-century doors tended to be low, with wide casings, the effect is of a very pronounced frame, often with little extra space within it.

- She catches a view of herself with the artist's manikin in a mirror.

- Vermeer (a nearly mute Colin Firth) allows her to view the picture he's working on through his new toy, a camera obscura, which captures the image through a lens (something she's never seen) and mirrors.

- Vermeer, half-hidden by a door frame, watches Griet with her hair undone as she prepares to put on the blue scarf that famously appears in the painting. The partial revelation emphasizes the voyeuristic quality of his profession and their relationship. (See also, Hitchcock.)

- When the climax arrives and Catharina storms the ramparts to demand to see the painting, Vermeer removes the painting on which he is currently working. In so doing, he reveals Griet, who is standing in front of a wall of paintings, through the lattice of his tripod. She suddenly goes from a girl standing in front of paintings to an image of a girl standing in front of paintings.

- Once she is dismissed from service in the house by the jealous Catharina, her exit is a series of framed shots. She walks slowly (she does everything slowly in the film) through a door and into a room. To her left, through one open door and in front of another, we see her fellow maid, Tanneke, look up from her sweeping at her departing friend. The shot is *composed* like a painting, lest we miss the point: in the foreground, just before the doorframe, a small, dark chest with a parrot on the stand; slightly beyond that, a circular table with a bright cloth and a candelabrum, then the door, and then Tanneke, sweeping. Griet then moves to the stairs below the studio, where we see her, predictably, from the upper hallway, through yet another aperture. Again, the shot has a very painterly quality—the girl with a bundle under her arm stands before a sturdy balustrade, and beyond that, a large, translucent window. It's a terrific shot. The one we don't get to see, though, would be with one or both of them framed by the studio doorway; she goes to the door, caresses it, but does not open it, while he remains, tormented but predictably silent, within. Even then, she is framed by the corner the wall makes with the frame, and by the sliver of light coming through the barely open door, the lesser shadow that is the wall, and the greater one that is the door itself. It is a highly Vermeer scene. At the far end of the hall, she pauses and looks back one more time, with the same POV as the earlier shot, only this time she is on our level and not below. The last framing of her departure takes place not indoors, as so many have, but on the bridge over the canal, with the houses on either side closing off the view anywhere but straight ahead, toward Griet's departing form.

• Griet's final framing is in the kitchen door of her new house, presumably that of her husband and his father, the butcher. She is seated when we first see her, but rises as Tanneke arrives with a memento: a package containing the cornflower-blue head wrap and the pearl earrings that caused all the fuss.

All of this makes perfect sense: she works in the house of a man whose entire life is devoted to capturing images in frames.

Again and again, we see Vermeer seated in front of a frame, a work in progress of one description or another. We see the painter and his wife view the offending portrait with very different eyes. Griet herself has studied many of the paintings in the studio. And when, at the movie's end, Vermeer's patron, the lecherous Pieter van Ruijven (Tom Wilkinson), sits before the titular work, his response is both appraising and creepy—which is probably the way a great many works of art have been viewed down the years.

On the other hand, who says frames have to be rectangular? One of the most famous is a pointed arch, and it's perfect. Even in movies with the most expansive canvases possible, John Ford manages to carve out human spaces by placing his characters in frames. Sometimes those frames are transparent: stagecoach windows, jail doors or barred walls, exterior or interior doorways (open). Sometimes they are solid: walls of rooms shot so as to encompass the human activity in front of them, spaces between buildings shot from oblique angles so that the side wall of the far building seems to close off the alley, barn or livery interiors. There is even the malleable example of swinging doors of saloons, which can reveal or conceal as the moment demands. Anything to provide a livable scale in the vastness of the desert Southwest. For my money, however, his finest frame has nothing to do with Westerns. Unless we mean the West of Ireland. The glory of *The Quiet Man*, of course, is Winton Hoch's cinematographic love affair with the County Mayo countryside in and around the village of Cong (changed to the more euphonious Innisfree in the picture). But even with all those streams and rock walls and rolling landscapes, the thing that makes the picture are the framing shots: the runaway wife Mary Kate (Maureen O'Hara) peering out the train window, then slumping down and almost out of view from her searching husband, Sean Thornton (John Wayne); the two of them in a tiny cottage with the wind raging in through windows and doors; the crowd parting to make way for Mary Kate at the start of the fight sequence, then forming and re-forming around Sean and Mary Kate's brother, Will Danaher (Victor McLaglen), proving that frames can be mobile and ad hoc; and the bar and the header over it framing the combatants while they take time out for a glass of porter. And doors and windows and low ceilings seemingly everywhere.

Topping them all, however, is the arched window of the ruined abbey. Like a couple of kids, although neither is played for youth, Sean and Mary Kate bolt away from the marriage broker who is chaperoning their stroll from his slow horse-drawn carriage by commandeering a tandem bicycle, then race away until they come to a small stream. In order to ford it, Mary Kate removes her silk stockings, a gesture much appreciated by Sean and that raises the sexual tension between them, and then they race onward, along the way foolishly tossing off their hats—there is a great deal of hat-and-cap business in the film, probably enough for a seminar paper or three in some graduate program. Just as they finally embrace, the unforeseen storm hits, sending a branch down that narrowly misses them. Sean puts his suit coat over Mary Kate's shoulders and they race for the cover of the roofless abbey, hoping the walls will afford some protection. Soaked to the skin, they finish their embrace, adding a passionate kiss, directly in front of the pointed arch of the old monastery's window. With his sodden white shirt and her flaming red hair reduced to soggy curls, they resemble, if only for a moment, a painting that Dante Gabriel Rossetti or some other pre-Raphaelite forgot to paint. Perfect.

Equally effective if somewhat less exulted are the many framing shots in Lawrence Kasdan's *Body Heat*. I mentioned earlier the French doors encompassing the now-suspicious lovers after the murder, one on either side of the open double frame. In some ways, the other shot I mentioned, of Matty serving Ned a drink, is even more interesting. Shot from the outside looking in through floor-to-ceiling windows, it takes in the lovers and reveals, beyond them, French doors opening to the outside in vain hope of catching some cooling breath of air—the utter absence of air-conditioning in contemporary South Florida is one of the great mysteries of the film, but it affords better photography. Throughout the movie we are treated to all manner of framing devices, windows and doors of all shapes and sizes as well as the boxy enclosures of consultation rooms and interrogation rooms. Not for nothing is the bomb Ned uses in an attempt to destroy the evidence of his crime placed behind a door, nor the bomb that seemingly kills Matty behind another door. Utterly fitting, don't you think, for a movie in which one main character is framed by another?

Here's the thing about placing frames around the action: you can accomplish almost anything you want with them. Sometimes directors use them to restrict the real estate of the screen, closing off much of it to focus our attention on a smaller portion. Sometimes they go the other way and expand the frame until it takes in virtually the entire screen. You can push characters farther away by putting the frame between them and the camera or pull them nearer by placing the frame behind them. The size of the frame relative to the characters also conveys information. Here's an experiment you can try on your own: stand two people close to each other and shoot them inside frames of different sizes. For the first, shoot them through a narrow opening so they pretty much fill the frame. For the next, find some considerably wider space and photograph them again. You can expand the project, placing them nearer or farther away from the openings, then moving the camera closer or more distant and keeping the "characters" in the same space. This research requires willing accomplices and patience by all parties, but you will be amazed by your artistry.

What does it tell us if the frame lies completely between two characters? Sounds downright unfriendly, doesn't it? And the farther outside the frame they stand, sit, stroll, lie, or lumber, the more the distance between them will be magnified. Or if the characters are off-center within the frame (not merely on the screen, but within the device that further defines the space). Every such decision conveys critical information about characters and the relationships between or among them.

There's nothing magical with these examples. While I would urge you to see these movies, don't worry about seeing them simply for the examples. Every film has plenty—good ones if it is competently done. What we need to do on our journey toward mastery of the medium is to recognize and understand those devices when they appear. Which is pretty much all the time.

In the course of this book, there is a lot of discussion about film technique. It may not be all that technical, but inasmuch as the aim is to analyze how filmmakers communicate with us, how they use their language to bring us stories that compel, it is about technique. From time to time, however, it behooves us to consider just what that language can accomplish. Movies, you see, rarely stay inside their frame. One way or another, they leap or inch or lurch out into the broader cultural conversation, making points about history or ideas or politics. One of the functions of technique, that is to say, is to get beyond itself, beyond "mere story," to something of larger significance. An example, you say? Sure. Try this:

In *The Grand Budapest Hotel* (2014), director Wes Anderson

offers up a madcap, surrealist version of life between the two great wars. But he does something else very particular: he shows us, visually, the extremely circumscribed life of the inhabitants of that world. Everything about this situation is narrow. Great cars carrying notable guests arrive via a passageway that barely permits their entry. Zero Moustafa (Tony Revolori), the lobby boy, sleeps in a room scarcely wide enough to contain his single bed; later, we find that the concierge, M. Gustave H. (Ralph Fiennes), sleeps in a room scarcely larger and takes his evening meal in an even meaner, smaller space, in his underwear. That pretty well strips away any illusion of grandeur projected by his public persona. In his nightly review of and pep talk to the staff, M. Gustave speaks from an alcove scarcely wider than his lectern but also containing brooms and ash bins, emphasizing its smallness. This alcove appears to be set at right angles to the dining area, equally narrow, so that speaker and audience evidently do not see one another but are each confined in a tiny space. We see Zero and M. Gustave in the tiny elevator with guests, Zero pressed against the back wall; the two of them framed by a railway car, one on either side, while the fascist authorities (who in this fictional world prefer double Z figures to the Nazi SS insignia) occupy the center of the carriage, even as they are framed by the door; Gustave with his accountant and lawyer framed by a tiny window whose frame seems in danger of bursting by the three large heads that fill it; various characters seen within automobile or railway windows; Madame D. (a hilariously made-up Tilda Swinton), one of the elderly ladies for whom the omnisexual M. Gustave has provided special "services," in her coffin; and, well, everywhere. There's hardly a scene in which we are not reminded, in one way or another, of the puniness of these merely human, and delightfully wacky, efforts. In fact, when Gustave is falsely arrested and imprisoned, the tiny spaces and weirdly continuous architecture of the penitentiary don't seem all that different from the Grand Budapest. The uniforms are more drab, but otherwise ...

So what does all this business with tight spaces mean? On some level, of course, anything the movie suggests to you. The two of us, however, don't know each other that well, so I'll limit myself to what I see going on in that constricted space. The movie gives us plenty of hints. The action takes place between the world wars, which was itself a brief moment in history, and even shorter if we consider the interval as lasting not from 1919, with the Treaty of Versailles, until the open outbreak of hostilities in 1939, but as instead ending with the accession of the National Socialists to power in 1933, which is really the first domino in a very long chain of calamity. Beyond that, Gustave is a man hemmed in and limited by the class system. He possesses the bearing and some of the trappings of the upper classes, but he is still stuck in the servant class, however elegant his service may be. We see this conflict in the sudden swings of his behavior from the debonair and obsequious to the crude and boorish. Although he does acquire a fortune late in the film, he is never a member of that blessed group, the Truly Fortunate, those born into wealth and power and ease. In part, naturally enough, that's because he spends only moments of screen time in that lucky state.

Even more than that individual level of restriction, everyone in the film is imperiled by the rise of the heavily uniformed, totalitarian presence represented most clearly by not one but two intrusions of authority into railway carriages in which Gustave and Zero are seated. One is violent but ultimately comic; the other proves fatal. This is a world very much like the actual world between the wars: personal freedom is a scarce and fragile commodity that will soon be snuffed out by a series of menaces that figure in the film (the hotel resides in a mythic country that, like so many others in Eastern Europe, would fall to another brand of absolutism following the war). And that leads us to the final correlative to the physical constraints—time. At the end of the film, the elderly Mr. Moustafa (F. Murray Abraham) says that he believes that Gustave's world had vanished even before he was born into it. Be that as it may, it is certainly true that the five-star, old-line hotels and their upper-crust clientele—indeed, even the sort of privilege conferred more generally on that class—are doomed to a fate as sure and nearly as swift as that of M. Gustave himself.

As the movie progresses, there are sprints down vastly long corridors and up and down staircases that miss M. C. Escher recurring-loop standards by a mere architectural hair and entries into a series of boxes—rooms, to be sure, but boxes nonetheless. The surrealist and absurdist elements build and build on those initial shots of straitened spaces. But neither surrealist nor absurdist art grew in a vacuum: the first developed after and at least partly in response to World War I, the second somewhat more directly out of Nazi occupation and the various resistance movements that tried to subvert it. How else to explain that so many of the existentialists and absurdists—Albert Camus, Samuel Beckett, Eugène Ionesco, Jean-Paul Sartre, Simone de Beauvoir—had direct experience of either fighting against or living under the Nazis? Anderson, something of an absurdist by nature, picks up the connection along with themes of entrapment, meaninglessness, pursuit, and fear, if not quite fear and trembling. And he does so in bizarrely inhuman settings: a transfer of the hunted and their rescuer that involves switching cable cars over a dizzying drop, stairways that lead to stairways that lead to still more stairways, a gunfight across an atrium in which hundreds of shots are fired to no effect but noise, mazelike passageways. That may or may not look like political commentary to you, but in a literary universe in which Ionesco's version of people getting caught up in political mania showed them first denouncing and then turning into rhinoceroses, it works for me.

We've been talking here about frames in particular, but it's worth mentioning that those are only a small part of the larger screen geometry: how bodies and objects move through space on the screen, how they are arranged in terms of each other, how they are presented for maximum effect. Is a character in front of or behind the main action of the scene? Part of the key group or off far left or far right? Seen from above or below? In other words, all those sorts of shots we've talked about. Frames aren't the whole story, but they are a major piece of the story. If you can see frames at work, the rest of that geometry becomes pretty obvious.

13

Highly Generic

QUICK, NAME THAT CATEGORY: *High Noon*, *The Sands of Iwo Jima*, *Star Wars*, *Bringing Up Baby*, *The Big Sleep*, *Annie Hall*, *Scarface*, *Goldfinger*. Give yourself fifty points if you said, Western, war, sci-fi (also accepting space opera, today only), screwball comedy, mystery, romantic comedy, gangster, and spy, although some of our judges place that into a separate category of "Bond, James Bond." Very exacting, those judges. Extra credit, of course, if you put your answers in the form of questions.

Almost every film fits into some familiar category, and each of those has its own set of rules. When a movie is genuinely original and outside genre, it is often genuinely beyond its audience. We know that movies tend to look like other movies, so it comes as little surprise that they fit into a fairly limited

set of categories. Add to that the fairly limited way of thinking about most moneymen (and, to be fair, moneywomen) in
Hollywood—standard movie meeting pitch: "It's *Easy Rider*
meets *Wall Street*," or whatever combination you like—and
you get an idea of why it is that movies look like other movies.
Or part of the reason, anyway.

And now for the tough one: *Blazing Saddles*. Or *Spaceballs*.
Okay, those may be a separate genre called "Mel Brooks," but
in terms of their cinematic family, what are they? Is *Blazing
Saddles* a Western or a comedy? I can hear the truly savvy
among you shouting that it's a parody, which generally means
it is comedic in structure and intent, and that the thing it parodies is the Western.

Genre is just a scary-sounding word that we use in literary
discussions for "type" or "category." Its fear factor comes not
from meaning but from pronunciation (how hard to hit the *g*
and is it "-ruh" or "-er" at the end?), and that, naturally, we can
blame on the French, from whom we lifted it. If, on the other
hand, we use it as an adjective, we are not at all frightened by
generic, which has morphed into good old American pronunciation, and which we use all the time for things not remotely
literary, as in, "He's just a generic politician," meaning he's just
like all the rest of an indistinguishable lot. We don't mean *genre*
in that way, necessarily. For best results, even birds of a feather
have to fly separately. Films may need to be of a type, but they
can't *be* the type, not if they hope to have any staying power. A
detective story that simply repeats all the clichés of every other
detective story is pretty much doomed.

So now that we have the hard part out of the way, let's think
a bit about film genres. What does it mean for a movie to fall
into one? What we usually mean is that it follows certain con-

ventions for telling a certain kind of story. You want to tell a
Western? There are rules and guidelines. Nobody, so far as I
know, ever wrote them down. They filmed them. As we went
from movie to movie with men, horses, six-guns, and tumble-
weeds, a set of practices emerged. Of course, it would matter if
your planned film involved a trail drive, revenge, cowboys and
Indians, or a brave-lawman-against-the-odds. Each of those
subgenres has its own specialized elements. The trail drive
allows you to assemble a motley cast of hands (played by guys
with names like Sheb Wooley), each with his own backstory,
conflicts accruing from their differences, one stampede, two
rattlesnakes, danger from rustlers aimin' to cut out part of
the herd, and gunplay among large boulders. Always with the
boulders. Each type had its own rules, yet they all adhered to
some common elements having to do with the type of hero
(strong, silent), methods of justice (rough), visions of landscape
and sky (big), and quality of chuck wagon coffee (terrible).
If you watch long enough, you'll see a fair bit of variation,
but also a huge amount of sameness: **Genre is a scaffold
that can be both a blessing and a curse.** Yes, that scaffold
provides the familiar structure on which you can drape your
vision, but that very structure is also a curse that limits your
moves. People who know the genre will expect to see certain features—"what do you mean, the coffee is good?"—and
won't be happy if you go mucking around with things.

A funny thing happens, though, with genre. Sometimes a
genre will run its course and die out by virtue (or maybe by
vice) of its own popularity. That is what happened, eventually,
with the Western. But sometimes a visionary comes along to
reinvigorate it. At a time when not only the Western but even
the revisionist Western seemed to have run their courses, Mel
Brooks came out with *Blazing Saddles* (1974), replete with elements no previous tale included, like the connection between

all those beans and flatulence around the campfire. No one said visionaries couldn't be crude.

What we hope for and even sometimes get is a film that expands its genre, showing new possibilities in an old and sometimes tired form. Think of *The Godfather*. By 1972 the gangster film had long since played itself out, and for good reason. Traditional gangsters were largely one-dimensional beings, toughs who ruled with an iron fist until they got their come-uppance in the last reel. They were played by professional tough guys—Edward G. Robinson, James Cagney, George Raft. They were beset by mannerisms and nervous tics, about which we shall talk later. They were unmoored from normal life. But then Mario Puzo and Francis Ford Coppola gave us Don Vito Corleone. First of all, he's not played by a professional thug but by very likely the greatest actor of his generation, Marlon Brando. He is not portrayed as the conventional hard case. Don't get me wrong: he is capable of plenty of violence (in many ways much more violence than the old crowd). But he's a family man. He has kept one son, Michael, free of the family business, hoping to launch him in a legitimate career. He takes care of his community, of his extended "family." No, it's not altruism, but he has a sense of responsibility to those he "pro-tects." Most important, he seeks peace among the Five Families of crime lords of New York. And *that* was not something the gangster flick had seen before.

So can genres die? Maybe not forever, but on some level, absolutely. Consider the Western. If you're under the age of, say, forty, how many have you personally ever seen at the mul-tiplex? That's what I thought. There was a day, however, when the cowboy was king. We had cowboys cleaning up tough

towns, cowboys subduing Indians, even cowboys finding a
way to get along with Indians (although this was rare), cowboys facing down their nemeses, and sometimes even cowboys
herding cows. But let's face it: there are only so many things
you can do with cowboys, and after the industry has made, oh,
say, ten thousand Westerns, those have been done. And done.
And done. This realization set in around 1960 or so, when
Hollywood made one of the last of the truly great Westerns,
The Magnificent Seven. Of course, the studios didn't all get
that memo. John Wayne had a number of films in the sixties
in the same, tired vein of his greatest movies, some Westerns
and some disguised Westerns with Wayne as, say, a cop or a
soldier, but it wasn't until his films changed things up that his
movies got interesting again. His two Rooster Cogburn films,
True Grit (1969) and *Rooster Cogburn* (1975), along with the
late Westerns *The Cowboys* (1972) and *The Shootist* (1976),
bring out possibilities in the form and in Wayne that few of
us might have suspected. Yes, he had been involved in revising
the Western since at least the mid-fifties with *The Searchers*, but
filmmakers kept reverting to form with him, going to the well
once and twice and ten times too often.

The Shootist, his last film, is particularly telling. The story of
a dying gunfighter played by an actor who had already had
his brush with death when his entire left lung was removed in
battling cancer in 1964 and who knew his own time was limited, it is full of references to the past—Wayne's and the Western's, which, much as it may seem so, are not always the same
thing. The movie boasts roles by Jimmy Stewart (*The Man
Who Shot Liberty Valance*), Richard Boone (*The Alamo, Big Jake*),
Harry Morgan (*Big Jim McClain, How the West Was Won*), Hugh
O'Brian (longtime friend and the last man the Duke ever killed
on-screen), and most notably perhaps John Carradine, another
passenger in the stagecoach Wayne rode to stardom. It also has
a young Ron Howard, still early in his stint as Richie Cun-

ningham on television's *Happy Days*. One of these things is not like the other. Which is the point, really. Or sort of the point. If the presence of Ron Howard among these grizzled veterans suggests nothing else, it signifies that times have changed on the outside of the film. On the inside, too. Westerns in 1976 can never be as simple and clean as they were in 1915 or 1939 or even 1951. There's too much baggage from all that slaughter in all those movies. *Stagecoach* had clear-cut good guys and bad guys. Sure, the Ringo Kid has broken out of the penitentiary, which means he was in it, but he has a good reason, and anyway, it turns out he was framed. *High Noon*, too. There's never any doubt who's the good guy there. Gary Cooper's face registers his character's distaste for the task at hand in almost every frame. Here, not so much. Wayne's character, J. B. Books, is trying to find a way to die quickly and honorably. He eventually finds that way in a group gunfight in the saloon, settling old scores and new challenges with three other gunfighters, whom he kills but not before being mortally wounded. The fatal shot, however, is delivered by the barkeep, who sneaks up behind Books and shoots him in the back. It falls to the callow Gillom Bond (Howard), to take up the old shootist's revolver and kill the assassin. Appalled, Gillom flings the gun away, earning an approving nod from the expiring Books. It's 1901. Books arrived at the final gunfight via trolley, Richard Boone's Mike Sweeney in a Curved Dash Oldsmobile, which only appeared earlier that year. Books has even given away his horse to Gillom. They don't make 'em like they used to.

Maybe they never did. Or maybe we eventually learned the lessons contained in all those shoot-'em-ups. Whatever it was, the Western changed. Throughout the latter half of the sixties and all of the seventies, we got what were known as revisionist Westerns, films that skewered the myth of the Old West. A revisionist work is one that revises or reimagines the form it employs. The foremost exponent of these revisions is, of course,

Sergio Leone. What Leone in particular did with his "spaghetti Westerns" was focus our attention on that ambiguous nature of good and evil in that myth of the West. His heroes, whether Clint Eastwood's Man with No Name or Charles Bronson's Harmonica, may work on the right side of the divide, but they are by no means "good" men, whatever that might mean. They are as willing as anyone to take unfair advantage in a fight, and their motives are hardly ever clear. In the climactic three-way shoot-out at the end of *The Good, the Bad and the Ugly*, for instance, Eastwood's character stacks the deck by having stolen the ammunition from one of his opponents, knowing that he had only to worry about the third man. Gary Cooper never did that. Leone also takes other Western tropes and upends them, often by stretching them to preposterous lengths. If the cowpoke hero is taciturn, his versions are silent. We find ourselves wanting to scream at them to just talk, for crying out loud. If pauses are central to the shoot-out dynamic, he elongates them to unbearable lengths. The opening to *Once Upon a Time in the West*, as I discuss elsewhere, could be subtitled, with apologies to John Cage, "Seven Minutes of Silence." It is followed, of course, by three seconds of mayhem. In short, the Leone treatment calls into question just about everything on which the classic Western is based.

But others got in on the act as well, from George Roy Hill (*Butch Cassidy and the Sundance Kid*, 1969), Sam Peckinpah (*The Wild Bunch*, the same year, about more or less the same folks), Robert Altman (*McCabe and Mrs. Miller*, 1971), and Clint Eastwood, who absorbed enough of the new genre through Leone's "Dollars" trilogy (*A Fistful of Dollars*, *For a Few Dollars More*, and *The Good, the Bad and the Ugly*) and then his next few films to become its most accomplished director. He directed the morally troubling foursome of *High Plains Drifter* (1973), *The Outlaw Josie Wales* (1976), *Pale Rider* (1985), and *Unforgiven* (1992). For many directors, that would be a good career. For Eastwood, it barely scratches the surface. In those movies, we learn that the less said, the better, that violence is bad but gratifying, that people with noble motives sometimes do terrible things, that evil is always present and taints even the innocent, that help can come from surprising sources, and that Clint Eastwood mystery men can vanish and reappear at will.

As does the form itself. So what if, say, Quentin Tarantino did his own revisionist Western? What if he turns the strong, silent trope on its head in his late horse operas, which are self-conscious revisions of the revisionist Westerns? We'll just avoid labels at this point. In both *Django Unchained* (2012) and *The Hateful Eight* (2015), as in so many of his other movies, characters talk their heads off. With few exceptions, these are the chattiest terrible people you'd ever care to meet—or not meet, given their murderous intentions. Tarantino has long been known for his fondness for genre pictures as platforms on which to build his not-quite-genre pictures. The former film is a revenge tale set in pre–Civil War Mississippi, with Jamie Foxx as a former slave bent on liberating his wife from a particularly despicable slave owner (Leonardo DiCaprio) and who learns the Way of the Gun in order to effect that rescue. *The Hateful Eight* is a new take on the spaghetti Western: not a single one of the scoundrels and lowlifes provides a character to root for. The title may recall John Sturges's *The Magnificent Seven*, one of the early revisionist Westerns that moves the genre toward its Italian reimagining, but there's no magnificence here, except in the landscape. Tarantino, moreover, has alerted us to see his film in terms of its Italian antecedents by enlisting Ennio Morricone, the man who gave Sergio Leone's films their sound, to compose the first full score for any of his movies. Or maybe film is the wrong place to look for antecedents. Maybe the correct precursor here is Luigi Pirandello's play *Six Characters in Search of an Author*. The film does have that sort of existential-crisis element, with characters concerned with matters of being and nonexistence amid whole-sale slaughter. Part of renewing a form is to make it strange once more, to cause viewers to look at it again with new eyes, to see possibilities it never before possessed.

As Tarantino's example shows, what dies can be reborn. Once upon a time in the movies, buckles were swashed. Mostly by Errol Flynn, but there were others. *Captain Blood. Fortunes of Captain Blood. The Son of Captain Blood. The Sea Hawk. The Sea Hound. Scaramouche.* Yes, novelist Rafael Sabatini was implicated. Frequently. But others, too. *The Scarlet Pimpernel. The Count of Monte Cristo. The Man in the Iron Mask. Against All Flags. Treasure Island. Long John Silver. Return to Treasure Island.* Remakes of *Treasure Island.* Remakes of *Return to Treasure Island. Son of Return to Treasure Island.* Okay, I made that last one up, but you get the idea.

They started right away. D. W. Griffith made *The Pirate's Gold* in 1908, and J. Searle Dawley followed in 1912 with the first adaptation of *Treasure Island.* Once they started in earnest, Hollywood hit chasers made about one pirate escapade a year through the thirties and forties, then kicked things up a few notches in the fifties, with three each in 1950 and 1951, a whopping ten in 1952, and on and on. And eventually, they exhausted the genre. Oh, pirates kept hitting the big screen, but the formula had suffered beyond the point of indignity. When you reach the stage of *The Son of Captain Blood* being played by the son of Errol Flynn, you pretty much know the form is a goner. When *Peter Pan* becomes *Peter Pan and the Pirates* and then *Hook*, it's pretty clear there is no end to Hollywood's lack of inventiveness. And when the Muppets arrive on the scene, all hope is lost. But things are funnier. Parody becomes parody of the parody. So imagine my enthusiasm when Disney, with a long track record of repackaging Flubber and Volkswagens, announced it was going to make a movie. About pirates. Based on a ride.

Seriously? Another pirate movie? A trilogy, no less. Based on a five-minute ride. What were they thinking? You must be joking. They weren't, although the films are pretty jokey. So what *were* they thinking about? About four billion or so.

But here's the thing: *Pirates of the Caribbean* is not your father's buccaneer movie. It has pieces of all of them but deploys those pieces in quotation marks, as it were. Here are some of the things that audiences have always loved about those movies: elegant ships, winds and salt breezes, thrilling if slow-motion chases, colorful and seedy characters, grog, wenches, cannon fire, boarding, swinging from ropes, swordfights, eye patches, peg legs, hooks, parrots, and really cool outfits. Who has not at some point wanted those tall, tall boots, those shirts with blousy sleeves?

The problem is that, as with most things, pirates on film reach a saturation point. What do you do when you—and Joe and Roberta and Jim and Mary and Michael Curtiz—have done everything there is to do with pirates? You repeat yourself. Endlessly. How many planks can be walked, how many enemy ships boarded before we've seen every trick that a plank or a grappling hook knows? Same with Westerns: after a while, the gunfights all look the same. How many trickles of sweat, how many twitchy trigger fingers, how many steely stares had we all seen when the genre finally rolled over on its back and pointed its feet skyward? The problem is that at a certain point—and that point often comes fairly early in a genre's history—the form is reduced to self-parody. Pretty soon, everything that happens on-screen takes place in invisible quotation marks. For a while, that's okay, since it makes viewing easy and comfortable for audiences. But when that happens in enough movies (say, all of them), the form is a goner;

Figure 7. Errol Flynn as Captain Blood.
Licensed By: Warner Bros. Entertainment. All Rights Reserved.

there ceases to be any originality, and the films just seem tired and sad. Self-parody, especially if it occurs unself-consciously, can be the death knell of an artistic form, whether cinematic, musical, dramatic, visual, or literary. Eventually, we don't need more Impressionist paintings, whatever Sotheby's might wish.

At those times, parody is exactly what a genre needs to expand its horizons—or shut it down for good. Before we discuss particulars, a small definitional moment is in order. When we use *parody* in ordinary discussion, we generally mean a warped copy of an original involving brittle humor and a topical focus, which gives the copy, therefore, a limited shelf life. Yes, Weird Al Yankovic making a hash of Michael Jackson's "Beat It" with "Eat It" or turning Madonna's "Like a Virgin" into "Like a Surgeon" certainly qualifies as parody—and embodies nearly all the qualities most of us associate with

Figure 8. Johnny Depp as Captain Jack Sparrow.
Courtesy of Jesse Grant / Getty Image Entertainment.

the term. Literary critics, however, take a somewhat different view of the word. Following the great Russian formalist
critic Mikhail Bakhtin, they generally take parody to mean
any use of source material for purposes other than the original
intention. By this definition, Weird Al's oeuvre (the imitative
portion, but not his original comic songs) certainly qualifies.
So would Woody Allen's *Love and Death*, which puts the fun in
War and Peace. Allen uses many conventions of not only Tolstoy
but several of the great Russian novelists in order to upend
them. But so would the revisionist Western or the neo-noir
film, a genre so perennially popular that it is in constant need
of repurposing.

Consider film noir. From Mervyn LeRoy's *The Public
Enemy* (1931) through Carol Reed's *The Third Man* (1949),
the genre was huge. For about a generation, it packed theaters
and charted a rebellious course during the restrictive, Hayes
Office censorship period, frequently building on the suspense,

menace, and general dim view of humanity seen in the novels of James M. Cain (*The Postman Always Rings Twice*), Dashiell Hammett (*The Maltese Falcon*, *Red Harvest*), Raymond Chandler (*The Big Sleep*; *Farewell, My Lovely*), and Patricia Highsmith (*The Talented Mr. Ripley*, *Strangers on a Train*). The *noir* in *film noir*, from the French for black, is generally taken to allude to dark settings and dark film stock used to film the early examples, but it could also refer to the dark view of human nature, dark actions, and dismal prospects for outcomes for the protagonists. Roger Ebert, in defining the genre in an entirely tongue-in-cheek—although less accurate for that—entry in *Roger Ebert's Journal* from 1995, says that one of the hallmarks is that no one involved, audience included, is able to harbor any illusions that this movie will end happily, adding that such a bleak genre is the most purely American form since it could only be created by a nation "as naïve and optimistic" as ours. Other elements he identifies are fedoras and heavy mascara (not inevitably on the same characters), plunging necklines, cigarettes, fear and betrayal, murder, doom, fate, "women who would just as soon kill you as love you (and vice-versa)," and use of black-and-white film or color that looks as if it should have been black and white. Not the most theoretical analysis, but you'll not find a better list.

Golden eggs, however, can spell doom for the goose that provides them. Noir had pretty clearly run its course in the forties and fifties. After some time off, as in a couple of decades, a new generation thought maybe there was some life in the old gal after all. Not surprisingly, one of the leaders of this particular parade was the selfsame Woody Allen, who has a nearly unerring radar for targets for comedy, in *Play It Again, Sam* (1972), in which a recently single man gets help with his sad-sack love life from Humphrey Bogart, the über-star of the noir era. Go straight to the top, right? A much more serious reenvisioning of the form came two years later in Roman

Polanski's *Chinatown*. As with Sam Spade and Philip Marlowe in earlier movies, the film's hero, if that is the word, Jake Gittes (Jack Nicholson), is a private eye drawn into a case under false pretenses. The case devolves into lies, betrayals, a beautiful and dangerous woman (the great Faye Dunaway, who could be the right woman in pretty much every noir film ever made), some very grisly violence that never could have made it into the scene under the Production Code, and some frankness about sex (ditto). Gittes has some disadvantages, among them his name—is it one syllable? Two? And the sound is just anemic next to Spade and Marlowe—and a lack of the hypercompetence of his famous predecessors. He's always about a step slow, and when he finally figures things out, his success proves ruinous.

Throughout the seventies and eighties and beyond we saw a cascade of neo-noir films, from remakes like *Against All Odds* (1984; original *Out of the Past*, 1947), *The Postman Always Rings Twice* (1981; same name, 1946), *Body Heat* (1981; *Double Indemnity*, 1944) to new imaginings, or at least adaptations of new sources, such as *Klute* (1971), *Shaft* (also 1971, breaking the "color line" for noir films), *Taxi Driver* (1976), the Coen brothers' *Blood Simple* (1984) and *Fargo* (1996), David Lynch's *Blue Velvet* (1986, showing just how frightening Dennis Hopper could be), Quentin Tarantino's *Reservoir Dogs* (1992) and *Pulp Fiction* (1994) and pretty much everything else, *Basic Instinct* (1992), and *Road to Perdition* (2002). There were also, following Allen's example, comedies and parodies including *Throw Momma from the Train* (1987; *Strangers on a Train,* 1951), Carl Reiner's *Dead Men Don't Wear Plaid* (1982), and *The Cheap Detective* (1978), as well as sci-fi/noir mash-ups including *Soylent Green* (1973), Ridley Scott's *Blade Runner* (1982), and *Minority Report* (2002). Whew! And that's only a few.

You're obviously not going to sit still while I natter on about all these films, so let's focus on just a couple. Since we've already mentioned *Body Heat*, let's stay with that one for another moment. The film introduced us to (and made major stars of) William Hurt and Kathleen Turner as well as Ted Danson, soon to shoot to fame on *Cheers*, and a skinny, motor-mouthed Mickey Rourke. The lone veteran of note was Richard Crenna, far from the hayseed comedy of *The Real McCoys* television series as the husband (and victim in waiting) of Turner's Matty Walker. Of perhaps greater significance (if anything can be greater than the debut of Kathleen Turner) was the attitude the movie displayed toward its famous predecessors, *Double Indemnity* and *Out of the Past*. Kasdan has shown himself to be not just a brilliant writer and director but also a great film reader and historian. His Indiana Jones movie (although he only wrote the screenplay for *Raiders*) catches every nuance of the Saturday afternoon adventure serial, including both the fedora and bullwhip, both cribbed from various postwar movie heroes. The result, however, is anything but the low-rent, throwaway installment films of childhood memory; certainly Steven Spielberg's direction helps, but between the two of them, the whip, the hat, the hair-raising escapes, and dotted-line maps fairly scream out their status as cultural artifacts being self-consciously employed in service of a postmodern sensibility. His later *Silverado* (1985) similarly uses almost every signifying aspect of the Western to make a movie that is a "Western," with the quotation marks clearly in evidence.

So what elements of film noir does this film exploit? All of them, including possibly one or two no one had previously noticed. Let's begin our list with cigarettes. As Ebert mentioned in his list, you simply can't make a noir without smoke, but who knew that smoking (and even smoking hot) could be so darned funny? Cigarettes form one basis for the affair between Matty (Turner) and Ned Racine (Hurt); the other is rather more obvious. Beyond that, however, *everyone* smokes. With

two exceptions. One of those is a child. The other is the pros-
ecutor, Peter Lowenstein (Danson). At one point, a meeting is
convened around a conference table. When the group is permitted to light up, every single one of them does except Peter,
who on being offered one demurs, saying that he'll just breathe
in smoke from the rest of them. Smoking rates were still somewhat higher in 1981 than in the early twenty-first century, but
even so, finding that many tobacco users in one group, outside of the offices of R. J. Reynolds, was pretty dubious. The
distance between the film's release and the era of classic noir,
when around half of adults did in fact smoke, permits sufficient
perspective to poke some fun at the convention. So too with
sweat. In the classic noirs, people are always sweating; that's
how we know they're hot and bothered. Achieving this level
of personal overheating would seem a problem in the modern
sexy thriller, yet *Body Heat* takes place in a contemporary South
Florida that, as I mentioned earlier, has conveniently forgotten about air-conditioning. The movie starts with Ned's latest
coital playmate complaining about the heat, saying that she has
just stepped from the shower (a fact we can confirm) and is
already sweating. In the eighties, you would have to go a fair
distance down-market to find a Florida motel that didn't have
conditioned air. Later, Matty and Ned go through a lot of ice
to cool themselves off after trysting, as if the fifties had never
ended. Just another wonder of the Dream Factory.

Then there's the matter of the femme fatale, the woman who
kills with sex. *Les femmes fatales* in the classic era were vamps, to
be sure, with mystery, sexuality, and danger aplenty, but parts of
their makeup (and their persons) had to be hidden. Hard to let
out one's inner harlot from inside all those constraints. And I
don't mean foundation garments. Seriously, open-mouth kissing was one of the forbidden displays under the studio system's self-censorship. If you couldn't show *that*, what hope was
there for nudity and sex? Right? Happily, Kathleen Turner was

under no such constraints. Or much in the way of garments for large chunks of the movie. We know how sexual she is because we *see* how sexual she is. No need to extrapolate from the mass of molten gunk that was once Ned Racine's brain. She is able to be frank and open in her performance, and she makes the most of that liberty. There will always be those who say that such matters work best when more is left to the imagination. Maybe, but I very much doubt it. She's as sexy and devious and farsighted and just plain wicked as any femme fatale you could ever hope to meet. Or be afraid you might. Moreover, what every femme fatale needs is a hapless male, and few in film history are as hapless as William Hurt's Ned. A man who thinks he is a player despite all evidence to the contrary, Ned has no idea as to the depths of his cluelessness. The late critic Northrop Frye described a type of character, the *alazon*, the bumbling but self-important type who is easily fooled, as someone "who doesn't know that he doesn't know." That's Ned right there. If only he had any awareness at all of his limitations, he might be able to save himself, but he hasn't and so he can't. This may be a match made a few steps south of heaven, but it's wonderful for the movie.

Speaking of sex, does it strike anyone else as odd that an entire film genre could spring up around the one thing that it couldn't depict? In the heyday of noir, it was mostly clear what the couples were getting up to, but the Production Code allowed none of the stuff that would convince us they were really *that* hot to trot. No problem in 1981. The end of the movie code meant that Matty and Ned could be as overtly sexual (and the sex could be as overt) as such people really would be, thank goodness.

Then there is the dialogue. Characters in noir films don't talk like ordinary people. Their language is elevated, supercharged, fraught with meaning and subtext. The dialogue in *Body Heat*, as with most neo-noir films, is highly stylized:

Matty:	My temperature runs a couple of degrees high, around a hundred. I don't mind. It's the engine or something.
Ned:	Maybe you need a tune-up.
Matty:	Let me guess. And you have just the right tool.
Ned:	I don't talk that way.

Ned's line, delivered deadpan, is the funniest, since from the beginning of the movie that's the only way we've heard him talk. The risk with this sort of dialogue is that not everyone gets it. Not long after its release, I sat in on a screenwriting class in which an otherwise intelligent student opined that the film wasn't much good. His reason? That the dialogue wasn't "realistic." Of course not, someone else (not me) fairly shouted, "It's stylized." That led to a short explanation of stylized dialogue's salient features. In the original films, language had to be stylized to talk about the things that couldn't be spoken of directly. That is no longer a problem, and neo-noir films can (and do, especially if directed by Tarantino) use blunt Anglo-Saxonisms for sex and the relevant body parts, so that we're not entirely surprised when Peter says, "Ned, someday your dick is going to lead you into a very big hassle." Never heard Fred MacMurray say *that*.

My favorite neo-noir film? It has a femme fatale, plenty of bad behavior, a flummoxed detective, a lot of serious danger, a truly villainous bad guy, and an entirely goofy lead with long ears. When *Who Framed Roger Rabbit* came out in 1988, what everyone noticed first was that not only did it mix live characters with animated ones but that all of them lived in a world where living humans interacted with cartoon characters on the same plane of existence. In 1947 greater Los Angeles, cartoon characters, called Toons, live in Toontown, near Hollywood, interact with humans and animals as near-neighbors would, and go to work making movies just like humans, although the

contraptions they drive through the studio lot gate are sometimes a little wacky.

Less noticed was the way director Robert Zemeckis and
screenwriters Peter S. Seaman and Jeffrey Price integrated
all the characteristics of noir drama into a world of cartoon
comedy. Rather than hide the conflicts in genre, the film
emphasizes them. Eddie Valiant (Bob Hoskins) is a Toon-hating
detective who nevertheless takes a job for studio head R. K.
Maroon on behalf of Toon star Roger Rabbit because he needs
the money. The gig is to tail Roger's wife, Jessica, who is voiced
by an uncredited Kathleen Turner and drawn in a way that
puts Barbie dolls to shame in the improbable anatomy department, because Maroon fears she's playing patty-cake (hey, it's a
cartoon) with someone else. As with any good noir movie—
and many bad ones—the case soon becomes something else
when the owner of Toontown and the Acme Corporation,
one Marvin Acme, is found dead, with Roger as the prime
suspect. Predictably, this throws Eddie together with the most
toonish of Toons, Roger, whose antics push all of the grumpy
detective's buttons. Eddie was once friendly with the Toon
community, until some years earlier when his brother was
killed by a Toon who, in a standard cartoon trope, dropped a
piano on him. Toons, as the Brothers Warner taught us, can be
squashed flat and bounce back instantly; humans, not so much.
The case, then, proves a severe trial for the unhappy Eddie,
trying to save a character whom he spends most of his time
wanting to throttle. Add to the basic setup a sex siren (Jessica)
who may or may not be a femme fatale, a lot of stylized period
dialogue, including some tough-talking bullets (again, anything
is possible in Toontown), some bad-guy antics from a predictably over-the-top Christopher Lloyd, and you've got yourself a
bona fide noir send-up.

Much of the dialogue is priceless, combining the best, or at
least the most clichéd, of both genres. A truly great line comes

by way of apology from Jessica Rabbit, who in explaining herself says, "I'm not really bad, I'm just drawn that way." That same husky whisper of Kathleen Turner says similar things in *Body Heat*; indeed, it could explain every femme fatale character from the beginning of time.

Every once in a while some performance comes along that makes you seriously reevaluate what you thought you knew. Such a moment came in the late sixties when Sergio Leone cast Henry Fonda as the villain in *Once Upon a Time in the West*. Henry. Fonda. We're talking about the man who was Wyatt Earp, Mr. Roberts, Tom Joad, for crying out loud. Turns out, he was quite convincing as a soulless killer. With 2002's *Road to Perdition*, we got not one such performance but two: Tom Hanks as mob hit man Michael Sullivan and Paul Newman as his boss, mob leader John Rooney. That would be Forrest Gump murdering people at the behest of Butch Cassidy. Worse, by that point, Newman was best known to a younger generation as the foody-philanthropist head of Newman's Own products. Needless to say, this was a stretch, more for viewers than for the actors. And the film they find themselves involved in is full-on noir. A little shy on femmes fatales, but otherwise possessed of all the tropes. There are murders, chases, ambushes, betrayals, double-crosses, and double-double-crosses. Sullivan, raised as a son by Rooney, eventually has need not only to kill Rooney but to wipe out his entire entourage. He, in turn, is killed by another hit man (Jude Law), whom he disfigured in fighting off a previous attack, but not before killing the hit man to protect his son both from being killed or becoming a killer in his turn. Indeed, Michael's love for Michael Jr. is his sole good quality, which gives him one more than any other adult in the movie. The role of Rooney may not have been such a stretch for Newman, who had played mystery writer Ross Macdonald's Lew Archer (renamed Harper) twice, in *Harper* (1966) and *The Drowning Pool* (1975), although even in these noirish films he plays the hero. And of course he played a number of edgy or compromised heroes over his long career. Tom Hanks, on the other hand, was cast clearly against type, stretching both the actor and the genre. A service to both. He's no crook with a heart of gold. Rather, he plays a cold-blooded killer who is nevertheless a family man and determined to protect the one remaining member of that family. We find a morsel to admire in an otherwise contemptible man. In a genre where even the heroes are seriously flawed, that's about all we can hope for.

So there you have something like sixty or seventy years of movie history in which noir features prominently, from *The Maltese Falcon* in 1941 or *Little Caesar* in 1931 forward to *Road to Perdition* right after the turn of the millennium. Nor does the noirish machinery slow down very much. Much of the work of the Coen brothers—*Fargo, The Big Lebowski, The Man Who Wasn't There*, even *No Country for Old Men* (although we could argue all evening about whether that one is a noir, a Western, or a noir-Western)—and Quentin Tarantino—*Reservoir Dogs, Pulp Fiction, Jackie Brown*, even *Inglourious Basterds*—has been informed by noir. *The Big Lebowski*, in particular, offers clear insights. The Coens have said that the movie was inspired by Raymond Chandler's mysteries and by *The Long Goodbye* specifically. There are numerous parallels here: the crime that is not a crime (kidnapping this time, murder in the original), danger to the protagonist despite the hoax, numerous misleading and strange characters, and a final unmasking of the hoaxster. Yet Chandler could not have imagined the Dude (Jeff Bridges) or the nature of the action, in part because what passed for kinky in the forties couldn't possibly contend with the kinkiness of a half-century later. And while he could be wry in his humor, he is rarely laugh-out-loud funny in the way *Lebowski* is. We could probably compile a very long list of contemporary noir films, or at least those with significant noir elements, from David Fincher's *Girl with the Dragon Tattoo* to

Robert Rodriguez's *Sin City* and on and on. Like so many of its heroes, it's a tough genre to kill.

The history of film is full of genre reinvention. Often, that has meant the path of revisionist Westerns or noir films, in which important forms are revived, but at other times it has involved rescuing some lightly regarded form from the scrap heap of movie history. From the position of the twenty-first century, it may be hard to recall that at one time, serious filmmakers wanted nothing to do with science fiction, particularly of the space-opera variety, and they believed that Saturday serials of the Cisco Kid or Flash Gordon sort (proving that there was overlap with sci-fi in the prejudice) only existed to fill the time between the cartoon and the feature—or maybe the time until the ascendency of Saturday morning television. But then George Lucas and Steven Spielberg came along to give us two of the most successful franchises in cinema history, the Star Wars and Indiana Jones sagas, after which it became impossible to imagine the world without lightsabers and bullwhips. In a very different arena, a raft of newer creative minds—among them Rob Reiner, Norman Jewison, Nora Ephron, Mike Nichols, and Garry Marshall—reimagined the romantic comedy during the eighties and nineties. Among them, we might say that without Nora Ephron's contribution, the romantic comedy might have remained an occasional place to visit and not a genre sufficiently robust to have its own nickname, the rom-com. Sure, there were others even beyond the ones we listed, but the woman who adapted her own novel *Heartburn* as a Meryl Streep–Jack Nicholson vehicle (1986) and then wrote *When Harry Met Sally . . .* (1989) for Rob Reiner to direct, then went on to write and direct a number of other movies in the genre, most notably *Sleepless in Seattle* (1993) and *You've*

Got Mail (1998), was clearly a trailblazer. What she and others saw were the possibilities that shifting sexual mores and politics permitted: greater frankness about sexuality meant things could be said and shown that had never been available in the genre's initial heyday. It is impossible to imagine the restaurant fake orgasm scene from *When Harry Met Sally . . .* in any film starring Spencer Tracy and Katharine Hepburn, even *Adam's Rib*, with its racy (for 1949) scenes of the married characters giving each other bare-skin massages. For this new freedom we must credit *The Graduate* (1967) and director Mike Nichols, who stands as one of the few links between the "end" of the classic era of rom-coms and the beginning of their renaissance. Predictably, the genre has become raunchier during the new era as filmmakers endeavor to find new ground. Perhaps this is simply a balancing of the scales against all those movies from the classic era that pretended that in all that romance there was no role for sex. More to the point, the experimentation with the form is necessary; without it, as we have seen again and again, genres become moribund.

Sometimes, a movie or series can become its own genre. The various Star Wars movies aren't really like anything else in the cinematic universe. The same can be said for the Jurassic Park series. Nobody ever quite did *that* with dinosaurs before. And then there's life and death on the road. There had been road pictures before George Miller. Post-apocalyptic pictures, too. I suppose if we pushed hard enough we could find a post-apocalyptic road picture somewhere, at sometime, by someone. But there had never been anything quite like *Mad Max*. Miller brought to those existing genres a gothic imagination and an inventiveness about modifying vehicles—imposed by limited finances—both of which developed further in subsequent installments. Both the vision and the execution led some early reviewers to dismiss the first movie as some sort of trashy B-movie. By the time he arrived at *Mad Max: Fury Road*, not only had his vision matured and deepened, but both the automotive creations and the action sequences in which they feature had become considerably more baroque. Indeed, it was suggested in some reviews that the movie is one long chase sequence, and while that isn't entirely accurate, it contains enough truth to give readers a sense of the movie. What the post-apocalyptic road becomes, however, isn't merely one long shoot-'em-up, although that element plays an outsize role. Rather, it stands as an instrument for character development, social commentary, environmental engagement, and gender politics. It shares that depth of development with its famous predecessor in the human conveyance road film genre, *Stagecoach*, even if the two seem superficially to have nothing to do with one another. In each, after all, a disparate and even nominally opposed group of characters are thrown together in an incredibly dangerous situation (and there's even a pregnant woman in each) during which they are allowed to grow, develop, or fail to do so. There are numerous occasions for nobility, cowardice, courage, and self-sacrifice. And you thought it was just dust out on the road! George Miller is not John Ford, however, and his vision expresses itself in quite different ways.

Here's the thing. Every genre has its conventions. Those may develop over time, ossify into cliché, wear out their welcome, become available for parody and satire, but they exist because they are used, and they become a sort of shorthand for the type of movie we're currently watching. Those conventions vary widely; we would hardly expect to see those of the Western show up in a romantic comedy or of a space opera in a monster mash-up, but savvy creators can sometimes borrow from other genres to startling and hilarious effect. The key is to know that genres exist and to begin noticing the conventions and how they apply. From there, anything is possible.

14

Novels into Films

Now, class, for this exercise you will need a sheet of paper divided into two columns. In one column, name all the great films that have come from great novels. In the other, name all the disappointing movies and outright failures that have come from great novels. Take your time; I've got all day.

What's that you say? You only need one column?

A bit harsh, don't you think? There have been, to be fair, a few great movies to come out of great novels. Probably more than it seems at first blush. Of course, to establish that fact, we would have to agree on what constitutes a great novel. And a great film. We'll come back to those points in a bit. For now, though, let's just consider what happens when the page hits the screen.

What we want to consider, ultimately, is how to think about movies that grow out of books—novels, memoirs, histories, biographies. What happens to them on their way to the big screen? How should we think about those changes and the films that result? Is it possible to have a perfect adaptation? In order to answer these questions, we need to look at the process of adaptation itself.

Sometimes it works, sometimes it doesn't. What's the difference, and can we predict the outcomes? It's not always about literary quality. In fact, hardly ever. In that special category of movie Hell reserved for comprehensive failure of vision, work done in bad faith or bad understanding, we must put the terrible or ludicrous or wholly misguided attempts to bring excellent novels to the Odeon. And here, I'm not talking about the failures that are due to exigencies: the director dies mid-shoot or money runs out before everything can be accomplished or any of a hundred shocks to which Hollywood flesh is heir. No, here we must mean the shallow or halfhearted takes on novels, the venal attempts to capitalize on a title, the star vehicles for stars wholly unsuited to the material. In other words, the great mass of adaptations, since, like the great mass of everything, they're terrible. If 90 percent of everything is dreck, and you know it is, it stands to reason that the same percentage of movies from books will be, too. There are so many ways to go wrong.

On the other hand, there are a great many ways to go right. And it's hard to generalize. I can offer a rule, but it won't be much help: If you want to adapt novels into movies, be John Huston. A fairly solid argument can be made for Huston as the most accomplished, and almost certainly the most prolific, adapter of novels into movies. We've already mentioned him at length—yes, that one about the falcon, but also *The Treasure of the Sierra Madre* (1948, another "genre" novel, although the genre in this case is "B. Traven," the author, whose work is not quite like anyone else's), *The African Queen* (1951), *Under the Volcano* (1984), and even his final film, *The Dead* (1987). And in between, lots of movies drawn from books. Not every one is a gem, of course, but there are plenty of polished stones on that beach. Of course, no one can be Huston, nor can we necessarily learn a great deal by his example, except this: he understood and respected his source material like almost no one else. Sometimes that understanding and respect took the form of complete fidelity, as in the case of the virtual transcription of *The Maltese Falcon* from book to screenplay. At other times, it manifested as knowing when and why to depart from the original. The elements he adds in *The Dead*, for instance, play as if they occur in James Joyce's story, so much so that those of us who know the story intimately may find ourselves unsure if a scene or speech is from the story or is an addition made in the film.

At the far end of the spectrum, Wes Anderson claims for *The Grand Budapest Hotel* only that it is "inspired" by the stories of Stefan Zweig, which is to say that it captures something of the spirit and a little of the action of the originals, but no one who knows the one will see the other as anything like an adaptation. Which is fine. What matters is how successful the finished product is, and on that score, the film more than passes muster.

As do many contemporary adaptations. In fact, I am about to say something shocking, so hold tight: we are living in a Great Age of movie adaptations. See? You didn't faint. Of course, you're right—there are some lousy films made from really good books out there. Always true. But that may not be about adaptation so much as simply a statement that someone, somewhere, is always making a lousy movie. Source material may matter less than execution in most cases, even though our sense is that the film wrecked the book we love. But there are also a whole lot of good movie adaptations over the last few years. Some really good ones. And a few outstanding ones. We'll name names in a moment. For now, keep this little fact in mind: of the eight films nominated for the 2016 Best Picture Oscar, seven began life as books. Only four were novels, but the centrality of adaptations is beyond dispute.

First, however, I want to make a more outrageous statement: we have always lived in a Great Age of movie adaptations. I thought about putting in earplugs before giving you that provocation, but that seriously curtails our ability to have a conversation. In any event, I need to offer evidence for what will strike some of you as a pretty shaky assertion.

Let's begin with a definitional matter. We need to establish just what is meant by a Great Age. We could take that to mean an era that produces more excellent films than any other, or at least produces lots of them. If we do that, though, we'll get hung up on rating and ranking and be here forever without convincing one another of anything at all, which is just not productive. So let's think of it differently. How about an era in which a huge number of works that appear on-screen began life in a different medium? On that basis, every cinematic age is a Great one, and for a couple of very basic reasons. For one thing, the Dream Factory has an enormous appetite for product. You can't crank out hundreds of movies every year without burning through a lot of stories. Now, a great many of those stories have ever and always been originals, works imagined by screenwriters specifically for the movie at hand. But the world of books provides a vast library of preexisting stories—some fictional, some based, as they say on the movie posters, on real events—that await transformation into film. Which brings us to the second reason. Those works already have a track record. If you were a producer and someone came to you with a story of marital betrayal and crime, would you be more impressed if it were a two-page treatment for a script or *Gone Girl*? Yeah, me too. And this is quite apart from the merits, literary or otherwise, of Gillian Flynn's novel; its real merit, strictly from a monetary viewpoint (remember now, you're a *producer* in an industry where, historically, seven out of ten films lose money), is that it comes with a huge potential audience. The same can be said for *Lord of the Rings* or *Harry Potter and the Sorcerer's Stone* or *American Sniper* or *The Hunger Games*. Or *Frankenstein*, for that matter. Which is probably why folks keep going back to reimagine that novel, although I wouldn't discount not having to pay a copyright holder. But even if a novel or memoir isn't a mammoth bestseller, it still has a track record: somebody chose to publish it, and a number of other somebodies elected to read it, which means that there will be word of mouth about the finished product even before it is seen. And word of mouth, or word of social media these days, is still a great marketing tool. So we're starting to get a handle on the appeal of books as cinematic fodder. Sometimes reinventing the wheel is more appealing than inventing a new wheel.

Not that the reinvented wheel is all sweetness and light. No less an authority than Woody Allen once said that, given the chance to live his life over, he would do everything the same way again, "except for watching *The Magus*" (1968). Ouch. The 1966 novel by John Fowles is terrific—and was wildly popular when it came out. By most accounts, including that of the star, no one in the Michael Caine vehicle seems to have understood the novel they were filming. It is difficult. We'll skip the particulars and only say that, if a movie based on such a widely read novel can sink without a trace, there's no such thing as a sure bet.

The art of adaptation is fraught with all sorts of difficulties. Adding material is rarely among them. More commonly, the screenwriter and director grapple with a source of massive headaches: what to cut. Even a modest novel has much more material in it than a lengthy movie. For instance, how is it that, in a set of films as long as Peter Jackson's adaptation of *The Lord of the Rings*, a character as interesting as Tom Bombadil can completely vanish? And how is it that we don't particularly notice or care? Steady on!; yes, some of you care. Some of us care. My recollection of the trilogy, admittedly fuzzy, was that he was among the most intriguing of the books' inventions, so I was wondering how Jackson would represent him. I did sort of notice that Jackson finessed the issue by not representing him at all, but noticed mostly because someone, a far bigger fan than I, had pointed it out to me. On reflection, it sort of makes sense: Tom Bombadil is a narrative back road, and film, even an immensely long film or set of films, is an expressway. He takes away focus from the main issue, which is getting Frodo from the Shire to Mount Doom, and that takes quite long enough as it is. Besides, his absence gives lovers of the books another point to quibble with: "if I were making it, I would have made Tom Bombadil . . ." and so on. Probably not Jackson's point, but we should accept it as an unintended gift.

Jackson's decision points to a frequent complaint. One aspect of adaptations that we almost all object to are the liberties that filmmakers take with the "facts" of the novels. We can all cite instances of our favorite books that didn't show up in the movie versions—or that were mangled beyond all recognition. And of course we're right. But many times those changes are essential. You cannot cram three or four or five hundred pages into a hundred and twenty minutes. The math simply doesn't work. So changes must be wrought.

Here's an example. By almost universal agreement, one of the best adaptations of a literary novel ever is David Lean's *Great Expectations* (1946). It features outstanding performances by a very young John Mills, Alec Guinness without capes or exotic makeup, the radiant Jean Simmons, Valerie Hobson, and a host of terrific character actors. It has great atmosphere: the opening scene, in which the young Pip races through the marshes along a levee populated with gantries that look forebodingly like gallows and to the graveyard where his parents lie buried and where he meets the frightening Magwitch, is worth the price of admission all by itself. It's all darkness and wind and barren landscape and shadows and danger. Those components will persist throughout. This movie has everything. Except Orlick. He's the book's chief villain, the one who, the scary Magwitch and creepy Miss Havisham aside, represents the chief danger to Pip. Late in the novel, he waylays Pip by chicanery and then force, holding him captive so an associate can thwart Pip's plans to save Magwitch. Much earlier he kills Pip's sister, Mrs. Joe Gargery, with a hammer. But he's not there in the film to do the deed. And Orlick or no, Mrs. Joe has got to die. Instead, Lean carries her off with a voiced-over sudden illness. Purists can't be happy with that. Still, it must be done.

So why the change? Necessity. Movie logic. Clean narrative lines. Call it what you will, it is both inevitable and different. In this case, Orlick is simply unnecessary. That's a strong statement in connection with vaporizing a major Dickensian villain, not to mention a significant plot element, but it's true: Orlick is not essential to the *Great Expectations* that Lean is making. The story he wants to focus on is Pip's growth and development among the various grotesques—Magwitch, Miss Havisham, Estella, Jaggers, Wemmick. We've got a bloody-minded convict-benefactor, a fanatical, jilted woman living in her bridal gown amid the ruins of her wedding feast decades after the nonevent, a beautiful but pitiless young woman groomed to break men's hearts, an attorney who keeps death masks of the clients he's failed to save, and his clerk, who's merely a little odd and therefore hardly noticeable in such august company. Plus, there are the gloomy marshlands, the gloomy crumbling mansion, the creepy law office, the gloomy Thames waterfront—did I mention that this movie has a certain gloom? With all that, of what purpose is a mere villain? Given the time constraints, he would be a distraction from the main narrative: in five hundred pages, distractions are good, so long as they tie in eventually (and Dickens, sometimes to our consternation, ties everything up by the end in every novel), but in two hours and change, they just distract. So then, Orlick is released into the narrative ether, and Mrs. Joe is seen off to the hereafter in a single dismissive sentence. And the film works.

The moral? Change is inevitable. Go with it.

Liberties?

How about a five-foot-seven (maybe) Tom Cruise playing Lee Child's thriller hero Jack Reacher, who is ten inches taller? It happened after many years of an ongoing "bizarre conversation" in Child's words, "saying, well, this guy who is eight inches shorter than Reacher is better than this other guy who is eight and a half inches shorter than Reacher." He said on a National Public Radio interview that getting the "internals" of the character right matter a great deal more, and that physicality is always a problem in adaptations: "A book is entirely in the realm of imagination: my imagination and your imagination. But then if you turn that into a movie, it is fundamentally real: people in a real physical space and so you're limited straight away to the real people available." Can't say it better than that.

Fidelity to the source, as we know, is not the point. Movie quality is. Actually, sales may be, but quality figures in somewhere, sometimes. For faithful adaptations, your best bets are likely to be films by John Huston, mentioned a little while ago, who may very well be unsurpassed in his sensitivity to the written word. If anyone can top him, it would be the creative team of director James Ivory, producer Ismail Merchant, and screenwriter Ruth Prawer Jhabvala, herself a novelist of great accomplishment. Their work over thirty years with novels by Henry James and E. M. Forster and Kazuo Ishiguro and Jhabvala herself stands as a testament to what sensitive filmmakers can do with literary material. Had they done nothing else, their version of *A Room with a View* (1985) would place them in the pantheon of novel adapters. But they did so much more.

Here is a contrast in styles of successfully adapting novels for the screen. Horton Foote was as faithful as a screenwriter can be in adapting (1962) Harper Lee's *To Kill a Mockingbird*, as generations of high school students, having been subjected to both versions, can attest. Foote totally nails the novel. It helps, of course, to have material so friendly to the screen. Please don't misunderstand. No one could accuse Lee of writing for the screen (that moldy-oldie complaint about facile, superficial fiction seemingly designed for a role in the movies). But her narrative is sufficiently straightforward and concerned with surfaces—in a good way—that it lends itself to cinematic transformation.

That would not be true of John Fowles's playful, arch, postmodern masterpiece *The French Lieutenant's Woman* (1981). When we heard it was being adapted back in the early eighties, nearly all any of my acquaintances asked was, "How are they going to handle the two endings?" Because it has them, you see. True to the Victorian models and also to his own literary gamesmanship, he provides one ending, then has a surrogate version of himself wind a watch back fifteen minutes, and then provides a second, nearly opposite ending. You just know how that would go over in the movie house, right? Film is too linear to be forgiving about that particular gambit. As I mention elsewhere, this book had the good fortune to fall into the hands of a theatrical genius, Harold Pinter. And part of his solution is to have a character ask, almost as soon as we were comfortably in our seats, exactly the question we all had already posed: what's up with the two endings? It may be true that you can't give a story two endings in the movies, but you can have two story lines of which each has one of them. His solution is to create two sets of characters played by the same actors, in this case, Meryl Streep and Jeremy Irons. In one story line, they play Sarah Woodruff and Charles Smithson, Victorians who have an illicit affair that has quite profound effects. In the other, they are Anna and Mike, the actors who are playing Sarah and Charles in a movie version of the novel. The solution neatly handles the ending, of course, but also a number of other elements, especially a lot of background and commentary about the Victorian age that Fowles employs in the novel to distance us from the "reality" of his tale. While such material would be poison in a straight adaptation, it plays very well coming from actors researching their parts. The conceit also provides some droll moments, such as the wonderful Leo McKern as the actor who has played the worldly and aging Dr. Grogan in the inner film dancing at the wrap party with Lynsey Baxter as the actress who has played Charles's simpering fiancée, Ernestina. They and the rest of the cast are thoroughly enjoying themselves, unaware of the private drama upstairs that is tearing Mike and Anna apart, just as it had so tormented their Victorian characters. So, Charles and Sarah get one ending, Mike and Anna the other, but I'll not tell you which. What kind of monster do you think I am?

The answer to the question of fidelity is that there is no answer. Every novel needs its own treatment, which is to say it needs its own peculiar alchemy of writer, director, producer, cinematographer, and actors. If there is a weak link anywhere in that chain, it is doomed. On the other hand, sometimes we get a miracle. Here is one such case, when I had mentioned that I would be discussing adaptations of novels, well over half my conversation partners mentioned the same film as the chief (in some cases only) instance of a film being better than its print predecessor. The movie? *Jaws* (1975). There's the wisdom of crowds in action.

We've spent a fair bit of time talking about what is lost when novels move to the screen, but what is gained? There must be something; otherwise we wouldn't shell out all that money for tickets. Here's what I think it is: magic. When we see that shower montage in *Psycho*, the shock effect is like nothing we can get from reading: it comes all at once and as a complete surprise, changing the nature of the film we're watching. In mere seconds. The horrors of the Hunger Games spring off the screen at us in the first installment. And no amount of print can present the manic energy of Gatsby's parties as well as pretty much any film version; the screen, whoever directs, is always jam-packed with activity and crowds and noise. We believe that these are truly revels.

Rather than talk generalities, let's look at one example, *Harry Potter and the Sorcerer's Stone.* Actually, any of the Harry Potter movies would work, but this was the one that introduced us to all those elements that would become so familiar and so loved. From its opening frames, the movie captures not only the magic of the magical world but the contrast with the Muggle world. Almost the first thing we see is a strange-looking chap we'll come to know as Dumbledore capturing the light from the streetlamps as his group of guardians drops off the baby

Harry at the Dursley household. Bet you never saw that in your neighborhood. The horrors of living as an orphan in that household are equally vivid. Whatever the perils of Hogwarts and the magical realm, they will be as nothing compared with living with that odious family. From there forward, everything is touched with wonder. No description can quite prepare us for the shifting wall in Diagon Alley or running through the pillar at Platform 9¾. And at the first grand dinner at Hogwarts, we are treated not merely to the wonder of the candles floating in the air but also the awestruck delight with which the young scholars view the enchanting scene. And there is the secret of the film: everything at this impossibly old place is so, well, new. New to the students, new to the kid viewers, and almost certainly new to the adults. This could well be the most bifurcated audience in film history: virtually every child knew the novel intimately, having read it and by many accounts reread again and again, while the majority of the adults had not. That fact explains why there were so many conversations around the exits with kids explaining things about Harry and his milieu to their parents. Excitedly.

So what's the point? Just this: as we've mentioned several times, film is a separate medium with its own language. Because of that special language, it acts on us in very particular ways. Those ways are neither better nor worse, only different. More immediate. Visual. And visceral. As a medium, print is great for conveying complex ideas, things that need to be teased out over a period of time. Movies? We can get a little lost in complexity. That, in part, is why none of the great philosophers of modernity have used film as their medium of choice. On the other hand, if you want something to really have a kick, film is terrific. Movies are unsurpassed for action, which partly explains the enduring appeal of spandex at the Cineplex. Spiderman swinging between buildings can never be as thrilling as he is on the big screen. Or, to use our current example, when

we watch Harry Potter have his wizard's duel with Draco Malfoy, we feel it in our gut. Our hands grip the arms of the theater
seats a little tighter. Or think back to the first time you saw the
Quidditch match with all those broom riders swooping and
climbing and banking. The real-life audience was as breathless
as the one in the movie, right? The beauty of books is that they
not only allow but force us to use our imaginations in order
to see ... anything. Characters. Action. Danger. Joy. Fear. Love.
None of those come to life unless the reader vivifies them,
breathes life into them via his or her imagination. The beauty
of film is that those same entities are given life on the screen
in front of us. The people and their actions are instantly alive
via a technological miracle and a vast amount of hard work—
but not on our part. It is tempting, at this point, to agree with
the frequently made assertion that film is therefore a passive
medium: all the audience has to do is sit back (or lean forward
in anticipation) and receive the movie as given. But we're not
made that way. We're making judgments all the time about
what the screen is presenting. In that Quidditch match, for
instance, Ron and Hermione become convinced that Snape is
using an enchantment to imperil Harry, whose broom is veer-
ing out of control. Hermione dashes over to set Snape's robe on
fire, knocking over Professor Quirrell in the process. The kids
are convinced that they have spotted the villainy and stopped
it, but we are free to have our doubts. Which will later be confirmed. We similarly wonder about nearly every element of the
film: Did he really do that? Can that be right? Is he working
for Voldemort? There are little signs we might read that Quirrell, not Snape, is the problem, but we can easily ignore them,
given the kids' insistence that Snape is the bad guy. Okay, a
Harry Potter film is likely to be more heavily weighted toward
these sorts of questions, but every film gives attentive readers
something to do besides—or along with—emptying that vat of
popcorn. Nothing passive about it.

Overall, the movie is quite faithful to its original. Pretty much has to be when the audience is full of pint-size critics expecting to see *their* book. In truth, there are quite a few changes from the novel, most of them minor and nearly all made in the interest of streamlining the narrative. Peeves the Poltergeist, for example, is absent from the film. Interesting as he may be, he doesn't advance the plot and can therefore be dispensed with. Similarly, Harry doesn't meet Draco Malfoy until the arrival at Hogwarts, whereas in the novel they meet at Madam Malkin's in Diagon Alley and then again on the train. Yet one need only meet Draco once to know he's a bad actor, and the meet and greet at the entrance to the school is sufficient to that task. Hagrid is rather more in evidence than in the book, as when he and not the Dursleys takes Harry to King's Cross Station. His presence here, as elsewhere, serves as a device for exposition: backstory, needed information that happens naturally on the page as part of the larger narration but can more or less happen in film only by a character saying it. We've discussed before the pitfalls of voice-over narration, right? That only leaves dialogue. And Robby Coltrane's Hagrid is so charmingly unaffected that he can get away with a lot of exposition.

These are the sorts of changes that matter. Are they made in the service of creating a better film? On the whole, definitely. Other changes may be more happenstance. Some absolutists may disagree, but do we really care that Dudley and Aunt Petunia Dursley are brunettes and not blondes? Yeah, that's what I thought. It may well be that the actors who best fit the parts were not fair-haired. Or, most likely, that Harry Melling was a better actor than anyone else of the right age and body type for the role of Dudley. That's the explanation we always hope drives movie decisions: Do you want a blond Dudley or the best one? And occasionally it even does.

Sometimes the changes are neither gains nor losses but merely differences dictated by the shift from print to film. *No Country for Old Men* feels more like a fable than a realistic novel, and with good reason. The subsequent film (2007) plays closer to realism. Before going on, it is worth noting that the film is in most ways highly attentive to the book, and this difference is not a conscious decision—or even an avoidable one. Even so, many viewers and a number of reviewers of the subsequent film have expressed the feeling that Anton Chigurh is a figure of "pure evil," but that is in some ways a result of the nature of film. Those who have only read the novel might well see him as more of a cosmic force. Here's why.

The novel is Cormac McCarthy's "Pardoner's Tale." For those of you not up on your Chaucer, one of the pilgrims, the Pardoner (a clerical position circa 1384 that has long since been retired), on this trip to Canterbury Cathedral tells the story of a group of young men who, finding out that "Death" has taken one of their pals, go out to the forest swearing vengeance on the rascal. Rather than finding an actual being, much less a figure with a cloak and scythe, they discover a treasure. Their newfound wealth causes them to kill each other off, so they find death, if not in the way they had naïvely planned. There's a lot in that story that shows up in McCarthy's novel.

Wait, that's not what Llewelyn Moss goes looking for.

You sure? Why is he out there?

Um, he's hunting?

The purpose of which is what? See, he's seeking death, just not his. And he's also pretty naïve. What other construction can we put on his thinking he can get away with a case full of money when he stumbles across the aftermath of a drug deal gone bad? Just because the guests at this murderous party are all dead, it is foolish to conclude that no one is going to miss it. The day has not yet arrived when two million dollars can vanish and no one is going to notice or care. That single decision sets in motion a series of deaths of almost everyone associated with Llewelyn—and several unfortunates with no direct connection to him. In that context, Chigurh is beyond labels of good and evil; he is simply death. In all its randomness and suddenness, coming always as a surprise even to those who expect it, death. Hence the coin tossing, the quiet, even soothing demeanor, the lack of anger or visible malice. He is merely a force with a job to do. See? Cosmic.

Of course, cosmic forces are difficult to establish when portrayed by an actual living being on film. As viewers, we have a hard time seeing a person and not imputing motives. As a result, the film becomes something altered from the print version, almost a different genre. Less fable, more naturalistic narrative. That's okay. It's not a failing, just an inevitable product of a change of media.

But back to my contention that we are living in a Great Age of movie adaptations. Just consider: since the year 2000, viewers have been blessed with highly acclaimed and high-grossing film cycles based on two fantasy series (*The Lord of the Rings* and *The Hobbit*), a children's fantasy adventure series (*Harry Potter*), and a young adult dystopian series (*The Hunger Games*). There have been excellent stand-alone films of bestselling novels *Gone Girl* (2014), *The Girl with the Dragon Tattoo* (2011), *Mystic River* (2003), *Life of Pi* (2012), *No Country for Old Men* (2007), *Atonement* (2007), and *Never Let Me Go* (2010); memoirs *Argo* (2012), *American Sniper* (2014), and *Twelve Years a Slave* (2013); histories *Seabiscuit* (2003), *Black Hawk Down* (2001), and *Lincoln* (2012); genre novels *Red* (2010), the *Bourne* trilogy (2002–07), *The Martian* (2015), and *Gone Baby Gone* (2007); even lesser-known novels such as *The Descendants* (2011), *The Best Exotic Marigold Hotel* (2011), *Sideways* (2004), and *Winter's*

Bone (2010). The movies have shown that they can do justice to both literary classics such as Henry James's *The Wings of the Dove* (1997) and literary trifles like *The Devil Wears Prada* (2006). Of course, status as a classic is no guarantee, as both *Beowulf* (2007) and *The Cat in the Hat* (2003) attest. A list like this, even ignoring stage plays as it does, strongly suggests that this has been an outstanding era for literary adaptations. But I suspect we could compile a list for any fifteen- or twenty-year period and make the same case.

Of course, there are inherent hazards, not least disappointing devoted fans of famous works. *Anna Karenina* (2012), adapted from Leo Tolstoy's novel by the great playwright Tom Stoppard, was criticized and praised in nearly equal parts for almost every element, from the casting of Keira Knightley and Jude Law to the nonrealistic elements such as setting the indoor scenes in an actual theater, then bursting the playhouse wall to take action outside. The inevitable difficulties of compressing six hundred or so pages into just over two hours mean that devoted readers will be unhappy, but the radical handling of the story to accommodate it to the cinema ensured controversy. So what should we think? Chiefly that we should see it for ourselves. And maybe appreciate the attempt, whatever we might think of the results.

Being Anna

Anna Karenina was far from the first time Tolstoy had received the adaptation treatment. Worldwide, there have been at least seventeen film versions, including English-language films starring Greta Garbo (twice, once silent in 1927's *Love*), Vivien Leigh, Jacqueline Bisset, and Sophie Marceau in addition to Knightley. The vastly longer *War*

and Peace has only been made into an English-language film once, in King Vidor's 1956 production starring Audrey Hepburn, Henry Fonda, and Mel Ferrer, which clocked in at a Tolstoyan three hours and twenty-eight minutes. Tolstoy himself gets the adaptation treatment in *The Last Station* (2009), a film version of the Jay Parini novel directed by Michael Hoffman. At least with that movie, critics were reluctant to grouse about the casting. Not when the leads are played by Christopher Plummer and Dame Helen Mirren.

But to the main point, what does it mean to live in a Great Age of adaptation? Only that a favorite novel or memoir or graphic novel may be coming to a Cineplex near you. And that we need to consider the differences in the media as part of our judgment about the adaptation of our darlings.

As I've been writing this discussion, I've been trying to come up with a set of rules that reader-viewers might employ for analyzing movies from books. Maybe *precepts* would be a better term, a set of principles by which we might best analyze adaptations. I started with a list for filmmakers, but it just boiled down to "Do no harm," and the doctors have that one all locked up. All of this presumes, of course, that we have read the book in question. If I've never read Andy Weir's *The Martian*, for instance, as either a serial on his website or the subsequent book, I'm perfectly free to enjoy the movie as if no prior text existed. Pretty silly to attempt anything else, really. So here we go:

1) First, a movie has to succeed as a movie. As much as possible, we should examine it with that in mind.

2) Don't set any a priori demands about what must or must not be included. Some of the best ele-

ments of adaptations have always been departures from the novels. And some of the worst.

3) At the same time, don't accept changes that are obviously stupid. This one you'll have to decide for yourself. In other words, judge the worthiness of any change—or any faithfulness—in terms of how it succeeds in context.

4) Develop two minds: the one where you keep your cherished memories of the literary original and another where you examine the cinematic variation.

That last one is the hardest. We have great difficulty letting go of *our* understanding of a book, and the more beloved, the greater that difficulty. So getting to that duality of mind can sometimes require a period of time. There were some things to appreciate and others to lament in Ken Russell's film of D. H. Lawrence's *Women in Love* (1969). My chief difficulty with the movie when I first saw it was the nude wrestling scene between Rupert Birkin (Alan Bates) and Gerald Crich (Oliver Reed). The scene is in the novel, by the way, so that wasn't the problem. For its time, the scene was shockingly homoerotic and without doubt the sexiest thing in the film. Surely, I thought, this isn't what Lawrence (a particular undergraduate favorite) had in mind. On reflection, however, I became pretty sure it was what he had in mind, that Russell's determination to shock us was necessary to make us reexamine the novel. I didn't get there right away; in fact, the process took months, until I finally got around to rereading the book. The printed scene isn't exactly the one filmed, but it's a lot closer than I thought before Russell made me see it with new eyes.

The bottom line here is that we go to the movies to see movies. We may prefer it when we can at least still find the book that was adapted, but if the movie doesn't work, how it treats the novel is moot. If we want to understand movies better, we need to examine them as if they are freestanding works of art while at the same time (here's that dual-mind thing again) analyzing the changes between the novel or memoir or history and the resulting film. Looked at dispassionately, what can we learn from the way the book is adapted? Does it perhaps tell us something about the mind-set of the filmmakers? Does it open up possibilities in the story that we hadn't seen before, that maybe the book doesn't even afford us? Adaptations offer an alluring opportunity to exercise our creative faculties, to read films actively and even aggressively. In fact, they virtually force us to do so since we can never unread a book. And as long as it's happening anyway, we might as well enjoy the game.

15

Movie Magic

YOU'LL BELIEVE A MAN CAN FLY! Remember that one? You would if you were around in 1978 when Christopher Reeve burst onto the scene as the Man of Steel. Prior to that Richard Donner film, flying men—and women, of course—looked pretty darned hokey. Those of us who remembered the Guy with the Spit-Curl and Cape from television went into the movie with visions of George Reeves (with an *s* and no relation) obviously suspended on wires with rear projection scenery flitting past. Which was okay when you were nine, but this was way cooler. *This* Superman looked as if he really were flying.

Filmmakers had been trying, of course, to achieve the illu-sion of flight ever since they began burning images into celluloid at eighteen frames a second. And of getting trampled by horses, falling from buildings, walking through walls, pretty much anything you couldn't achieve in real life (and survive) or onstage. They didn't get around to fighting with lightsabers until George Lucas brought them to the screen in 1977 in the original *Star Wars* (I refuse to submit to the renaming regime for the series; there is only one *Star Wars*; accept no substitute), but some sort of magic was always on hand. As near as I can tell, no trick in the history of film fired the preteen imagination quite like the lightsaber—this stick that emitted a beam of light that could be contained, controlled, and used with lethal efficiency. Okay, maybe the Winchester 73 and the Colt .45, but go with it here. The lightsaber's effect was achieved by means of rotoscoping—hand-drawing lines around the object (in this case, model lightsabers) on every frame in which the weapon appears, to create a matte, then fill in the matte and add a glow. You could fend off projectiles and bursts of murderous light, parry the best efforts of an assassin, cut a man in half, probably carve your Thanksgiving bird. I'm not sure there is a house in America that contained a boy between 1977 and, say, 1992 that did not possess, or maybe even still does, a plastic imitation. It helped if the Force was strong in you. Which was part of the magic. Lightsabers were only one element in a complete universe of enchantment, filled with exotic creatures, magnificent evil, really cool devices, mystical powers, and excellent gadgets. If you'd like, I believe I can show you every one of them in my basement. There is a (deliberately) cheesy diner in Kent, Ohio, that has a replica (suitably cheesy) of an X-Wing fighter outside the entrance; virtually no male patron of the appropriate generation can resist having his picture taken beside it as he leaves. You want to talk about the Force? There it is.

This is not, however, a chapter about special effects. It's about *movie magic*, which is different. Special effects are part of that magic, of course, but only part. And not necessarily the most important part.

So what do we mean by "movie magic"? Just this: that a film employs devices and techniques to draw us into the world that the film is creating. Those devices and techniques can be as simple or as complex as you want; what matters is that they convince us of the reality the film presents. Here's simple: you can have a group of travelers talk about the danger from an Apache attack all you want, but the moment we really buy it is when that first arrow lodges in the wall of the stagecoach. *Now* we understand the hazard. We can be fairly certain that, actors being somewhat expensive and a nuisance to replace even in the studio era, no one actually shot an arrow into the wall of the stagecoach, and yet it appears with all the emotional force of one that has come direct from an Apache bow. And complex: take us into a world where ten-foot-tall blue beings generated by motion capture and CGI move through a world that is computer generated and the whole thing not only looks real but does so in three dimensions. And in between? Well, there's a sea of possibilities in terms of both chronology and technology. And the thing about movie magic, broadly constituted, is that it is designed not to trick the eye—although that happens—but to use the eye (and the ear, of course) to convince the brain. Because the brain knows two things: first, that none of this is "real," and second, that it wants it all to feel real. Our thinking selves are always willing to be seduced by a movie's reality. And we will be, if the movie gives us a juicy slice of invention.

Before going on, let's stipulate that, yes, all moviemaking is magic, that we are watching stories that never happened (or never happened like *that*) to people who aren't real or, if real, not the actual persons. In other words, there is a great deal of magic in actors convincing us of the reality of unreal stories. A great subject, but not our concern at present. We are concerned, rather, with the panoply of techniques by which video information can be manipulated to trick, astonish, terrify, amuse, befuddle, enlighten, or otherwise enthrall us. Whether that video information is analog or digital, black and white or color, achieved with razor blades or computers, is immaterial. The point is that someone—cinematographer, director, editor, their designees, or a combination thereof—has fiddled with the information on or in the medium of the movie to achieve an effect, and that the effect, when successful, is indeed *special*.

The beauty of movies is that they can do things no other medium can manage. You can have effects that are impossible in the theater, that we can only imagine in books or on radio. Some of them are fairly simple parlor tricks. How about a bulleted list?

- If, for example, someone shoots a gun in a room and it bounces off any number of objects before coming to rest in the wall or the villain's thigh (it's a comedy), it's a straightforward procedure to show a series of extremely quick shots of those objects in the room deflecting the bullet before it thumps into the drywall or makes the bad guy yelp. Try that one onstage.

- You want Superman to stop a bullet with his chest or catch it in his hand? No problem. That's easy enough onstage (although a big yawn in a comic book), but at the Cineplex we can actually *see* the bullet being caught.

- In *The Matrix*, we see Neo bend out of the path of an oncoming bullet—or several thousand of them. We see him, see the path of the bullet, see the hair's-breadth escape in vivid terms. In fact, the moment succeeds only because super-duper-extreme slo-mo, or the effects that create the illusion, allow us to "see" all that happening. Which is pretty cool.

- In *Stagecoach*, John Ford's motto was no bullet left behind. Every time John Wayne's Ringo Kid fired his Winchester, an Apache fell. Actually, his horse fell. It's a record that still stands. About what was done to the horses to achieve that effect, the less said, the better.

The history of movie effects, "special" or otherwise, is a long story of invention and innovation. What often drives innovation is vision. A director wants to tell a certain story in a certain way and can't do so with currently existing means. The result is that he or she then searches for some new means or some new combination of existing techniques to achieve this vision. Let's say that he wants to re-create a stunt no actor can possibly accomplish, the shooting of which would prove fatal in the physical world, between two structures that don't exist but whose appearance is universally known. And make

Figure 9. Stop bullets? No problem for Keanu Reeves in The Matrix. *Licensed By: Warner Bros. Entertainment. All Rights Reserved.*

it look absolutely real. Put like that, the effort sounds slightly demented, doesn't it? To be fair, so was the original effort. On August 7, 1974, young Frenchman Philippe Petit walked across a two-hundred-foot high wire eight times and became the talk of the world. What made the feat newsworthy wasn't the length of the stroll or stunts like lying down on the wire mid-transit but the fact that the wire was suspended between the Twin Towers of the World Trade Center, a dizzying 1,350 feet in the air. There hasn't been an actor since Charlie Chaplin who could begin to replicate that performance, and there's no production company willing to risk its star and no insurer that would underwrite such a venture. Even if there were, other images of the Twin Towers have supplanted those of Petit traversing the gap between them. So how to film? For Robert Zemeckis, director of *The Walk* (2015), it's a combination of the highest of high-tech, old-fashioned set building, and athletic training by his star. To begin with, Joseph Gordon-Levitt, who plays Petit, underwent intensive training with the man he portrays, until he was able to take his own walks on an admittedly lower wire. In filming, Zemeckis re-created the top two floors of the towers on a soundstage and strung the cable twelve feet off the floor. Even that is daunting, as Gordon-Levitt told *USA Today*: "It's not so high compared with what a high-wire walker would do, but you'd be surprised how scary it is twelve feet in the air," which is twice the height at which he trained. Even the safety harness provided only limited comfort: "Your body still tenses all the way up. The only thing that allowed me to get past that terror was just the time spent with Philippe."

That's the human element. The tech portion kicks in with green-screen shooting and CGI re-creation of the towers and their surroundings. Green-screen shooting is just what it sounds like: the scene is shot in front of a green screen, which is replaced with chosen images in postproduction. Anything else you want to vanish is also green—which is why TV meteorologists never wear green: the weather maps and related imagery appear compliments of green-screening, and no meteorologist cares to appear as a disembodied head. In the case of our movie, at times the "wire" is actually a green plat-form, with the wire inserted later; you can hardly expect your lead actor to stand around for hours on a strand of woven steel. Shooting on such a stage also got rid of an inevitable prob-lem of shooting at heights: in a real setting, the star would be blown off the wire by the prop wash created by the helicopter holding the camera. This technique is hardly new; since the beginning of film, scenes of great heights have routinely been shot either on soundstage re-creations of outdoor settings or, less commonly, in the actual settings but with some sort of net just below the line of sight. When Harold Lloyd performed his very funny business with a clock in *Safety Last!* (1923), he was truly high in the air, although not on an actual skyscraper façade. Rather, he climbed on a wall constructed on top of a skyscraper and located near enough to the edge that, when shot from above, it hid the building on which it stood and gave the illusion of a truly dizzying altitude. The difference between his performance and Gordon-Levitt's is chiefly a matter of scale, of whether we believe the character is ten stories off the ground or one hundred and ten. And with how the trick is achieved. Lloyd achieves his effect with careful camera place-ment. Had he lived in 2015, he might, like Zemeckis, have used computer-generated imagery, or CGI.

The CGI element for *The Walk* was created by scanning thousands of images of the World Trade Center and surround-ing lower Manhattan, along with the Manhattan skyline. The place has to look like 1974 New York, after all, and not 2015 New York with two anachronistic towers. And the pictures of the WTC include both the interior as well as the more familiar exterior. The lobby and even stairwells also ceased to exist in

2001, so the filmmakers had to depict them as well. (Anytime you're tempted to daydream about how glamorous it would be to work in the movies, consider those poor blighters sifting through hundreds of thousands of photographs, many of them with no real visual interest at all, for the mere tens of thousands needed to fill the computer with images so that shots can be generated later on. Honestly, stairwells.) The sky is still the sky, of course, but it, too, is inserted digitally. This is all a tremendous amount of work, naturally, and of a very different sort from the traditional cinematic practices of set building and rear projection. The results are spectacular. The stock promotional shot that appears alongside virtually every article and review of the movie shows Gordon-Levitt as Petit lying on the wire, shot from above, with the towers receding down toward the ground and a very detailed image of the old WTC plaza simultaneously very far away and very clear. Add to this technology the use of 3-D projection and you have a stomach-churning experience of vertigo, especially to those of us with acrophobic tendencies. Critics were split on numerous aspects of *The Walk*, but there was near-universal agreement regarding the technical achievement of its centerpiece.

And the payoff? Even knowing absolutely everything about how the images were generated and the effects accomplished, I found the results terrifying.

At the far end of the effects spectrum, some of the best magic is only possible with lower technology. Angels, for instance, work best in black and white. At least one does. In *The Bishop's Wife* (1947), Cary Grant's angel, Dudley (sure, strange name for an angel, but work with me here), has a couple of enchanting parlor tricks. He has come to Earth in answer to a prayer by Bishop Henry Brougham (David Niven in a rare hyperserious role) asking for guidance. Henry thinks he's asking to win approval and money to build a cathedral, but what he really needs is help getting his values straight and getting over a bad habit of ignoring his wife, Julia (Loretta Young). It's okay about the wife; he's Episcopalian. Just not ignoring her. That he's capable of taking Loretta Young for granted is evidence of the depth of his need for divine assistance. In order to free up his afternoon, Dudley manages to complete his fling in a matter of moments, tossing the cards toward their destination and, with a wiggle or two of the fingers, directing them in several streams into the appropriate boxes. He reprises this trick with the decorations on a rather forlorn Christmas tree, although it takes him two attempts to make it magnificent. Watching him remove the lights and tinsel is almost as much fun as watching him put them on. Now, we all know that these feats are managed by some creative editing (in this case, by shooting the destruction—blowing the cards out of the box or knocking the ornaments off the tree, then running the film in reverse to get the desired effect), but we just don't care. What matters is that we see the results of his work and ignore the intense labor of cameramen and tinsel wranglers and editors. That business of ignoring is somewhat easier in monochrome analog cinema than it might be in super-duper-high-def digital, 3-D fabulousness. In some ways, it is more charming precisely because of the distance created by the older technology. And maybe because of the charm of its star: it would be hard to name a movie in which the hero moves with as much grace and coolness as does Cary Grant.

Having said that, the most magical moment in the movie requires nothing special at all, merely a bit of sleight of hand. An angry Henry summons Dudley into his office to have it out with him. To make sure they are not disturbed, he locks the door. When the interview is over, Dudley simply opens the "locked" door and exits with a devastating smile, leaving

Henry flabbergasted. When building a set, it is the simplest thing in the world to construct a door with a keyhole but no actual lock, but that doesn't matter. The movie has spent an hour establishing Dudley's bona fides as a miraculous being, so when he opens the locked door, we *believe* that he has done the magical. Well, someone has, but maybe not the angel.

It's because of these stagy miracles that we believe Dudley when he pulls off his real stunt: putting the bloom back in Julia's cheeks (not easy in black and white) and the twinkle in her eyes (achieved by having Loretta Young stand a little straighter, walk with a little more bounce, and smile more), while making Henry sufficiently jealous to remember his love for his wife. That's what brought us to the movie in the first place, even if we thought we wanted the parlor tricks. The human element is nearly always the driving aspect of film. Hey, we're human and, as such, interested in how and why people like us move through the world, even when the world is made-up.

How to Not Burn Books

Occasionally even less is needed to trick the eye and brain. In *Indiana Jones and the Last Crusade* (1989), Steven Spielberg includes a scene of a Nazi book-burning reminiscent of the notorious real-life 1933 Berlin burning of "un-German" books. By all accounts, the idea for the scene was Spielberg's, along with the insistence that no actual books could be burned. The problem? Nothing but a book burns quite like a book. The solution? A couple of guys with paint rollers and a huge stack of phone directories. A few buckets of several colors, a few hours, and, voilà: a cultural atrocity minus the destruction of any intellectual heritage.

The master of getting the most from the lowest tech is, as with so many things, Alfred Hitchcock. His most important technological tool is the single-edge razor blade. Attached to an excellent film-editorial hand, of course. In his most notorious scene, which we've discussed already, we see many things: dress, wig, shower curtain, showerhead, naked body (or sufficiently suggestive parts thereof), knife, blood. The rapidity of the sequence of shots tricks our minds into believing— into remembering—that our eyes have seen a murder. If you slow down the montage to a frame-by-frame experience, you quickly realize that we have seen no such thing. But that's exactly why the trick is so good: we don't watch movies frame by frame. We see them at twenty-four frames per second, so a half-dozen frames comprising a mere quarter of a second will register with us without actually showing anything clearly. *Psycho* doesn't have to supply the connective tissue of the scene, since our minds are more than happy to undertake the task. Considered separately, the images don't make sense; collectively, we get the whole awful message. No novel could ever convey that message with such terrible economy.

Here's another thing books can't do. Woody Allen has always investigated the difficulties of communication between men and women, nowhere better than in *Annie Hall* (1977). His character, Alvy Singer, is—surprise!—a neurotic, Jewish comedian who has just broken up with the eponymous Annie, a specimen of that alien species, Gentile woman. One of their big issues has been communication, and as a block on that particular road, the ethno-religious matter is a pebble compared to the male-female boulder. One of the great techniques of the movie is the breaking of the "fourth wall," that invisible barrier that keeps characters in their proper place and speaking to one another rather than to us. He trots out a wonderful example early on: while waiting for a movie, Alvy and Annie are subjected to a monologue by the man standing behind them in line ("on line" for the native Brooklynite) on Fellini, film generally, the pernicious influence of television, and the theories of Marshall McLuhan. Finally, Alvy, who has been kvetching the entire time, can take no more and steps out of line to address us about his annoyance. The annoying neighbor then asserts his right to pontificate in a free country, to which Alvy responds that the dope knows nothing about McLuhan's theories. That claim draws a comeback that said dope teaches a course on media at Columbia, at which Alvy produces the real McLuhan from behind a sign to say that the man, indeed, doesn't understand his theories at all. A normal director might be satisfied with this sight joke as is, but Allen has Alvy break through the proscenium again to say, "Boy, if life were only like this." He has already done groundwork for this scene in his reminiscence of his early education when the adult Alvy appears in his elementary school classroom to defend his younger self's transgression (he kissed a little girl) by saying he "never had a latency period."

The stage is set, then, for what may be the pièce de résistance: subtitles. After their initial meeting at a tennis club, Annie invites Alvy up to her apartment for a glass of wine. They're both extremely nervous and clumsy—and self-aware. As they sip wine out on her balcony, they attempt to make light conversation, but what they say is not what they think. How do we know? Allen provides subtitles. When Annie says that she dabbles in photography, the subtitle reads, "I dabble? Listen to me. What a jerk." Moments later, while Alvy is saying that photography has yet to develop a full set of aesthetic criteria, he's thinking (as we see), "I wonder what she looks like naked." This exchange is one of the funniest in the movie

precisely because we know that it's true. The language of meeting and courtship is fraught with subtexts, but in real life we
can never see them. In film, at least in this film, we can. And
their subtexts are chiefly ours: insecurity, interest, doubts, and,
mostly, awkwardness. Indeed, if there is one moment in the
movie that encapsulates the whole, it's this one. The anxieties
and uncertainties of the relationship that the film explores may
here be writ small, but written they are.

The beauty of these inventions is that they require almost
nothing in the way of technical expertise. Imagine, a human
being popping up in an unexpected place! How hard is that?
And yet, they get at the heart of what makes the movies magical. Take the McLuhan example: you simply cannot do that in
a painting or a novel. Even in a play, it can't be the same. We
need the real McLuhan, who by definition is limited in time
and space. So even if you could have persuaded him to appear
in, say, the original Broadway production, he wouldn't be available for the road company, much less for all those revivals and
high school performances. In film, though, if you can get him
once, you have him forever. The subtitles, similarly, can function in only one medium. Onstage, we would have to either
have the characters hold up essentially unreadable signs or else
flash the subtitles up on a marquee or rear-projection screen,
either of which would outstrip the characters in size and,
therefore, relative importance. Only the movie screen can provide that curious mixture of intimacy, simultaneity, and scale
that allows the joke to work.

I don't mean to suggest that anything books can do, film can
do better. Anyone who has seen one of the meager attempts
at filming stream-of-consciousness novels knows that's not
true. On the other hand, it can find its own way of projecting
consciousness, as two more recent films demonstrate. In both
Birdman (2014) and *Woman in Gold* (2015), we see the main
characters experiencing their pasts. In the former, Michael

Keaton's Riggan Thomson is a washed-up actor who once starred in a series of superhero movies as the title character. Now, as he tries to mount a play, he is haunted, literally, by his earlier character: we see and hear the derision that Birdman directs at Riggan. In the latter film, Helen Mirren's Maria Altmann periodically sees her Viennese past before her eyes— and so do we. In each case, no special techniques are required. Characters are inserted into scenes (in the first) or entire scenes are filmed (in the second). Yet the results are genuinely magical. Whatever novels may have over film in the specifics of stream of consciousness, they can never do this with the same ease. To achieve the same level of immediacy—that is to say, by jumping directly to a character or scene that wasn't there a second before—the novelist will leave at least some readers confused. If she provides a transition—that is to say, if she mediates the shift—by definition the immediacy is lost. If, on the other hand, we suddenly see the fantasy sequences begin in *Birdman* or *Woman in Gold*, or indeed in *Black Swan* (2010), our minds can accept and process that shift. We can tell there has been a shift, but our eyes and brains have been trained to accept that.

Sometimes the best movie magic requires no camera tricks at all—just brilliant planning and incredible courage. For the most famous moment in *Steamboat Bill, Jr.* (1928), Buster Keaton reprised and improved a stunt he had first used in *One Week* (1920)—the falling wall trick. In this case, as a cyclone hits town, the infirmary in which young Bill is a patient loses its roof, then his hospital bed is blown hither and yon, including through a horse barn, finally landing him in front of a building whose front falls down around him, the star providentially saved by standing where an open window will land. Being wrong by mere inches would prove fatal. When the critical moment in filming came, even the cameraman, as he later confessed, had to look away from the possible disaster. As the finished film shows, Keaton emerges unscathed (not always true of his stunts) and, looking around at the destruction, abandons his customary stillness for a quick exit from danger.

So that's the low-definition end of the scale. At the other extreme, film has probably advanced more in terms of special effect techniques in the last twenty years than in the previous hundred. We can make this sound like a thriller and call it the Rise of the Machines, although the Rise of the Processors is probably more accurate. The work at studios like George Lucas's Industrial Light & Magic, Disney, and Pixar had been advancing the world of special effects for years, but it took one man's frustration to really push things forward. James Cameron, fresh from the massive success of *Titanic* in 1997, had a vision for a film that he could not realize with current technology. This one would be a sort of *King Solomon's Mines* for the digital age, assuming the digital age would get its act together. It took the better part of a decade for CGI and 3-D and motion-capture technologies to advance to the point that he could make the version of *Avatar* that he saw in his head. The result was eye-popping: whatever critics and viewers may have thought about the tale and its telling—although most responses were positive—the visuals completely blew people away. Turning human actors into ten-foot-tall blue Na'vi humanoids is an achievement in itself; having them ride on mountain banshees (something between a dragon and a horse with elements of a butterfly) through completely imagined spaces is one for the ages. The seamless mix of traditional and computer-generated cinematic elements caught everyone's attention. One of the great challenges of the digital age of filmmaking to that point was the sometimes glaring boundary between the computerized elements and those shot with standard technology.

Of course, progress had been coming throughout the decade. Peter Jackson's *Lord of the Rings* trilogy had demonstrated that CGI could turn ordinary humans into dwarves, giants, Hobbits, and at least one Gollum. Indeed, actor Andy Serkis's motion-capture performance as the Ring-obsessed blue maniac was the real star turn of the films. And the several Harry Potter films made great use of CGI in a host of ways. In fact, Alfonso Cuarón, director of installment three, *Harry Potter and the Prisoner of Azkaban* (2004), had wanted to use puppetry rather than CGI for the Dementors, but expense and technical difficulty ultimately led him to abandon the switch. He also made use of "bullet time," the slowing or virtual stopping of some elements—in his case, the Muggle world outside the Knight Bus that takes Harry to the Leaky Cauldron.

Finally, we should note that films can do magic because they *are* magic. Let's go to the limit on this one: no CGI, no special effects, not even any falling walls or subtitles. Just regular—if there be such things—movie shots. How, we might ask, can a man time-travel? How can he leave his own historical moment and, for however long an interval, travel back, oh, eighty years? I suppose that if we worked at it long enough, we could come up with a fictive time machine or time tunnel or Chinese box or something (and those have all been employed), but we'd be better off with the simplest of devices. How about if he just gets into a car?

In *Midnight in Paris* (2011), that's how Woody Allen launches Gil Pender, successful screenwriter and balked novelist, hapless future husband and hopeless, or perhaps hopeful, romantic, back into his idealized twenties, when the City of Light was full of artistic exiles. The device is simplicity itself: on the stroke of midnight, a 1920s Peugeot Type 176 full of party-goers in strange dress drives up the hill and stops. Shades of Rip Van Winkle! Gil then finds himself deposited among the beautiful and desperate of twenties Paris, meeting Zelda and F. Scott Fitzgerald, Ernest Hemingway, Gertrude Stein, Pablo Picasso, and Salvador Dalí, among a host of others. At his first stop Cole Porter is playing "Let's Do It." And not as in "Cole Porter is playing on the phonograph." No, no, no. *Cole Porter* (actually, Yves Heck as Cole Porter, the original being some-what unavailable in 2011) is playing the piano while singing his latest witty creation. One of the beauties of the setup is that chronology need not be strictly observed. The song, like the Peugeot, is from 1928, while Hemingway has only one book (and is still on good terms with Gertrude Stein), putting the year at either 1925 or 1926, since his second, *The Sun Also Rises,* would appear in October 1926. Evidently, being magi-cal makes an era somewhat unstable. Oh, and Gil also finds a fictive romantic interest (what would a Woody Allen film be without one?) played with incandescent appeal by Marion Cotillard. Whenever the car delivers him, Gil arrives in his cherished era. When he tries to hoof it, no soap. At one point, he is sitting in a bar with Hemingway but needs to go home and retrieve his novel manuscript so Hem can take it to Ger-trude Stein. He starts down the street, then does an about-face and attempts to go back, only to find the bar has become a modern Laundromat. See? Simple.

When Gil tries to get his fiancée, Inez, to travel with him to the past, she grows impatient and leaves just minutes before midnight. On the stroke of twelve, the magic auto again drives up the incline and whisks him off to further adventures. No special techniques are required of the filmmakers, and the only requirement for us is *the willing suspension of disbelief* (more in a moment), that time-out we take from our knowledge that, for

Figure 10. Why not? Gil (Owen Wilson) with Hemingway
(Cory Stoll) and Gertrude Stein (Kathy Bates).
©Gravier Productions, 2011. All Rights Reserved.

instance, the past cannot be accessed by means of an antique Peugeot. This is a movie; of course it can be. We have only to allow it to take us along.

This story leads us to a basic truth: here's the real magic of movies: they make us see things that never were. They show us stories full of death in which no person died. Only characters did. And yet we respond as if they had. When Butch and Sundance ran through that door for the first time into a sepia freeze frame and a hail of sonic bullets—the first time for me, that is—I felt many things—panic, grief, despair—at their loss. The one thing I didn't feel in the moment was "It doesn't matter; they're not real." I *knew* that, of course. How could I not, sitting in a car at a drive-in theater a good hundred and twenty yards from the screen? You can't get much more divorced from the action than that. Yet what we know and what we feel are entirely separate things. The film had made me—made us— care about those characters within the context of the story *as if* they were real, which brings us to the curious paradox of watching real persons play unreal ones. Here are some basic facts:

- Sylvester Stallone is not Rocky. Nor Rambo.

- Neither Greta Garbo nor Keira Knightley is Anna Karenina.

- Humphrey Bogart is not Sam Spade, Philip Marlowe, or Rick Blaine.

- Nor is Clint Eastwood Dirty Harry Callahan or John Wayne the Ringo Kid.

- Et cetera.

- Not one of the preceding facts matters when we watch their films. Only the imaginative and emotional truths of the movies themselves matter.

This is what Samuel Taylor Coleridge, who missed the movie age by most of a century, meant when he said that we willingly suspend our disbelief at the door of the literary work. We know better, of course, than to believe that an actor is really a made-up character, that a man can fly, that Hobbits and wizards exist. We have it within our power, however, to *choose* to accept that reality. We don't really have to believe in the reality (this sometimes causes difficulties for the excessively literal-minded, folks like totalitarian rulers); we have only to *suspend* our otherwise quite reasonable *disbelief* in it. The process works out to a sort of compact between artist and audience. If the makers keep faith with us by providing what the late novelist John Gardner calls "the vivid and continuous dream," if they don't let us down through faulty technique or failures of the imagination (bad dialogue, clumsy action, or Ed Wood–style, *Plan 9 from Outer Space* ham-handedness), we will keep faith with them by believing, for the time we are their audience, in their reality. We won't needlessly bring in our knowledge of the larger reality, our pedantry, our boundless rationalism. It's a square deal. Paul Newman didn't die. Robert Redford didn't die. They went on to make many wonderful and a few sketchy movies. But Butch and Sundance died. And in that moment, our minds are with them, not the actors who make us believe in them. If that's not magic, I don't know what is.

16

You Can't Step into the Same Movie Twice

Old joke:

Question: How many movies have been made in the history of film?

Answer: One. Then they remade it again and again. And again and again and . . .

Okay, maybe not. But you get the idea. How many times have you sat in a movie house and thought, How many times have I seen this? In a worst-case scenario, the question morphs into, How many times have I been forced to endure this? Or maybe, Can't they think of anything else to do? Well, guess what? This derivative business didn't just start.

Everybody knows about remakes, sequels, prequels, and even laterals. What you may not know is how much of movie-making involves raiding the vaults for everything from whole film concepts to individual stunts. The greatest film school, as everyone in the business knows, is the screening room.

Let's take a worst-case scenario. Let's call it, oh, I don't know, maybe, *Psycho*? In 1998 Gus Van Sant infamously did a shot-by-shot remake of Hitchcock's 1960 classic, with Vince Vaughan in the Tony Perkins role as Norman Bates, Anne Heche in the Janet Leigh role as Marion Crane, and, most disastrously, Van Sant in the role of Hitchcock. What was needed at the outset was for someone to ask a really basic question: How many ways are there for this project to go wrong? Chiefly, the answer only has to be "one." Sure, sure—Vince Vaughan is no Tony Perkins, Anne Heche no Janet Leigh, and while Julianne Moore may well be a better actress than Vera Miles, in the ways that matter to the film, she's no Vera Miles. None of that, however, really matters, because something, or rather someone, else looms over all. For all his brilliance, and Van Sant is sometimes capable of brilliance, and for all his indebtedness to the Master, he's simply no Hitch. To do *Psycho* requires a special touch, one that few directors possess. I'm thinking the number is right around one.

Here's the thing: if you're going to film a shot-by-shot remake, assuming that it is ever a good idea, you'd darned well better bring something new to the party. Which is nearly impossible. If an older movie is lousy, why reproduce it so exactly? And if it's a classic, what on earth would make you think you could do it better?

There is, however, one aspect of the remake that matched the original. The film stuck to the great Bernard Herrmann's score. In fact, the music was the same music that Herrmann had recorded for the original. Sometimes a complete lack of originality is a good thing.

On the other hand, there are times when the remake works. Really. There's plenty of reason to doubt, but I'll give you an example: *The Thomas Crown Affair*. First of all, let it be said that I really like the 1968 original. Steve McQueen, Faye Dunaway, Michel Legrand score, gliders, dune buggies, "The Windmills of Your Mind," the world's sexiest chess scene (or maybe the chessiest sex scene)—what's not to like? It enjoyed modest success with audiences if not with critics at the time and subsequently grew in popularity as viewers caught up with Norman Jewison's direction. Here are the basics: the eponymous financier, played by McQueen (just before costarring with a Mustang in *Bullitt*), finding his customary diversions—polo, dune buggy racing, glider flying, cheating at golf, all of which he does superlatively—insufficiently thrilling, arranges for a bank heist carried out by five complete strangers, who are instructed to leave the loot, all $2.6 million of it, in a cemetery trash can. Fresh from shooting up the screen in the previous year's *Bonnie and Clyde*, Dunaway as Vicki Anderson is an insurance investigator brought in on the case who almost immediately suspects Thomas, who for his part relishes the challenge of besting this obviously clever and persistent woman. They fall in passion, if not love, over the aforementioned chess game in one of the great seductions ever committed to celluloid. Despite the obvious heat between them, they stick to their assigned roles, Vicki determined to get her man (and not to the altar), Thomas to win this match of wits. Eventually, as she closes in, he arranges another, virtually identical, robbery with five different strangers, although in this version shots are fired and the implication is that things have gone wrong, although we're never entirely sure. He finds that she has betrayed him, which forces decisive action. Vicki lies in wait with police backup at the cemetery, but when Crown's Rolls-Royce pulls up, he's not in it. Instead, he has sent a note asking her to bring the money and join him in flying off to some uncertain but well-heeled future; failing that, she should remember him fondly and keep the Rolls. In tears, she rips the note to shreds as he takes off into an extradition-proof sky.

Well, when a movie continues to fire imaginations down the years, what are you going to do? Remake it, of course. I'm not sure what the statute of limitations is on remakes, but thirty years (actually thirty-one in this instance) seems about right. Still, when I heard that a beloved film was being remade and would star TV's Remington-Steele-turned-James-Bond, Irishman Pierce Brosnan, I had serious doubts. Very little in the action-figure performances I had seen suggested the sort of reserves necessary to play the enigma that is Thomas Crown. True, his Bond did a lot less mugging for the camera than, say, Roger Moore's, but still. Moreover, *Remington Steele* was typically vapid American television, asking little more of its title character than to show up and look beautiful, a task for which he was eminently qualified. Let's just say that hopes were not stratospheric. I've never been more pleased to be wrong.

One nice thing about this movie is that we don't have to

Figure 11. All kinds of cool.
Steve McQueen . . . Courtesy
of MGM/Getty Images.

Figure 12. . . . and Pierce Brosnan
as Thomas Crown. Courtesy
of MGM/Getty Images.

ask if the filmmakers were seriously reprising the original. For one thing, they use the same title. That one is sort of hard to deny. For another, the female lead in the 1968 classic, Faye Dunaway, speaks first in the new film as Tommy Crown's therapist. Then there are a host of quoted scenes and shots, including the golf match that displays the protagonist's desperate need for stimulation. The remake has a lot going for it. Pierce Brosnan and Rene Russo are equal in screen presence to McQueen and Dunaway, fashionable and charismatic in a turn-of-the-millennium way.

Why does it work? Because it is just similar enough—and different enough—in just the right ways. Let's consider a few of those. First, the heist: undertaken by someone clearly not in it for the money. In both films, Thomas Crown is immensely wealthy and successful. The leads are great looking—lots of high cheekbones all around—and generate a good deal of heat when together; we believe they could manage affairs even in this highly fraught situation. Each film develops a high degree of intrigue in its fullest sense between Crown and his hot pursuer: a mix of fascination, love of the game, suspicion, doubt, attraction, and buried hostility. A fear of being bored—or boring. In each film, the investigator knows she's got her man. Russo's Catherine Banning announces at their first encounter, a charity bash for the museum where Crown receives accolades for providing a substitute for the Monet that has been stolen (by him), that the chase is on. The last two-thirds of each movie is a cat-and-mouse game between Crown and his beautiful pursuer. So, plenty of friendly reminders that the folks making this film are fond of the original.

And then there are the differences. First of all, this one moves from Boston as its base of operations to New York. In the original, Thomas Crown is a mostly unspecified business tycoon; in the new one his firm is, in a nice touch, Crown Acquisitions. And we all know, even if it isn't inevitably true, that financier types hang out in Manhattan. More significant, the film is following Sutton's Law: in this case, go where the art is. Crown could certainly arrange for a fabulous painting to be stolen in Boston. Or Chicago or Detroit or Los Angeles or any of a half-dozen different cities in this country. But for the film to click, he needs not only to steal a fabulous painting but to take it from the most famous museum in America. That, of course, would be the Metropolitan Museum of Art. Plus, nowhere else looks quite like the Met, inside or out. It's the one museum on the continent that, even if people haven't been there, they have probably seen; it's the one that says, "Inside, there be art." Beyond setting, we notice pretty early on that, while Thomas has his name, "Vicki" gets a new one. Catherine Banning, although sharing numerous traits, is a different being: different tastes, different haircut, different mannerisms, and a way different laugh. She is more aggressive, even predatory, than her predecessor. She is more nearly out of control, so the fight within herself is more visible, and we probably see it coming sooner. And we see more of her than of Vicki. Her relationship with Crown is not encoded in a chess match: what stands for sex in the new version is not some board game but, well, sex. Panting. Moaning. Writhing. Nudity. Plenty of that last one (times two).

But mere differences are not enough. They have to be the right ones. As do the similarities. The point is, you can't simply say, modern films need their female leads to be more aggressive. Even if you could, how much more would be enough? Where's the line for "too much"? Which other activity says Crown is rich and a little extreme without saying he's off his nut? In other words, what sport suggests the mix of danger and control that we need to see in him. Sailing itself, probably not. Catamaran racing? Now you're talking. It also lets him go too far without dying—or killing someone else—so that Catherine can say, "I saw him wreck a hundred-thousand-dollar boat because he liked the splash." Or perhaps just the spectacle, because it is quite a show when it pitches over, with Tommy in the outrigger seat suspended, momentarily, seemingly as high as a masthead before pitching headlong into the sea. That mix of recklessness and precision is integral to his character and therefore to the movie. You couldn't achieve as much in three minutes of dialogue as in that single frozen image just before he takes the plunge.

And there's not a calculator in the world that can tell you which elements to keep and which to jettison in order to make magic happen. The only machine that can calibrate that decision is the human brain. Which, admittedly, often gets things wrong. Oh, but when it succeeds!

Beyond the remake, there's the category we should proba- bly call "reimagining." Say you've got a genre you just loved from the Sunday afternoon movies when you were a kid. For those of you who were recently kids, there was once a time when football was not on wall-to-wall on Sundays. And in those benighted times, there were often two options. You could watch Don Wilson, who was Jack Benny's announcer, hawking classical music in lush arrangements, or you could watch old movies, usually black and white (always, if you lived at my house). What about all those other channels? Well, out in West Cornfield, we could only pull two channels. But enough of walking to school barefoot in the snow uphill in both directions. The point here is that we were blessed, if the Browns weren't on, with an endless supply of movies from the 1940s and '50s, which were not that long before the time we watched them. And among those old movies were some clas- sics. Any given Sunday might offer up Stewart Granger in *King Solomon's Mines* (1950), Humphrey Bogart and Lauren Bacall in *The Big Sleep* (1946), Barbara Stanwyck and Fred Mac-Murray in *Double Indemnity* (1944), John Wayne in *Fort Apache* (1948), Rory Calhoun in a lesser Western, or Robert Mitchum in everything. I first saw *Zorba the Greek* (1964) on a Sunday. Better, because no one was paying much attention, I first saw *Never on Sunday* (1960) on a Sunday. And they say television isn't educational. By all the evidence I can see, the filmmakers of my generation were indoors on Sundays watching those same movies.

And sometimes they thought they could improve upon the original, or at least give it a new spin for a new generation. No one here wants another lengthy meditation on the revisionist Western, but I would like to focus on just one entry, the one that got John Wayne his Oscar as one-eyed drunken lawman Rooster Cogburn, *True Grit*. The by-the-book would-be hero of the piece, Texas Ranger La Boeuf (the year's hot property, singer Glen Campbell), is boastful and naïve, and he winds up getting himself dead, although even he is granted moments of heroism before the end. In some other era, La Boeuf, young, dashing, good looking, would be the hero of the film. Here, though, he is cannon fodder, skillful but ultimately destined for a death that makes a point larger than his character. And Cogburn, even if he takes his horse over a fence at the end, nevertheless is too old and fat, so that when Mattie Ross (played with annoying earnestness by Kim Darby) offers him the chance to be buried in her family plot (when appropriate), his reluctant acceptance is as much for his era—and his genre—as himself. For the little time that remained in his career, in *The Shootist* and *The Cowboys* (1972) and especially in *Rooster Cogburn* with a very prissy Katharine Hepburn—a sort of *True Grit*–meets–*The African Queen*—his work seems elegiac, a sort of nostalgic victory lap by the great cowboy. And this was one of his greatest performances, in a late and much-loved film.

Now, let's leap forward a few decades. Once the statute of limitations ran out, someone got the bright idea of remaking *True Grit*. At first blush it might seem that Joel and Ethan Coen would be odd persons to have that particular moment of nostalgia. In retrospect, they were just the right guys for the job. There's one thing you can't do with a movie that well known and that much associated with a gargantuan figure such as Wayne: you can't simply copy it. If audiences are to care about the film, you're going to have to bring something new to the table. In the case of the Coen adaptation, part of that newness was a greater fidelity to the Charles Portis novel. There are changes from that text, of course. Mattie Ross doesn't haggle with the undertaker over her father's burial in the novel, nor does she sleep among the bodies to save money on a boardinghouse, but those additions act in the service of character development: she's thrifty, spunky, and mentally tough. But the overall faithfulness extends to retaining the love of language and the humor in the novel. Those elements assure that there is less of a star-turn quality to the picture. That may be in part because Jeff Bridges as Rooster Cogburn mumbles his lines rather than growling them as Wayne did, but it is largely because he, a major star to be sure, is not the contemporary King of the Western. The other factor here is a change of genre. The 1969 film is a straight Western, while in keeping with Portis's original, the newer film is a sort of black comedy Western. The horse elements are all present and accounted for—if anything, this new one is more violent and, dare I say, grittier? But it is also much funnier than its forerunner. In other words, it's a Coen brothers film. It convinces us that there are some vicious people in the world, some ugly accidents, but it does so with humor and irony.

The characters are different, too, chiefly because the actors playing them are different. Bridges as Cogburn is more cold-blooded and damaged by life; both his drunkenness and his violence are uglier than Wayne's. Matt Damon as Texas Ranger LaBoeuf is given more to do; his role is meatier than that given to Glen Campbell, who lent a blond glow and almost superhuman callowness to the proceedings. Damon is also a bit friendlier and less rule-bound than Campbell in the part, as if some of Cogburn's warmer qualities had been handed off to LaBoeuf. At the same time, he is highly competent, capable of making a four-hundred-yard rifle shot at the critical moment. Without doubt, the Coens give us a movie that is honestly *True Grit* yet unmistakably their own. Tradition *and* innovation. That's what we want in a remake.

This discussion isn't really about genre but about specific borrowings from specific films. After all, every genre and, for that matter, almost every film by this late date in film history has its specific antecedents, and sometimes the new entry seems to have an earlier one in mind. Case in point, the flyboy adventure. I was at the world premiere of *Top Gun* in 1986. That would be the East Lansing, Michigan, world premiere. The late Jim Cash was the word half of a writing team with Jack Epps Jr., and he only traveled to Hollywood when it couldn't be avoided, so he hosted an advance screening and bash for colleagues and friends, which happily included me. This was the movie that cemented Tom Cruise's status as a bona fide movie star, lest there be any doubt after *Risky Business* and *All the Right Moves* (both 1983). It also provided our first really good looks at future stars Val Kilmer, Meg Ryan, Tim Robbins, Kelly McGillis, and Anthony Edwards. It has become even more of a big deal in retrospect than it had seemed at the time, and while it was in no serious danger of winning a golden statuette as best picture, it was a major success.

The movie was thrilling in the right places, the party swell, and the evening a smashing success. A couple of years later, a colleague and I were discussing the episode, when he mentioned that the movie drew heavily on the silent film *Wings* (1927). They are both about fighter pilots, World War I Army Air Corps in the earlier film, Cold War navy in the latter. In 1917–18, when *Wings* takes place, there was no possibility to land planes on aircraft carriers, so that was a major difference. Planes were a lot faster six decades on. Even so, the shots of air combat in the two movies were equally dizzying in their time. If the biplanes of *Wings* were slower, so was the pace of land travel. More important, aside from a few crazy daredevils, many of them holdovers from the aerial war of the previous decade, almost no one in the audience had ever experienced air travel. What, then, could be more exciting than a movie about war in the air featuring real fighter planes? As for *Top Gun*, George Lucas never thought up an X-Wing dogfight faster or more thrilling than the one between American F-14 Tomcats and Soviet MiG-28s. Everything about the action sequences is exciting. Not only had airplane technology advanced in sixty years, so had cameras and film, affording new shots and angles not previously possible. The film also appeared in the heyday of the MTV music video, when directors had dusted off all sorts of quick cuts and effects long disused in conventional moviemaking, including some not seen since the silent era. As a result, the movie has a much quicker, even jerkier feel than films of recent decades.

Speed, however, is one of the few significant differences between the two movies. Each is concerned with the nature of warfare, the giddy nature of flight, friendship and rivalry, guilt, and the search for self. In their different ways, *Wings*' Jack Powell and *Top Gun*'s Pete "Maverick" Mitchell need to grow up and find their mature selves. They need to work through enmities with colleagues, and they need to overcome the guilt they feel at causing the deaths of best friends. These situations are part of a very old story; nearly all warrior tales since *The Iliad* deal with these in some fashion. Substitute a chariot or a frigate or a cavalry troupe for the F-14A and you're there. These two variants, though, share something more. *Wings* set the template for what a dogfight looks like. *Top Gun* followed that template. In fact, with the distances at which modern jets fight, dogfight choreography becomes problematic: it doesn't really look like two pilots engaged in wing-to-wing combat. The director and cinematographer—and writers, to a certain extent—had to look back to earlier movies in order to give us something we could recognize *as* a dogfight. Ultimately, that goes back to the first aerial combat movie. What it comes down to is that almost any film about fighter pilots owes something to *Wings*, which, even though it was lost for many years, was known and remembered in Hollywood so that it really did set the model for future iterations. Sadly, I never got to ask Jim Cash about his specific debt to the earlier classic, but it doesn't matter. You can't film a dogfight that doesn't have *Wings* in its family tree.

As we consider remakes of established movies, we can hardly overlook the place of the franchise series. Critics of the series sometimes deride the phenomenon as a contemporary debasement of cinema—and have done so virtually since the inception of the movies. After the success of *The Thin Man* (1934) came a string of movies, the first of which was, unsurprisingly, *After the Thin Man* (1936). Audiences in the thirties and forties were treated to a series of Charlie Chan movies starring no fewer than three different lead actors. And of course, there's

Bond. James Bond. *Spectre* (2015) marks the twenty-sixth appearance of the superspy over fifty-two years, a remarkable durability, even when spread among six different actors. More recently, the Star Wars franchise, begun in 1977, stands at seven films and counting with 2015's *The Force Awakens*; what began as *Mad Max* has arrived at four films; the seven Harry Potter novels became eight films; *The Lord of the Rings* and *The Hobbit* tallied three films each under the direction of Peter Jackson; the Tom Cruise Mission: Impossible franchise is up to five films with *Mission: Impossible–Rogue Nation* (perhaps more commonly known simply as *MI-5*); the teen vampire Twilight Saga phenomenon finished up with five films from four Stephenie Meyer novels; *The Hunger Games*, having made Jennifer Lawrence a major star, four films from three novels; and on and on. Superhero franchises are even more difficult to keep track of, given that there are reboots and new stars and stories coming and going all the time. Someone can figure all that out, but at present I lack a graphing calculator. The amazing thing about all these series is that, contrary to the traditional wisdom on sequels that they invariably wind down, many of them have maintained consistently high quality and a few even got better. To be sure, there have been some that flagged over time. After three more or less classic films (now numbered IV, V, and VI), the *Star Wars* prequel trilogy was widely panned by critics and suffered through by fans, only to reward audiences with a stellar comeback in the J. J. Abrams–directed *Episode VII: The Force Awakens*, providing hope that the series can close out the nine films in high style.

This last film suggests some of the things that can make a sequel successful. First, fans look for some consistency in story from prior encounters. This movie knows what came before and brings back old favorites Han Solo, Luke Skywalker, Princess (now General) Leia, Chewbacca, R2-D2, and C-3PO, all played by the original actors. Their new backstories all cohere with what we might call their general mythos. At the same time, the movie belongs to younger actors and newer characters, as befits a leap thirty or so years into the future from *Return of the Jedi*. The major personal issues have been settled for our old friends during the course of the original three films, and movies live on personal stories. Happily, the future contains new characters with their own complicated lives. Rey (Daisy Ridley), an orphan with murky origins who survives by scavenging, and Finn (John Boyega), raised and trained to be a Storm Trooper before he goes over to the Resistance, not to mention Kylo Ren (Adam Driver), the new villain with a tough backstory of his own. Two of them appear to have paternal connections to the original threesome. Now these three have some issues to work out. That alone won't solve the riddle of the remake—a Jar Jar Binks can scuttle the best-laid plans of any director—but melding the fresh with the familiar is a good place to start. And it can't hurt to have Lawrence Kasdan (*Return of the Jedi*, *The Empire Strikes Back*), one of the great writers of screen dialogue, back at the word processor, although he can't be part of the plan for all sequels.

This observation brings us back to our Screenreading 101 course: while we can never predict what will make a movie succeed, if we study the earlier and later films, we can learn something about how and perhaps why the remake or sequel succeeds. And study, of course, just means watching with a bit of care. As anyone who has watched sequels or remakes at all knows, the secret to good ones is the closest thing to alchemy. So when you view one or the other, it's another one of those times to use the split-mind trick. Keep a memory of the earlier film(s) active against which you can play off the new work. How does the newer work honor the prior one? Or deliberately ignore it? Or subvert some element that had seemed settled? Any number of possibilities of that relationship may suggest themselves. At the same time, see the new film for what it is. Appreciate its strengths and weaknesses on their own terms. As with any other cinematic issue, what matters most is the quality of the movie in front of us. Ultimately, you'll want to bring those two perceptions together: How does the current film's fidelity to or departure from its predecessor influence its quality? How does it extend the series? Undermine it? Take us somewhere useful or down a blind alley? Then you can be an alchemist in your own right.

We could go on till kingdom come and never run out of examples of remakes, reenvisionings, prequels, and sequels. The point is that the men and women who make movies were fans of movies long before they ever thought of making one. They have seen, on average, whole warehouses full of old celluloid, and the films they've not seen were probably seen by the filmmakers they loved and studied, so that there's only two or three degrees of separation between any current film and its earliest antecedent. You can't rob a train on film and not invoke *The Great Train Robbery*. And after all, why would you want to?

A couple of weeks later, Dave and Lexi run into each other again. He has some explaining to do.

"Hey, Dave, you missed trivia night last week."

"I got a little busy. I've been watching the other *Mad Max* films."

"Really! How's that going?"

"It's interesting. Looking back after the new one, the original is sort of like a student film. Lots of similarities—you know, deserts and wild cars and chases and stuff—but it's so much smaller. It's just one man's story in a world gone crazy, which is okay. Then each one got bigger and more complex, until *Fury Road*, which is really about the crazy world and how people try to get through it. Max still matters, but there's no way he's carrying this one. It's so much fuller than the others. Lots of ideas but still plenty loud and wild."

"Wow, listen to you. Dave, the film historian."

"Just having some fun. Isn't that what movies are there for?"

17

Listen to the Music

ONCE UPON A TIME, movies didn't have music. Sort of. That is, they didn't have sound. Silent pictures, you will recall, weren't just pictures without dialogue. This wasn't Kabuki theater or something. Filmmakers lacked the technology to attach sound to those black-and-white frames zooming by the lens at eighteen frames per second. Even then, however, there was music. Musical scores, the printed kind, were distributed with prints of the movies, and each movie house had to find a way to produce the music. Many big-city movie houses, the fancied-up movie "palaces" especially, had their own orchestras. Other theaters a notch or so down might have had the mighty Wurlitzer Theater Organ, a work of art in itself and capable of all sorts of sounds. Obviously, while this was a manageable strategy in New York or Chicago, it was tougher to pull off in East Left-Out, Saskatchewan. So East Left-Out, like most smaller communities, would have had a piano. And it would have had an in-house pianist or two (it's tough work, after all, to tickle the ivories for multiple shows every day) whose job it was to interpret the score and make it work with the film. On the one hand, this system was great for musicians, who with the advent of the movies found a host of new job opportunities. Indeed, one of the arguments against the talkies when they came in had to do with all the musicians' jobs that would be lost overnight. And in ways no one could notice, it was pretty great for audiences whether they knew it or not. Every performance was guaranteed unique, since no pianist would ever hit exactly the same notes in exactly the same way, no matter how hard he tried, in any two screenings of a movie.

That second strength, alas, was also the weakness of the system. From the studio perspective, there was no quality control. Was East Left-Out's pianist any good technically? Did he understand movies enough to sync up his playing in meaningful ways? Was he sober? For drink was the downfall of more than one accompanist during the heyday of live music at the Odeon. Eventually, of course, we moved into sync-sound and put all sorts of local music types out of business. But the accompaniment did get more predictable.

I usually don't tell you what to think, but every once in a while, I make an exception if the outcome is really important. This is such a *once*. It has to do with best. You know, there are no bests of anything and "best" is subjective and all that, right? Well, no. Here's a best. There is one—and only one—best development of a theme. Why is it best? Because it cannot be bettered. Because it was adapted to a cigarette ad for about a thousand years and adopted by a Disney ride. Because, first of all, it was composed by the great Elmer Bernstein, one of the gods of movie music. But mostly because of how it was employed in the film.

Don't know the theme? Bet you do. Try this: bum-BUM-ba-bum, ba-ba-ba-BUM-ba-bum. Doesn't ring any bells? Still, you've likely heard it. If you are of a certain age, the only way you cannot know it is to never have watched television. You never saw the Marlboro Man without it.

It starts small. Themes often do, but this is different. It's missing some elements—a lot of elements. We encounter this stripped-down version when we first meet the hero. When he offers to drive the hearse up to the town cemetery because certain racist elements won't allow an Indian to be buried there, we get some rumblings in the percussion section of a still-unformed theme. A stranger, another hard case like our hero, borrows a shotgun from the stagecoach to ride along, the staccato brushings of the lower strings kick in, and when he walks across the street in front of the hearse, suddenly we have the sprightly woodwinds hinting at the lyrical introduction and telling us he's on the right side of this business. *Now*, we think, we're getting somewhere. But not just yet. There's some dark business, and a countertheme comes in heavy, dissonant, and in a minor chord. It tells us this adventure won't be a lark. But with resolve and a quick gun, our heroes get the body to the cemetery.

Later, it turns out some Mexican villagers have come to town looking for guns to buy—or, as our hero convinces them, to hire. Eventually, he decides he'll need several friends, a gang that can handle thirty or forty banditos. And he sets about trying to round up his posse. As he does so, we return to the theme, adding just a little bit more with each successive addition, no one of them completing the piece, each adding to it just a touch more, and each time the music swells again.

And again. And again. Until there are six of them riding with the campesinos back toward the village, and the theme is complete—almost. It's big and bold, it swells and bounces, it's terrific. But there's something missing. And someone. A youth, a villager who has rejected the life of a "dirt farmer" to become a gunslinger, unaware that the men he idolizes are already passé, desperately wants to join them. It takes a day and a night, but when he does, we are complete. The music fills in some missing parts in the middle and mounts to its full glory as we follow the—okay, seven—heroes; happy now? A great seven. In fact, *The Magnificent Seven*. Another thing that makes it great is that the initial theme accompanies Yul Brynner, whose mere presence will enhance any piece of music. Or film. In 1960 he was the toughest man in the world. At least the world of the movies. He deserved the most macho theme of them all, and he got it.

Here's the thing about *The Magnificent Seven* theme: it is pure, old-fashioned, almost anachronistic, unembarrassed music. It couldn't be anything but what it is. There has never been a period of popular music that would have embraced it without a movie attached. It shows not the slightest awareness that jazz had ever occurred; this is European tradition writ large. And yet, although it has been played by countless pops orchestras, it couldn't stand alone as a traditional symphonic score. Movie music is like nothing else in the known universe. Especially perfect movie music.

Sometimes, composers become associated with specific directors. Fairly or not. Bernard Herrmann worked with just about everyone in Hollywood at some point or other. He scored Orson Welles's first two—and probably best—films, *Citizen Kane* and *The Magnificent Ambersons* (1942), two by François

Truffaut, even Martin Scorsese's *Taxi Driver* (1976). Say his name around people who know a bit about film, however, and you will get one name—and one name only—back: Hitchcock. Always with the Hitchcock. They made seven films together, including some of the great ones: *The Man Who Knew Too Much, Vertigo, North by Northwest,* and *Psycho*. And what they will mostly know is something less than sixty seconds of shrieking strings as Norman Bates is stabbing Marion Crane in the justly notorious shower scene. Jack Sullivan, writing a Herrmann centenary appraisal in the *Chronicle of Higher Education,* called the moment "Hollywood's primal scream"; no one could say it better. In many ways, however, he is hitting his peak in the others, especially *Vertigo,* with its constant undercurrent of dread, and *North by Northwest,* which mixes foreboding, danger, and whimsy in just the right proportions. Director and composer were both famously difficult at times, yet they seemed to be in perfect harmony in their screen collaborations. Even so, to dismiss Herrmann as "Hitchcock's music man" would be to vastly underestimate his true range and his greatness.

Then what about Spielberg's music man? For the man who gave us Indiana Jones and a killer shark has worked with John Williams on all but two of his films. And because of his Spielberg/George Lucas connections, we sometimes think of Williams as the guy who cranks up the volume on epic adventure, which is true to a point. Had he done nothing but that heartbeat drumming for *Jaws* and the Imperial March theme for *Star Wars,* he would still be remembered for a long time. But he also has written the rest of the scores for those movies as well as for the Harry Potter series, *Lincoln, Catch Me if You Can, The Terminal, Angela's Ashes, Home Alone,* and films with dinosaurs, sharks, spaceships, and hidden treasures. What can we say about the scores for *Lincoln, E. T.: The Extraterrestrial,* and *Schindler's List*? That the composer shows amazing range?

That he writes to the nuances of the film? That he can do anything he sets his mind to? Yes, and more. In seconds he can slide from the ethereal Harry Potter theme, "Harry's Wondrous World," to the Voldemort theme as if it's the most natural thing in the world. When he scores *Schindler's List*, he opts for a sparseness that is almost skeletal—minor keys, very simple instrumentation, a main theme in which Itzhak Perlman seems to be playing a solitary violin and indeed is for stretches of it, with only the slightest accompaniment at other points— almost as if to say that any ornamentation or richness would be wrong for this story. Leave the bombast to the Nazis. Instead, Williams gives us clean, simple, sad. A requiem for a lost world.

It is true that some composers "get" certain directors. Erich Korngold wrote scores for such Michael Curtiz features as *Captain Blood, The Sea Hawk,* and *The Adventures of Robin Hood.* Come to think of it, maybe Korngold really got Errol Flynn. Some seem best suited to a particular genre. Maurice Jarre seemed especially suited to big, sweeping epics: *Lawrence of Arabia, Doctor Zhivago* (1965), *The Man Who Would Be King* (1975). You want music that swells? Jarre is the man for you. Others can—and do—work with everyone doing everything. Jerry Goldsmith received Oscar nominations for, among others, *The Sand Pebbles* (1966), *A Patch of Blue* (1965), *Planet of the Apes* (1968), *Patton* (1970), *The Boys from Brazil* (1978), *Chinatown* (1974), *Hoosiers* (1987), *L.A. Confidential* (1997), and Disney's animated *Mulan* (1999). Just let that sink in for a moment. Does your head hurt yet? And the only win he garnered was for *The Omen* (1976). Go figure. Or there is the case of Henry Mancini, who got around a good deal in his heyday but may well be remembered for a single theme, the jazzy little slow-walk of *The Pink Panther* (1964). As far as I can tell, it is the only live-action movie music ever to spark a cartoon series, although the cool pink cat traipsing over the title credits prob-ably had something to do with that. Still more specialized is

Marvin Hamlisch's arrangement and use of Scott Joplin's rags, specifically "The Entertainer," in *The Sting* (1973). What on earth would make someone look at a story of mostly white confidence grifters in the middle of the Great Depression and think, I'm gonna use ragtime music by a black composer from thirty years earlier? Only two answers present themselves: insanity and genius. I'll plump for the latter, because the score fit the movie like a glove. Who knew? Only Hamlisch.

Up till now we've been talking about musical scores and themes, that is, music written specifically for the movie in question. But over the last few decades there has been another trend: tunes cannibalized from other sources, chiefly popular radio tunes. Oh, there have always been movies that made use of popular song or even of classical or jazz melodies. *An American in Paris* is built around Gershwin's tone poem, which might make it the granddaddy of such movies. But we're talking about something a little different here, something we might call "jukebox" or maybe "record stack" movies. In Lawrence Kasdan's 1983 classic *The Big Chill*, a group of former hippie-activist thirtysomethings, now square, well, square but in denial, are reunited for the funeral of one of their number who has committed suicide. And one of them, Karen, has agreed to play one of the departed's favorite tunes at the funeral. She sits down with great solemnity and begins, in equally solemn organ tones, something we pretty quickly realize is "You Can't Always Get What You Want," and in a few moments, the organ gives way to the guitar strum of the Rolling Stones' original. It's a very funny scene, which even the mourners recognize, their tears turning to smirks and chortles. Throughout the film Kasdan brings in the music that a group of Ann Arbor collegians would have been hearing in the late sixties and very early seventies, from Three Dog Night's "Joy to the World" to Smokey Robinson's "Tracks of My Tears" to Procol Harum's "A Whiter Shade of Pale." Nor is he the first to do this. In films ranging from the counterculture (*Easy Rider*, 1969, and probably the first really concerted effort), to *The Strawberry Statement* (1970, and a cautionary tale about the music overshadowing the film), to war (*Coming Home*, 1978), to, um, the rather odd (1971's *Vanishing Point*), Hollywood had been interlacing contemporary music into movies at a pretty fair clip. But what *The Big Chill* points out is that the technique may work best for nostalgia. You doubt? Then I have a question for you.

Where were you in '62?

Yeah, I know where most of you were. Or weren't. The question is rhetorical. And from a movie poster. The film that wanted an answer was by a young, unknown director named George Lucas, pre–Darth Vader, pre-pretty-much-everything. And one of the actors was an unknown Harrison Ford, who would later be Lucas and Spielberg's favorite gun-and-whip slinger. But this time, he's just a hot rodder out in the Valley. The film, *American Graffiti* (1973), is full of future stars of various levels: Cindy Williams, Richard Dreyfuss, Charlie Martin Smith, Mackenzie Phillips, Paul Le Mat. In fact, there were only two name brands in the cast. The featured one was Opie. This was to be his breakout picture, the one that moved him beyond Mayberry. It did, and right into *Happy Days*. The star who really made *American Graffiti*, however, played himself: Wolfman Jack. The most famous DJ in America played, of all things, a DJ. He seemed to have psychic powers, something he had in common with Cleavon Little's Super Soul in *Vanishing Point*, the record spinner with a seemingly mystical connection to Barry Newman's hopped-up driver, Kowalsky, sending him messages for alternate routes and looming nasty surprises. Wolfman Jack also seems to see what goes on in the long night of the film, and manages to pull the exact right record at each moment. These records are not all from 1962, ranging from Bill Haley & His Comets' "Rock Around the Clock"

(1954) and Buddy Holly's "That'll Be the Day" (1957) to Booker T. and the M.G.s' "Green Onions" (which is actually from 1962) and the Beach Boys' "All Summer Long" (1964). Everybody's at the party except Elvis, who was too expensive. And the movie also has the distinction for its day of having zero original music. By the time the studio (Universal) paid all the permissions, there was no money left for any music written and performed just for the film. Happily. Nothing new could have kept up.

Here's what's really special about *American Graffiti*: it's pretty much the first time that all the music is being pushed through radios so that the characters hear it. This isn't our soundtrack; it's theirs. What that means is that the music can color their experience, and also that they can speak back to it, as when Big John Milner (Le Mat) says of the Beach Boys, "I don't like that surfer shit." One may agree or disagree with the sentiment, but it adds to character revelation. When the theme for *The Magnificent Seven* plays, by contrast, all Yul Brynner's Chris hears are hoofbeats.

Let's consider one more—or maybe two—instances of in-movie music. I've mentioned the two major adaptations of *The Great Gatsby* a couple of times now, from 1974 and 2013. Here's a question you've probably never asked yourself but someone had to: how do I convey the sound of that era of excess to an audience fifty (or eighty) years later? There are many possible answers, but here are the two chosen. In the earlier Redford-Farrow vehicle, bandleader Nelson Riddle acted as musical selector, choosing various period songs and connecting them with his own incidental compositions. In the more recent film starring Leonardo DiCaprio and Carey Mulligan, Baz Luhrmann and Jay Z opted for contemporary music that captured the mood, rather than for any authenticity. Indeed, the one concession to period music, Gershwin's "Rhapsody in Blue," almost feels like the anachronism when it turns up. Otherwise, the music is penned or performed by (sometimes both) Jay Z, Beyoncé, André 3000, will.i.am, Amy Winehouse, Bryan Ferry, Jack White, Lana Del Rey, Emeli Sandé, and Florence + the Machine, among other current powerhouses. The mix of hip-hop, rock, power pop, and contemporary swing sounds nothing like the music F. Scott and Zelda Fitzgerald would have heard when they were the Jazz Age power couple, but it conveys a sense, a feel for the era being invoked. These two approaches combine to form a question: what's the right way? And the truth is, there isn't one. The right way is the one that works. Neither I nor anyone else can tell you which of these is better. Oh, I can tell you what I think, but that's only what's better for me. The only way to know for sure is to watch for yourself. More important, to listen for yourself.

Music often informs us not only of the meaning of a moment or scene but of how multiple moments fit together. In *Mr. Turner* (2014), we watch painter J. M. W. Turner (Timothy Spall, Wormtail from the Harry Potter films) paint a seafaring scene in front of his academy colleagues with all the violence he can muster. He spits on the fresh paint, blows colored powder at it, stabs and grinds with his brush, and finally rakes upward through the freshly painted and still-wet smoky fog with his fingernails again and again, all the while looking over his shoulder, evidently wishing to see what sort of impression he is making on his confreres. As he does so, Gary Yershon's score relies on a highly agitated string section to enhance the sense of violence. The film immediately cuts to chalky cliffs—much the same color as the section of the painting we have just watched him attacking—at Margate, near the whiter and more famous cliffs of Dover. The camera pans nearer and downward, revealing grayer cliffs closer to us and, in the foreground, Turner bulling forward in his peculiar gait, somewhere between a march and a limp. A new, softer theme emerges with the start of the scene, but for the first few seconds, the agitated cello forms an undertone before vanishing. The implication is clear: Turner is getting away from the rush of his professional-social existence and settling into a quieter pace, almost as if the scenery is cleansing him of his previous aggression and competitiveness. Yershon's score was not universally praised, although it was nominated for several awards, including the Oscar; its chief shortcoming among traditionalist critics seemed to be that it didn't sound sufficiently like movie music—no big swells, no grand statements, and no nod to its nineteenth-century setting. Using minimal instrumentation, it employs a saxophone ensemble—the first notes of the film are played on a sopranino saxophone, whose existence, if you're like me, comes as a surprise—and a string quintet including double bass as it relies on discordant, jazz-oriented themes. Yet it is just that unusual element that serves to illuminate such an unusual man.

And the music highlights plot as well as thematic elements. Earlier, we have seen Turner hurrying up the stairway of the academy to a decidedly martial rolling of tympani. The message is clear: this space is a war zone. That proves to be the case, as time and again we are shown the backbiting, sniping, and outbursts of artists in competition with each other. In one key scene, Turner's sudden, seemingly impulsive insertion of brilliant red paint on the waterline of an otherwise neutral-colored scene provokes comment and criticism. What is he doing? Has he finally lost his mind? Turner's action is impulsive, but it is also calculated to score a victory. You see, the red paint is not his; it belongs to his colleague and rival John Constable. Turner's smaller, seemingly finished work is next to a more monumental scene on which Constable is still at work, currently placing splashes of red. Turner picks up Constable's brush and appears to deface his own painting with the large red dot, after which he immediately exits the hall. The action mystifies the onlookers but not Constable, who puts on his coat in disgust, saying that Turner "has fired a gun," which the uncomprehending audience swiftly denies. But he has. After a lengthy absence, Turner reenters the room, carves a curved line in the upper half of the daub, wipes away the lower half, and reveals—a buoy. His brilliant battlefield stratagem has carried the day.

The success of movie music is almost never about the quality of the music on its own. Some excellent songs have been wasted on dogs; they do not help and sometimes merely point out the inadequacy of the rest of the film. On the other hand, some musical dogs have dragged down the tone of otherwise exemplary films. And sometimes, whatever the quality of one or the other, the fit is unfortunate. An example? Figure out what on earth "Raindrops Keep Falling on My Head" is supposed to be doing in the middle of *Butch Cassidy and the Sundance Kid*. Burt Bacharach is a great songwriter, although whether this is one of his great songs is another matter. That issue, however, is moot; in context the song is just wrong. On the radio in its day, it was just another serviceable pop number, but with Butch riding around the farm on his newfangled bicycle . . . oh dear. Similarly, some scores or individual tunes that might be fine elsewhere are misapplied in terms of the movie they're supposed to be in service to. On the other hand, some merely adequate melodies have more than pulled their weight, and some that were not superb on their own, like "As Time Goes By" in *Casablanca*, which had a lengthy and fairly modest history before the movie, become strokes of genius with the right placement. You see, the question is never, or never merely, is this music any good, but rather, does this music make the movie better? And you know what the answer needs to be.

Homework Assignment

(A Very Short Interruption)

Do you want to learn more about how film works? Here's what I would suggest. Study it. Let's say you want to learn more about actors and acting. Rather than just watch a bunch of movies at random on the assumption that there's acting in all of them (perfectly true, but . . .), take one actor and follow that person through several films. If possible, get films of different types. The actor doesn't really matter, so choose someone you like watching. Joaquin Phoenix, Scarlett Johansson, Bradley Cooper, Jennifer Lawrence. Heck, get the collected movies of Bradley Cooper and Jennifer Lawrence and watch them interact in different settings. I thought of this exercise when watching, somewhat out of chronological order, *The Hunger Games* (2012) after *American Hustle* (2013) and *Silver*

Linings Playbook (2012). My first thought was, This young woman has a lot of range. My second, of course, was, She's using about 2 percent of it in this movie. Collectively, these films demonstrate the kinds of things she does with her eyes, her mouth, her body, her voice to bring characters to life. What the hey, throw in an *X-Men* movie, too. Nobody says homework can't be fun. Alternatively, you can take the same role and watch different actors inhabit it: Julie Christie and Carey Mulligan as Bathsheba Everdene in *Far from the Madding Crowd* or Greta Garbo and Keira Knightley as Anna Karenina. The actors and roles don't matter as much as developing a field of view by which you can analyze acting. Hepburn and Tracy in *Adam's Rib* and *Pat and Mike* and *Guess Who's Coming to Dinner*? Sure, great. Bogie and Bacall in *To Have and Have Not* and *Key Largo*? You'll have a blast.

Once you've got a handle on actors, turn to something else. Watch the work of one cinematographer or one director or one of whatever interests you. You'll learn a lot. Composers? Try listening to movies without looking, or only looking up when the soundtrack cues you to peek. I really came to love Bernard Herrmann this way. You can't shut out the dialogue, of course, but that's okay; you'll still pick up the music better if your eyes are elsewhere. Do anything you like. Just don't, please, watch *The Wizard of Oz* while listening to *Dark Side of the Moon*. You really won't learn all that much about movies, and I suspect it requires other sorts of stimulation that I really can't recommend.

The point is, you need to learn what you like about movies and in movies. We've established by now that you really do like them and want to learn more about them. I just think you should do it in the way that makes the most sense for you. And that gives you the most pleasure, which is what movies are really about.

18

Figuratively Speaking

FAVORITE STUDENT QUESTION: is that a symbol?

Favorite instructor answer: what do you think?

It might not be a symbol, though. Consider metaphor, metonymy, synecdoche, or any of a dozen other figures of speech and action. Plenty of options that are not precisely symbols. Like any literary form, film makes abundant use of our capacity for figurative thinking. We don't so much *understand* symbols and metaphors as *apprehend* them, and in a medium where they're gone in a heartbeat, apprehension is plenty. So what do we make of those figurative things as they go whizzing across our retinas?

We talked about images some little time ago and concluded, among other things, that movies are, give or take, a hundred and twenty minutes of images. Thousands of images, not that all of them implant themselves in our memories. Our question here, though, is different: how do those images become something more, begin to stand for something larger than themselves? To understand that process, we should begin with an example or three.

In *The Lion in Winter*, we might just notice a candle or two. Big whoop, right? It's 1183 and Edison is a few years away; the only light source is fire in one form or another—fireplace, torch, sun, candle. True enough, but there are candles and then there are candles. The ones I'm talking about get loving attention from the camera. For instance, in the fireplace scene between Henry and Eleanor that we examined earlier, there is a table in the foreground with three items. The two that matter to us at the moment are a very large candle and an hourglass. In the scene that immediately precedes it, Alais is lighting candles in a holder, and the one that gets our attention has numbered rings on it, clearly a way of marking off time. The candles Alais tends to, like the candle and hourglass, remind us of the importance of time even in societies before it rested on wrists or resided on phones. That is the image portion of the program. Since this is a movie about the movement of time toward death, the candles are about a good deal more than shedding light. Time is running out; their time is limited; Eleanor's time of freedom is nearly over; Alais's time as Henry's favorite paramour may be running out. For those who know their history, so is Henry's own time, destined as he is to fall in battle with those very sons he abuses in the film. So many possibilities. What we make of those possibilities, which of them we choose or ignore, is largely up to us. The film's creators have brought the images into being and, without a doubt, given hints about what we might understand them to mean, but viewers become the final arbiters as to their significance.

Sometimes, the images are so evident that we might almost

wish to ignore them, their suggested meanings a little too suggestive. But we can't. In *Annie Hall*, Woody Allen's sexually obsessed Alvy has a pronounced tendency to run into Diane Keaton's Annie with lengthy objects—the handle of a tennis racquet on their first meeting, a boat oar when they're trying to corral lobsters in the seaside cottage—that can only be described as phallic. This in a movie where almost the first substantive scene invokes Freud. Well, what do you make of that trope? And try not to blush.

While we're on the subject of blush-worthy moments, let me take you back through the ages, far back in film history, to the Time Before Sex. Okay, so there never was a time before sex. Romance and sex were of considerable interest almost from the moment the Lumière brothers filmed the workers leaving the factory. And for a little while in the late silent and early talkie era, things got rather, shall we say, heated on movie screens. And a number of off-screen sex scandals gave Hollywood an even worse reputation than it already had in much of this country. But then voices for decency and oppression got loud, and a censor's office was formed with President Harding's postmaster general, Will H. Hays, as its head. In truth, Hays gets a lot of unfair blame. He was in charge for only a few years before giving way to the much more inflexible Joseph Breen, but the Motion Picture Production Code was forever known as the Hays Code and the enforcement arm the Hays Office.

And why do we care? Because that office, and the a priori censorship of film it represented, was responsible for more figurative invention than any other single factor in the history of American film. In *The Maltese Falcon*, it is clear at one point that something is about to happen between Spade and Brigid O'Shaughnessy. We see her seated before a window at night and him bending over to kiss her. The next thing we see is daylight streaming through the same window and the curtains blowing in. I distinctly recall teaching this movie in the 1980s and having to explain to students what the curtains meant. Having come of film-watching age after 1966, their idea of what sex looked like in the movies was, predictably, sex. But for roughly thirty years prior to that date, it had not looked like that. The Production Code forbade depictions of nudity and sex, among other things deemed offensive such as getting away with crime or bleeding after being shot, so filmmakers found workarounds. Some realities couldn't be worked around, of course. Like double beds. Nick and Nora Charles in *The Thin Man*, who are recently married, by the way, sleep in separate twin beds. Endless heavy drinking and smoking and massive hangovers were no problem for the censors, but married persons sharing a bed, even for purposes of mere sleeping, no way. Unsurprisingly, both the folks making the movies and the ones watching them knew better, just as they knew that, as long as there are men and women in the world (it took a little longer for other pairings to be accepted), there was going to be both hanky and panky from time to time. It just couldn't be shown. So lots of other things were shown that, not sex in themselves, nevertheless encoded the act of coitus. Those curtains were not the only ones that ever fluttered in the breeze. The cliché we all know, even if we're not sure where we saw it, is waves breaking on the beach. That one occurs most famously in *From Here to Eternity* (1953), where Karen Holmes (Deborah Kerr) and Sergeant Milton Warden (Burt Lancaster) roll on the beach, kissing, with a wave breaking over them; they run up the beach, go horizontal and clinching again, we see another wave, and she says, "Nobody ever kissed me the way you do." That's some kiss, even without the postcoital dreamy eyes and tone. But it has those, too. For sheer variety, Tony Richardson employed the sexiest meal ever eaten in *Tom Jones* (1964) between Tom (Albert Finney) and Mrs. Waters (Joyce Redman), as they leer and slurp and slaver over their tavern meal and each other. For utter lack of subtlety, however, the champion has to be fireworks, employed by Hitchcock in *To Catch a Thief* (1955) when he wants to suggest what has gone on between John Robie (Cary Grant) and Frances Stevens (Grace Kelly). That's suggestive, all right. My absolute favorite comes at the very end of *North by Northwest*. In one of the great miracles, Hitchcock (again) gets Roger Thornhill (Grant, again) and Eve Kendall (Eva Marie Saint) down from the face of Mount Rushmore, where they are clinging for dear life. We cut seamlessly from Roger telling Eve to hang on and come up to him on the mountain to his same face saying, "Come along, Mrs. Thornhill," as he pulls her up into a sleeping berth on the Twentieth Century Limited, and then cut again to the train roaring into the tunnel. Now *that's* subtle. Of course, this was at the end of the Production Code era, and Hitch is pushing the envelope.

That same year, 1959, saw Otto Preminger's *Anatomy of a Murder* deal with rape and murder, and Joseph L. Mankiewicz's *Suddenly, Last Summer*, whose plot turns on paying for homosexual encounters. Curiously, those films received their certificates of approval after demanded cuts, but it was the one that didn't that hit the system hardest. The Production Code was dealt a hard blow in that very year by, of all things, *Some Like It Hot*, a saucy but hardly debauched comedy about two musicians who cross-dress to hide from the mob after witnessing a massacre. The Hays Office denied it a certificate of approval and crowds turned out in massive numbers anyway. Come on! Tony Curtis, Jack Lemmon, and Marilyn Monroe? Morality, shmorality. The death knell finally came in 1966 with Michelangelo Antonioni's *Blow-Up*, which dealt frankly with sexual matters and featured an extended scene of Vanessa Redgrave topless. It, too, found a large and ready audience. That it also featured youth culture and Carnaby Street fashion and the Yardbirds didn't hurt, unless you were the morality police. In any case, by the time my students got to me in 1986 or so, all that censorship noise was ancient history, and they had no idea how to decode old movies.

It needs to be said that not all figuration was about sex and gender topics. Film uses metaphor and symbol and all the rest about as much as any other literary art. Rain, for instance, often tells us something more than that it is wet outside. That poster of George Valentin that has found its way into the gutter in *The Artist*, for instance, would carry a different meaning were it not lying in a puddle with rain falling. The desolation is greater as filmed. Group dining scenes in *My Dinner with Andre* or *Babette's Feast* or *The Dead* carry the same implication of communion either observed or violated that they do in literary works; indeed, John Huston's film exquisitely captures James Joyce's original meaning in that last example. And how do movies achieve figurative meaning? By and large, much the same way as other artistic media. We begin with images, actions, conditions. A poster on the street in the rain. A group of old friends and acquaintances around a dining table. From there, it's largely a matter of what viewers make of the images presented—and how the director and cinematographer present them. Does the camera linger on the image? Zoom in to the exclusion of all else? Touch passingly? How does the lighting affect the image? The music behind it? Some elements are common to novels and poems and plays, but others are specific to cinema; you can duplicate them nowhere else.

Here's one such. It's a violin. Floating in a river. Not something you see every day, to be sure. On the other hand, if you are watching Roland Joffé's masterful *The Mission* (1986), there it is, plucked out of the water by a small brown hand, which in turn is attached to a naked Guaraní girl. She carries it over to a waiting dugout canoe, which is full of other naked Guaraní children, and they begin paddling upriver, farther back into the rain forest. Sounds almost paradisal, doesn't it?

Except that this is no Eden. It's a burned-out mission, the site of a recent massacre of Indians and priests by the combined forces of the Church and moneyed, slave-holding interests during the heyday of Spanish and Portuguese exploitation of the Amazonian borderlands, circa 1758. The movie is a wonder—screenplay by playwright Robert Bolt (*A Man for All Seasons, Doctor Zhivago, Lawrence of Arabia*), possibly the best score Ennio Morricone ever composed, terrific performances by Jeremy Irons and Robert De Niro—and it may be the best movie no one has ever seen. Despite winning the Palme d'Or at Cannes and an Oscar for cinematography, the film barely made back its costs. The details above will inform you that it is tough sledding, yet that should not keep away anyone with a genuine interest in the art of the movies. But back to our fiddle. The image of the floating violin and its rescue is just that, an image. We bring the knowledge necessary to give it meaning, as Bolt and Joffé know we will. We know, for instance, that the movie opens with the previous priest, who had tried and failed to convert the Guaraní, floating over Iguazu Falls tied to a cross, that Father Gabriel (Irons) risked terrible dangers getting to the mission and converting the natives; that he was accepted, loved, worshipped, even; and that the violin is a talisman of this murdered priest that the children are taking upstream, not down over the falls, and into their world. Watched in isolation, the scene tells us very little except that something very bad happened in this place. In context, it is incredibly rich in meaning.

There is a special category of figuration in film that has to do with characters and the objects associated with them. Example? Sure, try this one on for size—here are four items, from which you will name the character: tight coat, baggy pants, derby hat, and cane. What's that? You can't come up with a name? Of course you can't, because there isn't one. But if you're over a certain age (I'm guessing about eleven), even if you have never seen a film in black and white, much less without sound, you can identify those objects as belonging to—and defining—Charlie Chaplin's Little Tramp. We could have added a couple more talismans to his makeup, chiefly the outsize shoes and the little mustache, but those would make it too easy. He sprang, in a sense, fully formed onto the silver screen in Mack Sennett's 1914 Keystone comedy, *Kid Auto Races at Venice*, and remained intact, and silent, through dozens of short films and brilliant features up through the 1936 partial talkie, *Modern Times*. He stole audiences' hearts and, more often than not, won the girl, in such immortal features as *The Kid* (1921), *The Gold Rush* (1925), *The Circus* (1928), and *City Lights* (1931), although notably in the film that names the

Figure 13. City Lights—*the Tramp discovers that the Flower Girl is blind. City Lights* © *Roy Exports S.A.S. Scan Courtesy Cineteca di Bologna.*

character, 1915's *The Tramp*, he repeatedly saves the girl only to lose out to her fiancé. Part of his beauty as a character has always been that he does not invariably win.

Of course, those four elements do more than act to identify the character; they define him.

Q: Here's a question that may seem stupid, but we need to ask it: how do you know if someone's a cowboy?

A: It's not the cow. He has a horse.

Q: (hopefully slightly less stupid) How do you know what sort of cowboy he is?

A: What he's wearing?

Yes, that second answer may be in the form of a question, but it is an answer. Perhaps no movie genre is more shot through with codes than the Western. Good guys wear white hats, bad guys wear black hats, and so on. Or at least they did when Tom Mix was the good guy. Things got a little muddled later on, but the basic principles allowed and even caused that muddling.

I'm more interested in specific cowboys in specific movies. And one cowboy in particular. Shane. Alan Ladd's title character in the 1953 classic Western is defined by his accoutrements— and he is splendidly accoutered. Shane is a gunslinging dandy: fringed buckskin jacket and holster with silver rosettes on the belt, silver-plated, pearl-handled revolver. Only his hat, which is almost white, shows any appreciable wear.

Jack Wilson, his main adversary, wears a black hat. Seem accidental to you? Me neither.

The first of the truly great gangster films is Mervyn LeRoy's 1931 *Little Caesar*, the vehicle that not only made a star of Edward G. Robinson but saddled him with the mannerisms that impressionists would take to the bank for decades. Robinson's Rico sneers for much of the film and speaks in a sort of slide, where "Yeah" is spoken as "Myyeah," usually followed by a rising "see." You didn't have to be Rich Little to do a takeoff of Robinson as hoodlum, although Little did him very well. So did seventh graders in every schoolyard in North America. LeRoy has a tough job in the movie, trying to depict Rico as truly dangerous not in a way that would be worthy of our respect. He's violent, all right, but there's something slightly effete about him. Maybe more than slightly. He gets upset by the prospect of his best pal leaving the gang the way most people do at losing a lover; the feeling is entirely one-way. And then there's his grooming habits. He is identified by two items in particular. The first, his pistol, makes sense; the guy's a gangster, after all. The other one? A comb. It gets worse: he uses the comb far more than the gun. He's a dandy all around—snappy dresser, very concerned with appearance, good grooming—as befits someone hoping to rise in station, even if that station is as a lowlife. But the combing is a reflex in moments of stress and suggests an unmasculine (for circa 1931) obsession. The film overtly references the comb in its intertitles (those title cards with text that show up in the midst of old films), so it appears that LeRoy was attempting to lessen the peril or to ridicule the mob. That's mostly speculation, although the homoerotic subtext seems pretty clear. What is abundantly clear is that W. R. Burnett, who wrote the book on which the movie is based, was very unhappy with the change. He had written Rico as resolutely interested in girls and very masculine. To the extent that the celluloid character is less than that, Burnett felt his intentions were violated. The writer may have been annoyed, but audiences were thrilled. Even fifty years on, my students laughed at Rico's mannerisms even as they agreed that the movie is pretty taut otherwise. He's dangerous, but he's also a little foolish and conceited, not quite Al Capone material.

Now then, for the truly dangerous. How about a flat-topped

Stetson that looks like it's been through the wars? Nothing? Well, it doesn't add much. How about heavy stubble or a small beard? Still not enough. A well-chewed cigarillo that looks as bad as the hat? That narrows the field, but it remains pretty wide. Okay, what about a poncho? Now we're talking. That ensemble describes one character. Or three, since he's in that many films. He has no name, but he might respond to a fistful of dollars. In fact, that's where we met him, this Man with No Name, in the first of Sergio Leone's so-called Dollars Trilogy. He's a pretty ragged character—nothing like the traditional cowboy hero, as far as you can get from Alan Ladd's Shane as it is possible to be. In fact, I would describe him as the anti-Shane. They're both, in the peculiar subgenre of the Western, avenging angels, although our guy is hard to recognize as an

Figure 14. Not the Little Tramp. Eastwood in A Fistful of Dollars.
Courtesy of Getty Images/MGM.

angel. No fringed buckskin for him. No well-scrubbed look. His Colt Peacemaker and holster look like they've been used. A lot. Alan Ladd's look brand-new. As a point of information, Eastwood brought his boots, gun, and hat from his *Rawhide* days, when he had been a lot more well-scrubbed himself. He rides into town not on a sparkling steed but on a mule (okay, it's really a horse, but it's supposed to be a mule; casting issues, one supposes). And the poncho and shearling vest underneath look, um, lived in. Lived in, in fact, by the man who's wearing them.

Now, none of those items is merely a stage property or an emblem. They're not just window dressing. Rather, they are called into action. The revolver, obviously, plays a starring role in numerous action scenes. It is rarely fired just once. The poncho hides a multitude of sins. Our guy is not above shooting someone from inside it, the gun never showing. In *A Few Dollars More*, it will conceal a heavy metal breastplate that stops the villain's rifle bullets and provides the Man with No Name with the advantage he always seeks. But that advantage is never overwhelming power. It's surprise, anxiety, doubt, laughter, things that come out of hiding, out of the poncho. The little cigar offers any number of uses. The MwNN conducts lots of screen business with it, taking it out of his mouth and sometimes spitting an invisible fleck of tobacco from his tongue while letting a point sink in or waiting for an opponent to get nervous. It can suggest the passage of time, for it is almost always half-smoked. It lights a fuse or two when explosions are called for. It can attract or distract attention, as needed. It is perhaps the deadliest cigar in movie history. The hat, too, serves a host of cinematic functions, from keeping the sun off to taking a bullet aimed at its owner (this does not make said owner happy). The hat, moreover, tells a story of its wearer and the rough living behind its look. Taken together, this is one of the great ensembles, almost a character in its own right. We have only to see it from behind to know the man inside. What

Leone comes up with launches the look of a thousand unorth-odox "heroes." Think Popeye Doyle. Think Rambo. Different looks, same concept.

In fact, we only have to make a few changes to wind up somewhere else entirely. Lose the cigarillo. Swap hat styles for a fedora. Drop the poncho in favor of a much-worn leather jacket and some equally abused lace-up work boots. Most important, make the sidearm less explosive, something like, oh, maybe a bullwhip. You knew we were going there, didn't you? The world had already discovered in 1977 that cowboys transfer from horse operas to their space cousins and that Harrison Ford makes a more than passable space cowboy when the original *Star Wars* took us to that galaxy far, far away—and took ours by storm. Seriously, how many spaceship captains wear their gun that low on their leg, gunslinger-style? What no one could have guessed is how well they would transfer to the world of archaeology just four years later when Indiana Jones made his debut.

Images are everything, as we said earlier. They also tell us things. But what if the image is not one the character actually possesses? What if it is a desert or a mountain or a river? Or maybe the sun? After all, can anyone *own* the sun? Didn't think so. During one rural interlude in *Mr. Turner*, we watch Turner climb a ridge overlooking the sea. In the distance a lonely, abandoned structure occupies a promontory, but he never looks up at it. As he moves beyond the camera and begins his downhill walk, a line of wild horses climbs up toward the ridgeline from behind him, but he shows no awareness. His attention is all on the sea. Even if we haven't come to the film knowing Turner as a painter almost exclusively of seascapes, the action and the testimony (sometimes uncomplimentary) of other characters tells us so. But here is concrete evidence. Nei-ther the building nor the horses—perfect subjects for paintings in other hands—hold any magic for the sea-obsessed Turner.

Instead, it is the sea and the sun that fascinate. At the beginning of the scene, the low sun is shining through clouds to form an indistinct white glow familiar to anyone who has ever seen one of his works. He crosses the sun in a sort of top-of-the-world silhouette: this is his space, his setting. The scene's big payoff is that same white sun, now reflected off the water, forming a brilliant white line in the center of the screen in exactly the way the young John Ruskin (Joshua McGuire) comments on in another scene as being a defining feature of the paintings. As the camera travels the length of the light from its beginning to its end at the shore, it leads us to Turner, positioned directly in line with it and drawing it in his sketchbook. The scene then ends with Turner, again on top of the ridge, surveying the last light of evening, the sun now sunk behind the watery horizon. Throughout, the scene plays off a lone woodwind—oboe or alto sax—in a sad, slightly atonal melody against the prevailing strings, adding to the sense of aloneness and even movement against the general flow that characterizes Turner's life and work. The image of the solitary Turner silhouetted against a low sun appears in the very first scene and recurs periodically throughout the movie. Each time it appears, as here, we are reminded of Turner's status as a permanent outsider; this scene also emphasizes both his genius and its dazzling origin. You could make a case that Turner's talisman is his easel or his brush, but he is the artist who almost always places the sun or some equivalent at the very center of his paintings, no matter how dark and turbulent otherwise. No, our great artist here is a creature of the sun.

As every fashionista knows, accessories make all the difference. And sometimes not only the objects but how they are employed. Let us consider two drives to town. From the same story. Nothing really much going on, just a couple of guys making their way from Long Island to Manhattan. Could be anyone. Except that it's Jay Gatsby driving Nick Carraway in a fabulous yellow car. Those two scenes are from the Jack Clayton 1974 adaptation of *The Great Gatsby*, with Robert Redford and Sam Waterston playing driver and passenger, and Baz Luhrmann's 2013 version starring Leonardo DiCaprio and Tobey Maguire. On one level, the two drives are largely identical—semirural roads becoming more urban, the medal from "little Montenegro," Gatsby's too-well-rehearsed story of his life. Except that it's all different.

Redford's Gatsby takes a sedate, even stately, approach; the magnificence of the car, not the brilliance of the ride, is the point. You can think of it this way: he's dressed to impress. He's trying to soften up Nick so that later on, Jordan, as someone of Nick's social caste, can try to persuade him to invite Daisy, his married cousin, to a very private tea. The sequence is also very static. Gatsby shows Nick the car while it's parked in a bay of his garage, asks his question about what Nick thinks of him while they're standing on either side of the car. The driving scenes are minimal; we see landscape streaming past the talking heads. DiCaprio's Gatsby, by contrast, arrives with a roaring engine as he circles Nick's cottage again and again. Once en route, he drives like a teenage boy showing off for a pal, darting in and out of traffic, taking crazy risks, barely watching the road as he seeks to make eye contact with his quarry. His background "story" is all nervous energy and obvious lies, unlike the more studied Redford version, as his eyes dart to Nick for signs of disbelief or gullibility. Even the scenery is more jittery in the later movie. The party of young black men and women having a party "on a car" crossing the Queensboro Bridge is raucous and vibrant. Gatsby hands his get-out-of-jail card from the police commissioner to the motorcycle cop while both vehicles are still whizzing along the city's streets. The Clayton-Redford version is a slow waltz; this is full-tilt boogie.

Even the destinations bespeak the differences in character-ization. The restaurant where Redford's Gatsby and Water-ston's Nick meet Meyer Wolfsheim for lunch is quiet and approximately refined—soft music in the background, dig-nified waiters. The only uncouth thing there is Wolfsheim himself. In the Luhrmann version, the place is obviously a speakeasy—entered through a door with a sliding window—and the atmosphere lies somewhere between a jazz club and a stag party. The music is rowdy, the girls' costumes inspired by Josephine Baker, the action busy and a little jerky, the nerves a little jangly. Here's Wolfsheim (Amitabh Bachchan), garish and overstated but with none of the earlier Howard Da Silva's seediness, ruling like a pasha from his prime table. There is the commissioner, carousing with what seems an entire chorus line. And the music! As with the rest of the score, it's just like the original period, assuming Jay Z and Beyoncé had been alive then. On the one hand, the scene displays every sort of Luhrmann excess; on the other, it's exactly how we always hoped the twenties roared.

Really, though, can these two road trips, even with their destinations, really tell us what the main characters are like? Naturally, these competing sequences cannot fully reveal their respective Gatsbys in all their pied glory. At the same time, they can tell us a great deal. Remember, at this point in the films, we have barely met the title character. How he conducts himself around Nick, from whom he is about to request (through a third party) an enormous favor, speaks volumes. And that con-duct includes showing off his fabulous car. Redford's portrayal is cautious, measured, quite calculated. He can *almost* pull off this imitation of the aristocracy. Not quite, maybe, but nearly. We can almost believe that his restraint means that he really can be trusted with a wife's friend, as Wolfsheim says, although we also know that Tom Buchanan is no friend.

DiCaprio's Gatsby is vastly more dangerous. His mask of gentility keeps slipping, as if male power or animal instinct keeps overwhelming his less than fine-honed image. We can believe that he really did kill a man, that he is capable of ruthlessness, a quality we have to take on faith in the earlier adaptation. It's as if he learned how to play the millionaire but perhaps the final lesson was not provided. His driving is very nearly demonic; he can't quite contain himself; there are sudden outbursts of his inner gangster. Indeed, he can't stop himself offering Nick the chance to make a little money on the side, although he quickly recognizes that as a violation of the code in Nick's world, if not in his.

And we see all this in parallel trips in an automobile. The car is the same—thematically, anyway, although the first is a Rolls-Royce and the second a Duesenberg—but it's the driving that makes all the difference.

19

Masters of All That They Survey

A LUCKY FEW IN THE FILM WORLD, usually directors, have approaches so distinctive that their work constitutes a genre all its own. To say "Woody Allen" is to invoke a certain look, feel, sound of a movie, even though his aren't all *Annie Hall*. Or *Bananas*, for that matter. Very little in his previous work can prepare us for *Stardust Memories* or *Blue Jasmine*, films so much more bleak or desperate than his other movies. Still, there's a Woody Allen gestalt. Same for Hitchcock, Ford, Hawks, Kurosawa, Lucas, Wertmüller, Herzog, Bergman, Fellini. Their work is so immediately and definitively theirs, they don't require first names. So how do we read the special cases? And just what makes them special?

Sometimes it's the look of the film. John Ford's films look

a lot alike whether they're set in the desert Southwest or an Irish village. Before you ask, no, that's not because they all have John Wayne in them. Sometimes it's Henry Fonda. As we know, however, more than stars goes into the look of a movie. For one thing, there's landscape. Ford loved landscapes and hired technical people who could capture that love. Of course, he's most famous for the terrain he made famous: Arizona and Utah's Monument Valley. His films take us there again and again: *Stagecoach* (1939), *Fort Apache* (1948), *She Wore a Yellow Ribbon* (1949), and *The Searchers* (1956)—nine times in all. That setting alone marks a great deal of his "look."

But what about when he's looking elsewhere? Say, Ireland, as he does in *The Quiet Man* (1952), a place notably short on sandstone outcroppings and mesas. Happily, Counties Galway and Mayo abound in granite outcroppings, ruined stone cottages,

Figure 15. Monument Valley with stagecoach.
Photo courtesy of Shout! Factory.

stone walls, stone . . . everything. These served Ford's purposes
admirably. What the place lacks in dust it makes up for in rain
and mist, so while the atmospheres may differ, the atmospherics
are equally well suited to what he wants to do with landscape.
And a lot of what he wants to do is shoot long—very long. A
favored technique, first seen in *Stagecoach*, is to shoot from such
a distance that the human activity is utterly dwarfed by the
enormity of place. The west of Ireland affords no such vastness
as the Utah-Arizona borderlands, but its distances serve well
enough. We still see both the strength of humans and their
puniness in his Irish character study. Republic Pictures exec-
utives understood pretty well that they were buying the "Ford
method" when they green-lighted this film, as evidenced by the
fact that they required not only him but also stars John Wayne
and Maureen O'Hara to shoot a Western before they traipsed
off to Ireland. What Republic, an almost exclusively B-movie
studio, got was a Western (*Rio Grande*, 1950) that was better
than it had any right to expect and, two years later, the only
best picture Oscar nomination in its history. That film, maybe
because it steps away from the Westerns and army films that
dominate Ford's filmography, makes it easy to see the hallmarks
of Ford's style: directness, simplicity (although that is often less
simple than it appears), a love of faces, a seeming transparency
of style that translates into a sense of great honesty. Ford may
not be beloved by the auteur-theorists (those distrusters of
simplicity) in the way that his contemporaries Hitchcock and
Hawks are, but every film he ever made has his signature on
every frame.

   In some ways, his great heir may be Clint Eastwood. We
might expect him to be highly indebted to Sergio Leone,
under whom he starred in a fistful of spaghetti Westerns, and
to be sure his own Westerns owe a good deal to the renegade
Italian. But Eastwood has done a huge variety of films in just
as many styles. So here's my question: can you tell if you're

watching a Clint Eastwood film? How? And I think I know the answer: read the credits. Just consider: *Play Misty for Me*, *Midnight in the Garden of Good and Evil*, *Pale Rider*, *The Bridges of Madison County*, *Mystic River*, *Flags of Our Fathers*, *Unforgiven*, *Million Dollar Baby*, *J. Edgar*. Do you see a common thread there? A common subject matter? Aesthetic? Approach? I'm not sure I do. Let me rephrase that: I'm quite sure I don't. I'm still trying to get my head around the same man having directed *Space Cowboys*, *Bronco Billy*, and *Gran Torino*, and the truth is, my poor head hurts. Someone a lot more knowledgeable and subtle than I may be able to figure out the Eastwood style, but I have my doubts. He may be, in the words of my colleague Fred Svoboda, "a really good journeyman." He does not mean that, nor do I, as a term of derogation. Eastwood is both an old movie pro and a jazzman. You show up, do one, two, maybe three takes, and move on to the next shot. That's how movies were shot in the studio days, before directors became obsessive and self-indulgent, became, in other words, auteurs. So maybe he's our anti-auteur. Not that there's no technique involved. We know some things for sure about the Eastwood method. He hires really good and/or really interesting people—Morgan Freeman, George Kennedy, Gene Hackman, Meryl Streep, Sean Penn, Hillary Swank, Chief Dan George, Leonardo DiCaprio, Sondra Locke, Matt Damon—explains what he wants, and gets out of their way. He trusts their instincts. In other words, he works much less like Alfred Hitchcock or Ingmar Bergman than Dave Brubeck or Miles Davis, which probably shouldn't be a surprise from someone who loves and plays jazz. He loves faces, but then, what moviemaker doesn't? He trusts his talent, from actors to cinematographers to camera operators to, presumably, best boys and key grips. The result is more natural than naturalistic, more idea than ideology.

So what's the result? Does he have a style? Can we recognize it? Possibly. Oh, not in the way of some directors: we can see three frames and say, that's Hitch, that's Woody, or that's Pappy Ford. But if you see a whole movie, and it's clean, direct, swift, honest, and engaging, it just might be a Clint. Are they all great? Definitely not. There are a few cinders among the gems. Still, we should note that he finds a style appropriate for the genre. He doesn't try to make *The Bridges of Madison County* fit the template of *Pale Rider* or force *J. Edgar* to look like *Play Misty for Me* (a fact about which we can all be grateful). And it is true that he is a charter member of the less-is-more club, which can have its own perils. As with Hemingway, understatement at times can become as mannered as bombast or preciousness. But just look at a list of his great films: that's a fabulous career for someone who only directed. But he has acted, too, as we all know. Maybe that's his style, directing like an actor. In fact, he's one of the very, very few great directors who understand so completely the experience of being in front of the camera. I use the adjective carefully. Because he is a great director. Quite possibly the most significant American director of the late twentieth and early twenty-first centuries. And what more could we ask?

If we have doubts about the hallmarks of the Eastwood style, such is not the case with that ultimate auteur, Alfred Hitchcock. There are so many things to talk about here, but I want for the moment to focus on just one aspect of his mastery: efficiency. Hitch came up during the late silent/very early talkie phase of movie history, and he developed his style in a film world of tight controls on length. If the studio said that it wanted a movie to run between 92 and 104 minutes, they did not mean 138. Movies had to come in on budget, on time, and in time. Unlike the multiplex, where the only other filmlike product shown is an endless loop of local advertising, movie houses in the classic era showed, in addition to the feature, some combination of a short feature, an episode of a serial, a cartoon, and a newsreel, including up to three or four of those.

The speed with which Hitchcock can wrap up a movie will strike contemporary viewers as overhasty. Even such master-pieces as *Rebecca* (1940) end with a suddenness that can be disorienting: with the mansion ablaze, someone shouts that there is a figure at the window, and we see the specter of Mrs. Danvers at a window and then circling as if to avoid the flames and then standing stock-still as if welcoming the next moment, then witness the ceiling timbers collapse, and finally get a fleeting view of Rebecca's dress with its monogrammed *R*, and we cut to THE END. From the outcry to the title card is exactly a minute. In fact, only something like two minutes and fourteen seconds elapse from the time that Maxim de Winter (Laurence Olivier) sees the light that he at first can't identify as his burning mansion until he stops the car and discusses it with his friend, Frank Crawley (Reginald Denny). And during that brace of minutes we discover that:

a) Maxim can drive like a maniac when neces-sary;

b) The house is fully engulfed in flame;

c) The servants are safely out of the house;

d) Mrs. de Winter (non-Rebecca edition, Joan Fontaine) has escaped;

e) She has brought out the cocker spaniel (played by itself);

f) Mrs. Danvers has set the fire rather than see the new couple live there happily;

g) Mrs. Danvers is still inside, etc.

Those are a lot of data points in a very short period of time. To accomplish all this so expeditiously, of course, Hitch doesn't tell us anything (except that Mrs. Danvers set the fire).

Rather, we see a large number of persons milling about, and Maxim goes up to the butler demanding to know where his wife is. That question, asked of that person, establishes Maxim's horror over the calamity and fear for his wife's safety, who all these persons are (the butler standing in metonymically for the entire staff), and the general level of confusion and mayhem, all in about a quarter of the time that a lesser director would need.

Now, here's the nutty thing: he can do better. In *North by Northwest*, as I mentioned earlier, he dispatches the villainous henchman, arrests his boss, rescues the hero and heroine who are dangling from the face of Mount Rushmore, gets them married, and heads them back to New York on the Twentieth Century Limited in a whopping forty-three seconds. I was first reminded of this feat by screenwriter and novelist William Goldman's *Adventures in the Screen Trade*; the time elapsed is his calculation, but I've checked it repeatedly, and he's right. Here's how it plays out. Nasty sidekick Martin Landau is stepping on Roger Thornhill's (Cary Grant) fingers when a shot rings out and he stiffens and falls into the void. We cut to a small group higher up where his suavely vicious boss (James Mason) suggests to the authorities that the shot wasn't "very sporting," but they have him in custody and don't much care about his opinion. But Roger and Eve Kendall (Eva Marie Saint) are still hanging on, barely, by their fingernails, and he is encouraging her to come up, come up when, suddenly, while we are still focusing on his face, it morphs from concerned to smiling as he pulls her into the upper berth of their sleeping car. Cut to train entering tunnel and paste on THE END. I'm pretty sure it is some sort of record.

Hitchcock can achieve these miracles of compression because he perfectly understands his medium. He knows what it can do as well as why—and more important, how—it can be done. You don't need a chapel or a justice of the peace; you only need Mr. Thornhill addressing "Mrs. Thornhill," of whom the only model to this point has been his mother, to establish that a wedding has taken place. This tidiness follows on from Mason's Phillip Vandamm offering his quip while manacled. A bad guy in handcuffs requires no explanation that he has been arrested; we will assume that it is not part of some erotic game, particularly if said villain is in the company of Leo G. Carroll. Here's what Hitchcock knew in his bones and that the rest of us need to remind ourselves of constantly: **Pictures tell the story.** He tells us so, in what should be any film buff's favorite quote: "If it's a good movie, the sound could go off and the audience would still have a perfectly clear idea of what was going on." We might add, by way of explanation, because they tell the story faster than any other approach. I have left out a great amount of what makes Hitchcock one of the great masters, but this speed and assuredness alone marks him as a master of his craft.

Hitch is associated strongly with one or two genres, the suspense-thriller in particular, but sometimes a director develops what amounts to a personal genre. I said something a while ago about Mel Brooks being his own genre. The same could be said about Woody Allen, whom we'll get to presently. Yes, there are differences of type among his films, but with forty-some movies to work with (what week is it?), we could establish the constituent elements of his brand, as I do elsewhere. The same is true for several younger directors. Since I previously mentioned Joel and Ethan Coen as well as Quentin Tarantino, we should consider them not merely as extremely talented filmmakers but as auteurs with distinct personal genres. Coen films, however dissimilar they may appear from one another, have several identifying features. They use established genres but bend them to sometimes unrecognizable degrees (think of the standard prison-break film and *Oh Brother, Where Art Thou?* or the stock Chandleresque detective story and *The Big Lebowski*—you can see the original form, but as if it's reflected in a funhouse mirror). The resulting work is quite dark, as if a dim view of humanity or reality animates their vision; terms like "black comedy" come up frequently, and if there were such a thing as "black noir" (now even noir-er?), it would apply. They employ quirky humor—often lots of it—to leaven the proceedings—or to make viewers more appalled by them. And they often interlayer shocking eruptions of violence, as in the woodchipper scene in *Fargo*. The poet Marianne Moore once described poems as "imaginary gardens with real toads in them"; following her, we might say that Coen brothers movies are Mel Brooks comedies with real villainy in them. That may not be entirely accurate, but it gets at a sense of the deadly absurdism that animates much of their work. To get a sense of what is particular to their films, one has only to see the results when they write screenplays for other directors. Their screenplay for Steven Spielberg's *Bridge of Spies* (2015), for instance, reads and plays like a Spielberg film and not one of theirs. While there are surprises, they tend to be of the normal and even predictable sort: you can't trust your enemy and maybe can't trust your friends, you're just a small person in a very big world, but even so, you can accomplish great things, and so on. Not a surreal upheaval in sight. Unless you count the typical workings of the hidden world of espionage.

If their humor is quirky or absurdist, Quentin Tarantino's is just plain weird. And disturbing. That's something he works very hard to achieve. In fact, Tarantino has said on many occasions that he handles each film differently, using its particular materials to "get people to laugh at things that are not funny." He wants the comic elements to be as unsettling as his violence. Even sometimes be the violence. And the violence is plenty disturbing. In *Pulp Fiction* (1994), after the hit on Brent and his associates, Jules (Samuel L. Jackson) and Vincent (John Travolta) drive off with the lone survivor, but in an overly casual moment involving a hand cannon, Vincent accidentally blows off the head of the hapless passenger. The moment, like the cleanup that follows, is both horrible and ridiculous. We're not programmed to accept real violence (that is, violence not involving cartoon coyotes) as comic or silly, which makes our reaction doubly shocking. Tarantino's own noirish leanings tend to be in the direction of the revenge tragedy—or maybe fantasy, since they don't all lead to a terrible downfall for the protagonist. Still, they share with the Jacobean revenge tragedies of the early seventeenth century a macabre imagination, highly stylized portrayals of human characteristics, and a great deal of shocking violence. Jules's use of a passage allegedly from Ezekiel (and the very last bit is) about the righteous man and the iniquities of the world typically signals a barrage of gunfire, although in the final episode in the film, he breaks the pattern. Do we really believe that real-world hit men perform such antics? No, but it doesn't matter: we do believe that a Tarantino hit man, or at least this one, would. Dialogue is similarly stylized. Many viewers and critics have objected to the sheer volume of profane and crude language in his films, to which the director responds not that he is emulating the real world but that in his fictive universe, that's how his characters speak. Which is to say, it is appropriate to the worlds he depicts if not to the civil society we inhabit—or hope we do. Much of what he does is designed to disrupt audience expectations. Another aspect of that disruption is his manipulation of the story timeline. As in *Pulp Fiction*, he chops up the linear timeline to tell the story out of order, emphasizing not suspense or sequence of events but buildup of effect. By framing the film with the attempted robbery, he can withhold the key dialogue, Jules's decision to leave his violent life in search of something more fulfilling. At the same time, it allows us to watch one character's response even though we have already seen him killed earlier in the film (but not in the timeline of the film). This technique reaches back to the literary modernists, particularly to Joseph Conrad and Ford Madox Ford—whose *The Good Soldier* (1915) employs a similarly chopped-and-rearranged use of time and event—and their theory of *progression d'effet* (progression by effect), whereby the emotional response is heightened with each passing scene. Whether Ford and Tarantino would recognize each other as artistic kinsmen is debatable; what matters is that they are experimenting in similar ways with the manipulation of time in their works. It's safe to say that, while Tarantino will certainly have his imitators, no director will be able to do quite what he does without seeming entirely derivative. Tarantino himself, on the other hand, can use the components of his cinematic toolbox again and again without their seeming hackneyed. Part of being an original is having the capacity to reinvent yourself even as you repeat yourself. That's being your own genre.

Since I invoked Woody Allen at the beginning of this chapter, it behooves us to return at some point. I've been trying to come up with the hallmarks of the "Allen style"; I have also been signally failing.

- Hesitation, stammering
- A strong element of absurdism that allows the underlying existentialist angst to find expression

- Anxiety and hostility expressed rather than held in

- In keeping with his beginnings as a joke and comedy writer, an affinity for loosely constructed sketches rather than tightly organized plots. While his films generally have plots, a certain amount of patience is required to find them.

- Breaking of the fourth wall (already mentioned)

- Making free with the rules and conventions of cinema

- Following the internal logic of the movie at hand, not the logic of "reality," whatever that might be

- Very clean shots and scenes

- A general absence of bombast and overreach. In the filmmaking, that is. Characters can be plenty bombastic.

Allen's rule is, *Why not?* In a dialogue between two people flirting, how about showing subtitles? Well, why not? There's no *cinematic* reason not to, no rule against it. So, too, with sending an older person back to the haunts of his earlier Roman sojourn, where he sees other young people playing out a drama similar to his own.

Or this. It is probably true that every literary young—or not so young—person who has gone to Paris in the last seventy years has wished to have been there in the twenties, when Montparnasse was full of writers and artists reshaping the world. Just think of it: Hemingway, Fitzgerald, Archibald MacLeish, Gertrude Stein, Cole Porter, Djuna Barnes, Josephine Baker, Luis Buñuel, Salvador Dalí, T. S. Eliot, all of them milling around, and us with them. But, alas, we can't, can we?

Well, why not? There's no reason a modern character can't be transported back in time by a classic limousine full of revelers. In that case, by all means, let's try it. And off we go. In *Midnight in Paris* (2011), his protagonist, Gil Pender, is picked up in style and whisked away to the decade-long party where the people whose work he studied in school and has always revered behave like, well, people. Mostly drunken people, committing mistakes, running at life and crashing, making asses of themselves, suffering for and from their art, all while having a swell time. There's even a girl to fall in love with and, in the best Allen tradition, ultimately lose.

Allen has been down this path before, most notably in his short story "The Kugelmass Episode," in which Sidney Kugelmass, a humanities instructor at City College of New York, wants to have an affair with a character from a novel. He is transported into *Madame Bovary* when he and a copy of the novel are placed in a magician's Chinese box. Gil's mode of time travel, a 1928 Peugeot Type 176, is much more elegant. Both Kugelmass and Gil, in giddiness over their good fortune, remind themselves that they failed freshman English. One final similarity: final mayhem. Kugelmass suffers a tragic misdirection when the box misfires and the magician dies of a heart attack, sending him into a remedial Spanish textbook, where he is chased by the verb *tener* (to have) in the form of a large and hairy spider. Many introductory Spanish students who suffered through the verb's irregularities could relate. In the movie, while Gil is spared, the private detective who tries to follow him instead stumbles into the Sun King's Versailles, where guards chase him to cries of "Off with his head."

His follow-up to *Midnight in Paris*, *To Rome with Love* (2012)—after decades of refusing to leave New York, he's running through the great cities of Europe, having started with *Vicky Cristina Barcelona* (2008), so it will be interesting to see how he handles Zagreb—uses all the tools in his arsenal. He gets four story lines going that sort of parallel but do not intersect:

1) A famous architect, John (Alec Baldwin), back in Rome after thirty years, who meets architecture student, Jack (Jesse Eisenberg), who is about to have a relationship crisis when his girlfriend invites her best friend, Monica (Ellen Page), a highly disruptive actress, to visit. The situation parallels John's own relationship calamity from his student days there. John, Jack? Hmm. We should maybe keep an eye on that.

2) A young couple from a small town come to the city to begin their lives together. They become separated almost at once and find themselves caught up in sexual intrigue, he with a prostitute (Penélope Cruz) who shows up at the wrong room and must impersonate his fiancée in front of his censorious aunts and uncles, she with a famous film star who gives way to a hotel thief.

3) An office worker (Roberto Benigni) mistakenly identified as the hot new celebrity—for no reason. He quickly finds he is trapped by fame, then that he likes it, only to have it slip away just as quickly.

4) A retired would-be impresario, Jerry (Allen himself), and his wife (Judy Davis), who have come to see their student daughter, Hayley

(Alison Pill), and to meet her Roman fiancé
and his family. Unsurprisingly, the father of
the groom-to-be, Giancarlo (real-life opera star
Fabio Armiliato), turns out to be a fabulous
singer, but only in the shower. Allen devotees
instantly recognize that this absurdist twist cannot end well.

One of the complaints about the movie is that the series of
vignettes fail to cohere, and there is something to that. One
suspects that allowing the Italian characters to speak in Italian
may have added to dissatisfaction. Find an American who likes
reading subtitles. At the same time, the movie is an excellent
vehicle for studying the mature Allen at work.

- There is a good bit of stammering, most of it by
  Allen's Jerry.

- All four story lines have a strong element of the
  absurd. Man meets version of his earlier self, but
  not him; hooker walks into the wrong room; clerk
  plucked randomly for stardom; shower arias, etc.
  Ditto existentialist angst, again, mostly by Jerry and
  by Jack, who in an earlier era would have been the
  Allen character.

- Not only does the film have its own logic; so do the
  scenes. The vignettes don't even operate on a common timeline. The newlywed story plays out over a
  single afternoon. Both Jerry's operatic adventure and
  Leopoldo's sudden fame play out over many days,
  if not weeks; you simply cannot mount *Pagliacci* in
  an afternoon, however lengthy. Most interesting is
  the John/Jack back-to-the-future tale. Jack's growing
  infatuation with Monica takes several days, for which
  John is present. At the end of that saga, however,

John returns to the spot where he met Jack, and it is evidently the same sunny afternoon as when they began. Nice work if you can get it. Yet with all the different approaches to time, the movie cuts back and forth between the vignettes as if they occupy the same temporal space. Which they do—it's just ours, not theirs.

- Then there's the fourth-wall violation. We don't know quite what to make of Baldwin's John. Is he present in the young people's lives after the first introductions? Are they projections of his own memory and yearning? Is he a character or a one-man Greek chorus? When he talks to Jack, is he really talking to him or to the audience?

Jorge Luis Borges has a short story in which an old man, returning to Harvard, where he was a student, meets his younger self. He wishes to enlighten that prior embodiment in order to spare him pain and mistakes. The young man, naturally, will not hear of it and thinks the old man crazy. To prove his point, the old man hands his younger self a coin that, would he only look at it, cannot possibly come from the young man's era; the young man promptly tosses it into the Charles River. There is a similar sort of playfulness both with reality and with the possibilities of storytelling within the chosen form, in the movie. Indeed, there are ways in which Woody Allen, of all our filmmakers, comes closest to the magical realists of Latin America. His films, like their novels, are not fantasies; rather, they make use of fantastic elements erupting in an otherwise ordinary universe. His work and theirs obey the logic of the chosen medium, not the logic that we believe operates in our external reality. Gift coins from the future, like subtitles or choruses, are ever so much more likely in stories or movies than in everyday life.

Every director has his or her own idiosyncrasies. Quentin Tarantino can't resist an almost adolescent fascination with violence, so it erupts at odd times and almost invariably to excess. Robert Altman loved crowd scenes with lots of people all talking at once so that we never quite hear all of any conversation but may pick up fragments of several. Werner Herzog's films, including *Aguirre, the Wrath of God* (1972) and *Fitzcarraldo* (1982), often follow (and sometimes mirror) the obsessive's descent into madness and destruction not only of self but of those nearby. This interest explains his frequent use of Klaus Kinski, one of the great mad faces of modern cinema. If Herzog's films are often the stuff of nightmare, Federico Fellini explores dreams, fantasy, strange situations, and stranger people, and something like Jungian collective unconscious, whether in the fairly early *La Strada* (1952) or *8½* (1963), however different they might be in approach. David Lean, as I have mentioned several times, loves the sweeping panorama. Yet Lean can also work in almost claustrophobic enclosures; Fellini can work in something very like realism, Herzog in something approximating sanity. We can recognize trends in a director's oeuvre, but we risk falsifying the work if we insist too strongly on those trends. After all, we want our artists to be familiar to us, but we also like our surprises.

20

Put It to the Test

CAN WE TALK? You've been a great audience. Really. If you've
reached this part, I have nothing but respect for your perse-
verance and generosity of spirit. It's just that—how shall I put
this?—you've been a little passive. Oh, sure, you've wanted to
talk back now and then, probably wanted to throw the book
across the room a time or two, had your own view on certain
films or actors or scenes. I get that. But it doesn't change the
fact that the conversation has been a little one-sided. I mean,
did you actually throw the book? That's what I thought. Well,
here's your big chance. No, not that—you'll break a lamp or
something. But I'm asking you to get busy.

If we've accomplished anything together, it's time to put that
new knowledge into practice. Let's break down a film. First, a

confession: this isn't my idea. I got an email a few weeks ago from a reader of *How to Read Literature Like a Professor* that said he and his family, including children and grandchildren, were all going to sit down to watch *The Artist* and apply the principles gleaned from that book in analyzing the film. A day or so later, he sent me a report on their findings. One of their really interesting thoughts involved using their collective knowledge of other films: they agreed that the movie owes a great deal to *Singin' in the Rain*. That's a good insight. I had inclined toward *A Star Is Born*, but I also see those films as related to one another in a number of ways. He wrote some other things and asked me what I would see in the film that they hadn't noticed. My chief contribution (if it can be called that) to the discussion was to point out two images that seem significant. The first, which I mentioned earlier, is the whole mirror business. The second is the emphasis on stairways, especially the one big stairway where Peppy and George see each other a couple of times, once when he's on top and once when she is in the ascendant. It's a movie about highs and lows in entertainment, about rising and falling, so images of changes in elevation are significant. And one thing led to another, and it finally occurred to me (because I'm not all that swift) that you and I could play this game.

This next part is still a little one-sided. Obviously, I'm going to have to choose the film since it's beyond difficult to run a referendum to select a subject. And for obvious reasons, you will see my answer but I won't see yours, at least not within the pages of this book. I did something similar in that earlier book, and ever since, I periodically get an email with an analysis of Katherine Mansfield's "The Garden Party" from a reader who wants to point out what I missed. Which is great. They're always right: there are things I, or any reader, will miss or at least slide over in service to a larger argument. So here we go.

Sorry, *The Artist* is out. I've already addressed aspects of it, which will skew the results. That said, please feel free; it's a great film on which to try out your analytical skills. We could go anywhere with this, of course. Any halfway decent movie would suffice, but I think we can do better than halfway. Let's take another film from that same historical moment, Ben Affleck's *Argo* (2012). It's got everything we could want in a movie—characters in need, suspense, some laughs, a look back at historical events, plenty of bad hair, fashion, and huge eye-glasses circa 1979–80, conflict, and even a close shave or two. Did I mention suspense? Plenty of that.

So go ahead. Get a copy of *Argo* and watch it. Twice, if you want to do this up right. Then let it sink in for a day or so (you might just want to put this day between the two viewings; you'll see more the second time). Write out your analysis of the movie. Which parts are significant? What works? What doesn't? How does the film achieve those things it achieves? How does it use the camera? Space? Light? Whatever you find yourself focusing on, go for it. Whatever you do, DON'T PEEK. I don't want my reading corrupting yours. You may be tempted, but have a little self-control, for crying out loud. And don't worry about me. I'll just eat an apple or catch up on paperwork. Be right here when you get back.

★   ★   ★

Oh! There you are. So, how'd it go? Good, good. Okay, then, forward! Before we go, a word of advice. My version of the movie won't resemble yours in all details, perhaps not even in very many. That does not mean mine is better than yours. Nor particularly worse (although that's a distinct possibility). Only different. My predilections and obsessions are not yours, for which you should be profoundly grateful, so the sorts of things I notice are particular to me. Other readers may share some, reject some, veer toward others I haven't imagined. That's good. It gives us something to talk about over cappuccino. So no worries. All I insist on is that you own your reading of the movie. Really take charge of it and don't worry about what anyone else may be finding there. Your reading is identical to no one else's.

What, me?

Okay. Here we go. The first thing that strikes me is that, if I were giving advice, I would absolutely warn the aspiring screenwriter off using an opening like this one. I mean, seriously, a documentary-style voice-over history of Iran with still photos and drawings? I would probably tell you that your screenplay will be a corpse by the bottom of page one. And I would be dead wrong. One of the things that makes this attempt effective is that it uses storyboards, those sketches of movie shots that filmmakers use to chart the direction of not just the movie, but the shooting of the movie. In other words, the opening is using a movie device as a way of telling us that this film will be about, in some way or other, the movies. And we get it: those who know about storyboards think, Oh, right, that; those who don't still see drawings that effectively convey their messages. It's all good.

See, here's the thing about movies. The only thing you can't do is something that doesn't work. This works. Shouldn't, maybe, but it does. Same thing for the written statements at the end. The general rule is that writing on the screen gets viewers turning away even before the credits roll. But this does the job. Part of it is that we're dying to know what happened to these people after their ordeal. And star and director Ben Affleck buys our goodwill by showing us pictures of the originals along with shots of the actors who played them. Who can resist that stuff?

But back to that opening—it's only part of the opening. After it ends, we get the real drama. What's the first thing we see? A burning American flag, then a besieged U.S. Embassy, an angry crowd, a locked gate, all shot with a jumpy, handheld camera before pulling back to offer a more stable panorama shot. In the ten minutes that follow, we see almost everything we need to be able to follow this movie: frightened Americans, angry Iranians, barriers, locks, telephones, secrets (burned and shredded documents in this instance), portals (doors and windows), onrushing protestors displayed on closed-circuit monitors, television reports, escape. Those will all loom large in the rest of the film, and we'll get around to them in a bit. Yep, we have everything we need to make a movie.

Except a hero. Not to worry, we pick him up moments later, although not in the most heroic of poses. When we first see him, Tony Mendez is facedown on a bed, clothed, in a hotel room with sufficient debris to suggest slovenliness or a binge or both. He has to pull himself together to answer the phone call that's pulling him up out of sleep. From this first moment, and at pretty much every one thereafter, the film tells us that if Tony's going to be a hero, it won't be in the John Wayne/ Gary Cooper mode. He's a bit rumpled and disagreeable, a little surer of himself than he has a right to be. That's okay: this isn't going to be a Wayne/Cooper sort of movie. No horses, no six-shooters. This problem will be solved, if at all, by brainpower and guile and stealth.

From that initial moment, the remainder of the first act belongs to Tony. He has to be brought up to speed about events in Tehran; that is to say, that six potential hostages have escaped and found refuge in the Canadian ambassador's residence. At the meeting to plan a rescue, he rejects the ideas for exfiltration as unworkable and stupid, in the process rubbing everyone else the wrong way. He identifies the plan that becomes our movie and has to sell it to very doubtful superiors and competing interests, has to enlist makeup artist and sometime CIA collaborator John Chambers (John Goodman) and producer Lester Siegel (Alan Arkin) to help him sell the fake movie idea to the world. (As a historical aside, Chambers was a real person, Siegel invented for dramatic purposes; inside the film, they are equally present and vivid. This is a useful reminder not to take details from movies as historical facts.) Lester himself is resistant to the idea when John and Tony approach him. He seems not to welcome, maybe not even to hear, their arguments, until he gazes at the televised images of violence coming from Tehran and says, "We're going to need a script." That statement is the first plot point, arriving at thirty minutes and some seconds and pivoting the action from setup to activity. From that moment, the film begins building the story surrounding "Argo," the fake movie, before taking the show on the road to Tehran.

One of the challenges in this part is to tie the several time and story lines together: the "guests" at the ambassador's residence, the guards and hostages at the American embassy, the evidently tepid Washington response, and the Hollywood dream machine at full tilt. The result is an impressive juggling act. At a highly publicized table reading of the script for "Argo," a waiter carrying an empty tray on which Tony sets his drained wineglass walks into the kitchen and past a television showing an Iranian spokeswoman reading a prepared statement that the hostages are not diplomats but spies. We cut from that small screen to a bank of them at CIA headquarters, where a very disgruntled-looking Jack O'Donnell (Bryan Cranston), Tony's boss, is watching. Then we cut to the woman herself as she reads and is filmed by a phalanx of television cameras. John Chambers has earlier asked Lester if maybe all the anger emanating from Iran isn't just an act, so this scene plays on that. We cut briefly to the table read, where one actress is saying that the world as we know it has ended, and then quickly to the living room at the ambassador's residence, where the hostages are watching President Carter making a speech about not being held up by terrorists and blackmailers, then even more briefly back to the table read and a bad C-3PO rip-off character telling his captain that "there's not enough time." We pause ever so briefly at the Iranian student spokeswoman calling the CIA the "most terrorizing organization" just as we cut to some Iranian Revolutionary Guards rousting several male hostages out of bed for a mock execution. The film intercuts a couple more times among these scenes until we arrive at the end of the table read.

It's a great bit of intercutting, played for maximum irony. Is it likely that all these things were happening simultaneously? Of course not. But what the film is establishing is simultaneity not of events but of effect: these several scenes demonstrate a common element of events in Washington and Tehran and Hollywood, namely that all parties are engaging in some sort of theatrics. The fake movie is no more an act than the fake execution, no less than the spokeswoman's performance—or the president's. Everything about these events, the movie suggests, is *staged*. And therefore stage-managed.

This is a road film, a quest film, if you will. We're told as much early on, when Tony is asked if he's Moses, who will lead his group, however small, in an exodus. And if he doesn't part the Red Sea, he does at least part some red tape. And if it's not exactly a road picture in the Bob Hope/Bing Crosby/Dorothy Lamour vein, it nevertheless takes us many places as we follow our hero. We see Tony driving around Washington, then driving around Los Angeles with John Chambers and Lester Siegel, then flying to Istanbul, being driven into Tehran from the airport, driving around Tehran with his six charges in a rented Volkswagen Microbus, finally on the airport bus and then the plane out of Iran. During the trip to scout sites in the Microbus, the group endures ordeals, first when confronted

with angry crowds through which they must drive very slowly
while the van is pounded on by screaming demonstrators,
and again in the bazaar, when an ill-advised instant-camera
snapshot nearly starts a riot. That riot may have been staged, as
so much of the trip is, but it is nevertheless an ordeal for the
frazzled Americans.

It is fairly standard for road films to contain roadblocks, and
does this film ever have them! Remember what I said about
doors and other barriers in *Casablanca*? The Bogart classic has
nothing on *Argo* in that department. Doors and gates are wonderful cinematic devices. They open, they close, sometimes
they stay closed. People enter and exit, or sometimes they
halfway enter or turn partway through their exit. Doors have a
world of possibilities, and this movie has a world of doors and
related objects. Front doors. Office doors. Hotel room doors.
Sliding doors. Opaque doors. Transparent doors. Plus enough
gates to shake a wrought iron stick at. Not to mention people
who act as gatekeepers, holding characters back or allowing
them to pass through this or that physical space, this or that
bureaucratic impasse. How about some examples? Okay:

- The padlocked gate at the American embassy. Later, the
  front door of the embassy, which is breached through
  some bad judgment on the part of one of the guards;

- Entry to the embassy is gained by breaking out windows and grates;

- The consular worker in Istanbul;

- Tony's check-in at Tehran airport where a man is carried away screaming by guards;

- Tony's interview with the man at the Ministry of
  Culture and Guidance office; clearly, the official is a
  gatekeeper;

- The embassy gate opens for Tony and Ambassador Ken Taylor, then closes;

- As Tony walks toward the residence, he looks at the gate across the sidewalk;

- While the group is out on its scouting trip, the man from the Ministry of Culture and Guidance comes to the locked gate and talks to Sahar, the local woman who works at the ambassador's residence;

- After Tony gets the call that the mission is scrubbed, Cora Lijek (Clea DuVall) knocks on the door and then stands in the doorway as Tony lies to her, assuring her that they did well and don't need to practice further;

- After he leaves, Sahar goes inside, shutting the door, and leaning against it in a gesture of relief and fear;

- The front door of the residence that Ambassador Taylor opens to admit Tony the morning of the escape;

- The Swissair ticket counter, where the clerk discovers that Tony's ticket (and therefore the others) has not been validated; when she checks again, the confirmation has gone through;

- The hang-up at the terminal over the lack of white copies for the six passengers;

- Azizi checkpoint number three (Farshad Farahat), who accosts them in Farsi but turns out to speak perfect English, and who makes the call to Studio Six Productions, the fake production company. He almost doesn't get an answer because . . .

- The director's PA has been holding John and Lester back for the filming of a fight scene and doesn't even let them through before a second take, although eventually they burst through;

- The sliding doors being closed by a guard at the Swissair gate, seeming to promise the collapse of the plan;

- Azizi guards stopped by terminal's sliding glass doors, eventually shooting their way through;

- While on the airport bus, Tony looks out at the plane with its steep stairway and high, small (in perspective) door;

- Finally, the one they elude: the end-of-runway barrier that the plane just clears as it departs, while the pursuing cars and truck must turn back, thwarted;

- And one more door: the door to his house, on which Tony knocks when he has come home.

You can argue, and I won't fight back, that these are all real-life doors and barriers that anyone attempting to go from place to place would encounter. Absolutely true. What matters here, though, is not that they exist in the real world but that the director chooses to include them in this hurry-up-and-wait narrative of danger and escape. By its very nature, the film relies on these impediments as a way of selling the audience on the peril involved; the sheer number of barriers conveys that level of hazard, as almost every one of them can spell doom for the project and our seven travelers.

Along with doors, we have passageways and apertures, appropriate for people trying to make a very narrow escape. This trope finds an early, and perhaps its best, image in the arched entry to Istanbul's Hagia Sophia through which Tony walks on his way to the "secret meeting" with his British counterpart, OSS officer Nicholls (Richard Dillane). The arch is tall and narrow, ideal for framing first Tony and then the grand museum that has been both a basilica and a mosque during its sixteen-hundred-year history. Once he arrives in Tehran and clears a few hurdles, he leads the band of six to a meeting with a representative of the Ministry of Culture and Guidance at the grand bazaar. That trip is one long maze run, made more unnerving by the legendary crowding of the place. And that's before the conflict over the Polaroid. We know, although they do not, that they have been spied on and photographed during their trip, which will further narrow their prospects once the pictures are developed. Still later, we see them make their way down the passageway of the Swissair terminal and then in the terminal bus, itself a narrow space, toward the waiting airplane. Throughout their ordeal, Tony and the six "guests" are practicing a variant of *running the gauntlet*, a ritualized punishment or trial in which the victim is forced to walk or run between two lines of armed warriors. The point of the gauntlet is not always to inflict death (although in some traditions it was) but to humiliate and cause pain. In the movie, we actually see the guests flinch at times during the ordeal at the airport. And throughout, their available space is cramped indeed.

And that leads us to a related element: the film is filled with claustrophobic elements—confined spaces, secret hideouts. Early on, a helicopter passing over the ambassador's residence causes them to hurry for cover into a secret compartment, obviously well used, under the dining room floor. Their colleagues at the U.S. Embassy who were not so lucky are kept in tight stalls like so many cattle in a dark, seriously unfriendly basement. The VW Microbus that Tony rents, while technically able to handle seven adults, looks extremely cramped and uncomfortable as they drive through hostile and potentially dangerous streets. And the streets themselves add to that

atmosphere. Pretty much everywhere in Tehran there are traffic jams and crowds. The message is clear: there simply is no
space available. Even the shots are cramped. When the "guests"
are shown, they are often in such extreme close-ups that the
screen can't contain their faces: foreheads, chins, and ears are
cropped off by an unforgiving frame.

Here's a lesson in how different people can see the same
movie differently. As we rewatched the movie the other night,
about the third or fourth time we saw a poster of Ayatollah
Khomeini glowering at us, my Permanent Movie Companion turned to me and said, "Did you ever notice that when
a country plasters up pictures of its leader everywhere, the
place is never a democracy?" I have sort of noticed that, but
that wasn't where I was going. My response? Eyes. Watching,
watching, watching. Spies, photographs, observers official and
unofficial. The ayatollah, naturally, isn't watching, except from
the dozen or so posters that we see in various locations: the
consulate in Turkey, then at the airport in a sort of "Heil Hitler" salute, on random walls, including during the voiced-over
history at the beginning. He doesn't need to; he has people
for that. From the looks of things, nearly all of the people.
This watching thing doesn't just go one way, however. The
hostages/guests also watch. They watch the developing chaos
at the beginning. They watch the television (so does almost
everyone everywhere). They watch Tony Mendez very closely,
studying him to decide if they can trust him or not. And they
watch each other. Given their isolation and anxiety, what else
could they do? Tony, for his part, watches them watching
him, watches them for reactions, in fact watches everyone for
reactions. He is constantly appraising his situation, which is
accomplished most often through keeping his eye on people.

This all reaches its apex during the trip to the bazaar, where everyone is watching everyone else, the Americans with fear, anxiety, and caution, the Iranians with curiosity, hostility, and anger, Tony with nothing more than vague concern showing. I'm pretty sure there aren't a million eyes in the sequence, but it feels like there are.

Although we may rarely notice, music plays a very large part in the film. Why don't we notice? Because that's how Affleck and composer Alexandre Desplat want it. The music is largely atmospheric, lying comfortably (or maybe uncomfortably) under the action. For the most part, it doesn't rely on the big ups and downs of traditional "movie music," choosing instead to become part of the larger fabric of the narrative. For instance, when Tony and the guests are standing in the airport, as the first checkpoint tries to match their yellow "out" slips with the corresponding white originals, the music is a long single note on strings with a heavy bass note underneath. The moment is sort of the opposite of Bernard Herrmann's shrieking violins during the shower scene in *Psycho*. That one is designed for maximum fright. This one aims for the slow build of tension; by the end, we're dying for another chord to come along and relieve this one even if it is just as discordant. At the Swissair gate, music barely moves forward, sending a clear question: are they going to get away or be stuck here forever? That approach to the use of music is broken only when there is ambient music coming from radios or stereos. In those moments, the tunes are foregrounded and asked to provide commentary on the action. The clearest instance of this is after Tony takes the phone call from his boss, Jack O'Donnell, telling him that the White House has pulled authorization: the mission is scrubbed. This call takes place while the guests are having a last-evening party to celebrate what they assume will be their deliverance. When Tony gets off the phone, he looks back in on the party, where Bob Anders (Tate Donovan) has put on a Led Zeppelin album, choosing the cut "When the Levee Breaks." The song plays over or behind Tony passing along the information to Ambassador Taylor, walking around the fringe of the celebration, spiriting away a bottle of scotch, and more or less slinking away. We then cut to Iranian intelligence officer Ali Khalkhali (Ali Saam) leafing through photos of the guests taken at the bazaar earlier as the song fades out, replaced by more Desplat atmospherics, this one slow, adagio or lento, in a complex minor key. That melody will continue through Tony passing the burning car, driving to his hotel, drinking straight from the bottle, to a cut of the party, where the guests are having a fine time, unaware that higher powers have decided, in effect, to sacrifice them, and back to Tony smoking, drinking, capping the bottle, tossing it on the bed, and finally sitting on the bed. It carries us, in fact, through the night and to the muezzin's call to morning prayer that replaces it. But back to the song, the key line of which is the last one of the first verse, "When the levee breaks, I'll have no place to stay." We get it: this levee just broke, and the flood is about to hit. The irony of one of the would-be escapees selecting the record registers, but it plays as less heavy-handed than if the director imposed it from the outside. Plus, did *you* ever think of diplomats as Zeppelin fans? Theme plus character revelation: can't beat it.

We really can't appreciate this movie fully unless we consider the role of the telephone. This movie plays on our sense of the universality of cell phones. Even those of us who lived through the heyday of landline phones find ourselves frustrated by the sheer difficulty of communicating in an age when voices from afar relied on wires coming out of the wall. Telephones play a huge role in the film, especially the phone in the producers' office at the studio in the last act when Ali Khalkhali calls to make sure that an entity called "Studio Six Productions" actually exists. His first call fails when John and Lester are held up by the production assistant at the fight scene I mentioned earlier. Even after they break through, Chambers barely gets the phone answered before the intelligence officer hangs up. That's only the success or failure of the mission riding on that call. We also see phone calls back and forth across the ocean, at the American embassy in the beginning, at the CIA, at the White House, in various offices in Iran, at Ambassador Taylor's residence, including the time Tony gets the bad news. When the Iranian security forces later break in, that same secure phone, now broken, delays discovery just long enough to allow the escape. Not for nothing is the second plot point delivered by phone when Tony calls Jack O'Donnell to tell him that he's taking the guests out despite orders because "someone has to be responsible." This is a movie in which communication of all sorts—between offices, between underlings and their superiors, between Hollywood and the wider world, among Hollywood insiders, through the medium of television, via press release—is absolutely critical. And quite apart from its literal use, no device so completely crystallizes that theme as the humble telephone. Watching the film during the cell phone age really drives that point home, recalling a time when one could easily miss a call that might mean life or death.

Let's talk about the movies in the movie. At this late date in cinematic history, no movie gets made without awareness of films that have come before it. Beyond that general truth, this is a film, of course, about the power of movies, the way they can make us believe things that we know not to be true, the way they can dazzle us, distract us, even bamboozle us. It is significant that the one souvenir Tony keeps to give to his son is a poster board of a fight from the fake movie. So it should come as no surprise to us that *Argo* raids the history of film. Several times I had the sense that the film was quoting other movies. I wisecracked earlier about parting the Red Sea, but that feeling really is there, especially in the bazaar sequence. We get a Moses reference early in the film, and there is more than a hint of *The Ten Commandments* in this rescue effort, enough so that Tony is aware of it. Beyond that, this is every specialist movie you've ever seen. A *specialist* movie is a subcategory of action film in which the hero is called on to make use of "a very special skill set," as Liam Neeson's Bryan Mills is fond of saying in the *Taken* films. Often, as in that case, the specialist is called on to rescue someone or something. The ultimate example may well be *The Magnificent Seven*, where each of the seven brings a unique skill set to the party. Britt's (James Coburn) knife throwing may strike us as rather short-range in the wild gunfight that climaxes the proceedings, but it has its place. The real specialists here are John Chambers and Lester Siegel, the two old, jaded movie pros. Lester may not know about the Argonauts, but he knows how to sell a movie. But of course it's Tony's film, and maybe he is neither Moses nor Bryan Mills but that ultimate specialist, Indiana Jones. I know, he seems to lack both the swash and the buckle, but consider: he goes into hostile territory against overwhelming odds. He keeps his cool in the deadliest situations. He enlists improbable allies. He uses brainpower more than brawn. And come to think of it, sidekick/superior Bryan Cranston does look a little like Denholm Elliott. Most of all, there's this: the CIA clerk who receives and catalogs all of Tony's movie stuff, except the one storyboard he keeps for his son, rolls it into a seemingly endless warehouse. Now where have we seen that before?

One last bit, which requires a confession: I am a weather obsessive. That attachment to climatological matters probably comes from an adolescence of baling hay and mowing grass for income, but I always notice, and sometimes I give weather too much credit in films and stories. But not this time, I think. After his dark night of the soul, Tony is still sitting up when the muezzin sings out his call. The sky over the minarets is broken—ragged clouds interrupting a morning sky. Not the most auspicious of signs: things can go either way. Against that backdrop, he makes the decision to lead the guests out, against the orders of his superiors. The project has been stopped, the tickets not confirmed, lines of communication interrupted—what else could possibly go wrong? From that moment on, it is far from clear sailing, until the moment it is. Even on the terminal bus out to the plane, there's a bit of overcast. As that plane clears the terminal, however, the weather improves. We get a reverse shot from the streets below of the plane gaining altitude, and there it is in the background, blue sky with a few puffy, white clouds. And when they clear Iranian airspace, I'm pretty sure it's sunny inside the fuselage, too.

So what do we see here? A well-made movie in which the parts work together to make the whole thing stronger, in which the necessary plot components also carry figurative meaning, which deepens the film's significance. Yes, this is a spy thriller (to place it in its proper genre), but it is richer in meaning and tone than the garden variety spooks-and-secrets flick. This movie gets at the true nature of international intrigue, the nature of secrets and lies, the reality of working in a hierarchy, the importance of trust, the value of being true to your word. It brilliantly re-creates an era that is unlike our own in so many ways and yet is still informing our world. Is *Argo* a great movie? I don't know. Get back to me in a decade or two when some time has passed and we'll watch it again to see how it holds up. I do know that it is a very good movie, deserving of the critical praise it received and the numerous awards it garnered. In the short run, can we really expect anything more?

Conclusion

❉

Be an Auteur

I BEGAN THIS BOOK WITH A PREMISE: the thing that sets off film from other artistic media is that everyone is an expert. Now, don't get so defensive. I am not making fun of you. I did not, you will notice, put "expert" in quotation marks (until just now), and I don't mean it to have any. That would suggest that everyone believes himself or herself to be an expert, which is not what I mean at all. We're talking the real deal here. The average movie viewer will have seen more movies by age twenty-five than the average reader will read books in her lifetime. I'm figuring that beginning at age five, most of us see at least a film a week (averaged out over a year), times twenty years: $52 \times 20 = 1,040$ movies. This does not count the thrice-daily screenings of *The Little Mermaid* or *The Lion King* in households with young children but only what we might think of as discrete movie experiences. Even if some of the movies are indiscreet. That estimate, moreover, strikes me as quite conservative. A great many people see plenty more films than that.

So, let's say a thousand movies by early adulthood. You know how expertise is built? Time. More specifically, time-in-activity. Doctoral students in literature are given massive reading lists of books in their areas of specialization preparatory to taking what are called "comprehensive" or "qualifying" exams. These exams, and the lists that underwrite them, develop graduate students into "experts" in their field who are qualified to "profess" their expertise, initially in a dissertation and then in the world at large, whether in a university setting or in some other quarter. I am still in possession of my lists (modern British and American literature, contemporary—yes, there is a difference—British and American literature, and critical theory), and there are nowhere near one thousand books on them. That I am a person who would have kept the lists is another story entirely.

What we are asserting here is that viewing a thousand movies provides a level of expertise of its own, albeit without exams or, mercifully, dissertations. Yes, we freely acknowledge that not every movie was viewed in conditions conducive to study. We often sit through movies—or parts thereof—in social settings. I was in a rowdy fraternity house television den when we saw Roman Polanski's *The Fearless Vampire Killers* (1967, and no, I am not especially proud of the fact). It relieves me greatly to know that there will be no quiz. Even so, what we have absorbed in that amount of movie witnessing is astonishing: one thousand films times 120 minutes times 60 seconds times 24 frames equals—oh, good heavens! What a number! How could we not have learned a huge amount about the film enterprise?

It is also worth noting that not all expertise is the same.

There are, no doubt, experts in that noble subgenre, the gross-out comedy, just as there are viewers who have seen every blaxploitation movie. Five times. Well, who am I to judge? Many of us have a more eclectic approach: we watch what sounds interesting. Still others have a program: anything with subtitles; nothing with subtitles; rom-coms only (or everything *but* rom-coms); absolutely every film by a favored director along with any directors who influenced him or were influenced by him or merely resemble him in some almost-discernible way; whatever Turner Classic Movies sends their way. The system may not make sense to us, but it works for the person who employs it. Many men have sat through more romantic comedies than they would elect on their own; ulterior motives are suspected. The point is, movies have many uses, and given enough time, most of us will discover nearly all of them. All this helps explain why, when two or more persons are gathered to discuss films, disagreements break out—long before a specific movie can prompt argument—because of what sort of movie watcher each one is and why. The subject of the disagreement will rarely be so baldly stated, but that is what's going on.

And then we get to the movie itself:

"It's great."

"It's crap."

"You don't see what he was trying to do."

"I do see what he was trying to do. That's the problem."

"But that shot with the rooster and the motorcycle . . ."

"Utter crap. What's wrong with you?"

Which is why it is sometimes best to avoid cinematic discussions: they can be so dramatic. Oh, well, *de gustibus non est disputandum*, as they say. I'm sure someone said it. Pretty sure. And that he was a Roman, which would explain the funny spelling. It means, approximately, "In matters of taste there is no point in discussion." Which in turn means, best not to argue with someone whose taste is all in his mouth. Or to tell him so.

Which is also why you might as well take ownership of your reading, your interpretation, your understanding of movies. No one else will. Besides, we want to go beyond taste and value judgments: good/bad, best/worst, Top 10/50/100. Once we get past hierarchies and winners and losers, discussions become more fruitful and interesting. Not to mention less contentious. There are things on which we can all agree about a film: structure, technique, approach, shot design, score—stuff like that. But the real intrigue comes when we try to analyze how those elements affect the film's meaning. What does it say that it uses this old song redone by a new singer rather than by the original artist? That the scene is shot in a room with the door slightly ajar, rather than fully open or closed? That something in the shadows seemed to move in that one shot? These sorts of questions are where the fun begins. And fun is why we turn to the arts. We are interested in play, and the arts—movies as well as literature, poetry, drama and the theater, painting, drawing, music, dance—provide us with the occasion to play. So does thinking about them. I know, at some point in our education, we come to associate thinking with work, but that is chiefly because we have to produce evidence, whether essay, exam, or pop quiz, that brain function actually occurred. Those tend to be less fun. But you're on your own now and able to think your own thoughts. So think them. Be mindful of the thoughts you have, and take pride in owning them. They're yours, after all.

Do we really need to get bogged down in matters of, say, whether *The Sting* made better use of ragtime than *Ragtime*? Or if the expanses of *Lawrence of Arabia* are more expansive than those of *Doctor Zhivago*? Maybe, at some point, but not right off. There is a time and a place for matters of taste and value judgments, usually right after the show ends and we walk out saying, "What on earth was wrong with [insert Famous

Critic here] that she/he totally didn't get this movie?" Still, when we want to really think about movies or to discuss them intelligently, we don't want to stop at the yea/nay level. There is so much more to say that is so much more productive. Even then, stick to your guns. Who better than you to say what you think? There are bullies out there, people who try to win arguments through intimidation based on how many famous or old or obscure or foreign movies they've seen. Ultimately, it doesn't matter if you have or haven't seen Max von Sydow's Knight playing chess with Death in Ingmar Bergman's *The Seventh Seal* or you do or don't understand all the story permutations in Akira Kurosawa's *Rashomon*. What matters is that you bring your experience, your insights, your expertise to analyzing the movie at hand.

You will have noticed in the title for this farewell that I seemed to suggest that you direct your own movie. For a host of experiential, financial, and maybe existential reasons, this is not practical as a large-scale solution. Just think how overwhelmed we would all be if five or six billion of us started making movies of our own. True, when we use *auteur*, we are usually referring to directors of note, especially those whose work seems to cohere around style and technique. But to fully comprehend the implications of the word, we need to get back to its first meaning: author. The French critics who initially employed the term meant to suggest that the directors "authored" their films; that is, they were the creative authorities putting their particular stamp on the movies and that everyone else from the cinematographer down to the caterer's helper labored in obedience to this masterful vision. That view has pretty much won the day, as you will notice from my handling of film titles and director's names in this discussion. There's just one problem with it.

It doesn't go far enough.

To be sure, the director *authors* the product that appears on the screen. That leaves us with a question: what happens to it then? Does the audience passively receive that "text"? Or does it actively engage with the director's realized vision? I use the word *text* advisedly here. We read movies as we read books. Our meeting point, the surface where the authorial enterprise meets our imaginations, is the screen, which functions like the physical (or virtual) book with written literature. So here's the thing about that surface: it doesn't mean a thing on its own. Only when an audience enters the frame does the text come to life. Viewers, like readers, do more than merely complete a circuit. They develop meaning within that text. They decide what elements add up to signify what symbolic or metaphorical values. The creator may believe that this journey signifies a particular sort of quest (or whatever), but it isn't really true until a reader or viewer agrees with him. If the only audience a literary work ever garners is its creator, it essentially has no meaning, since an audience of one lacks judgment. It lacks life. But when that second member of the audience encounters the work, it begins to live. Not before.

That's a big responsibility, but I'm sure you're up to the task. Being a reader—of any creative work—is an act of the imagination. Of course it requires skills: understanding the form, knowledge of the language of that form, attention to detail, mental concentration. You've got all that covered. You've shown plenty of concentration to get to this point, and you have mastered the grammar of cinematic language. What remains is to apply your imagination along with your intelligence to the next movie you watch. It originally belonged to someone else. Make it yours. It won't be quite like anyone else's version of it, and that's fine. Better than fine. Own that movie.

You've got that one, too.

And what's become of our old pals Dave and Lexi? One of them has been off doing homework of his own, as he mentioned when they ran into each other at the coffee shop.

"Hey, let's go see another movie one of these days."

"I've been ready. Where have you been?"

"Watching a ton of movies. Trying to, you know, catch up a little bit. I can just about keep up now."

"It's not a contest, Dave."

"I know. But you've always been so smart, and I wanted to see if I could get up to your level."

"That shouldn't be too hard. So what have you discovered?"

"Tons, Lex. There's like this whole world in the movies, with its own rules and stuff. You remember when we saw *Fury Road*, right? I went back and watched the other *Mad Max* films. Wow, did that guy learn a lot about making movies! You've got his whole lifetime as a director there. And a lot of that stuff in the movie, guys jumping onto trucks and stunts like that? It's from all sorts of Westerns and pirate and other action movies. Which makes sense, I guess. It is sort of a pirate movie, isn't it?"

"Hadn't really thought of it that way, but now that you mention it, that makes sense. Lots of missing body parts in those, too. What else?"

"You know when Max and Furiosa have to take the truck through that canyon thing? That's in about every Western with Indians. The Apaches or Cheyenne or whoever always occupy that high ground and see their enemies down below and come racing down. This is like you're watching that same dance but with motorcycles and different natives. Even the rockslide looks borrowed. Not that that's a bad thing. It's always the same but also a little different. And the way he frames faces—I don't know where I've seen that before, probably lots of places, but it looks familiar and strange at the same time."

"Who are you? And what have you done with my friend Dave?"

"I'm still here. Just learning new stuff all the time."

"I'm going to start calling you 'Professor.' So what do you want to see?"

"I don't really care. Although I do still like things that blow up ..."

Appendix

✸

Cinematic Exercises,
or
Fun with Movie Stuff

MY USUAL PRACTICE AT THIS POINT would be to offer a viewing/reading list for your supposed edification. Having gotten this far, however, you probably don't want to hear any more titles from me. So I thought I might set you some homework assignments. Oh, relax! It'll be fun. How hard can it be when the basic assignment is to watch movies? Besides, nobody's going to see your work but you, and you can grade on a curve. I know I would. So here goes.

Novelistic Relativity

At one point, I had a long comparison of two movies with one title: *The Great Gatsby.* In fact, it got so long and so involved that it threatened to sink the whole enterprise, and shortening it didn't seem possible, so I did what any rational person would do—I killed it. Here's the problem that beat me down—neither the 1974 Robert Redford–Mia Farrow version nor the 2013 Leonardo DiCaprio–Carey Mulligan installment convince me that Fitzgerald's novel can really be filmed. It has to do with the centrality of voice in the novel and the impossibility of re-creating that in the adaptations. In fact, the more of the novel they quote, the more we see that it can't be done. Still, that's no reason for filmmakers not to try or for us not to watch the results. Those two movies (I freely confess I've never seen the Alan Ladd version from 1949, and it's not entirely clear that anyone else has, either) have their flaws, but they also have some moments of inspiration. One is stately and sedate, the other frantic and busy. Even the musical choices—period jazz versus hip-hop—underscore the sharply different approaches. So here's the assignment. First, obviously, watch the two films. Then, depending on your history, follow the appropriate path. My guess is that the vast majority of you have read the novel. For you, compare the two versions. How do they compare? Where do they differ? How, for instance, does Bruce Dern's Tom Buchanan compare with Joel Edgerton's? And how does the difference matter? Finally, which one works for you? For those of you who have never read it, DON'T (yet). Compare the two as stand-alone films. What do you like about each? What do you not like? And think about how they are or are not telling the same story. THEN read the novel and see what you think, having seen the films first.

Not a Fitzgerald fan? You can do the same with *Far from the Madding Crowd*, using the 1967 Julie Christie–Alan Bates film and the 2015 Carey Mulligan (there she is again)–Matthias Schoenaerts version. Any pair of films adapting the same novel, but these are all very attractive movies in their own right.

Longitudinal Acting

To see how actors adapt to different settings or adapt over time, watch several films starring the same performer. I've just mentioned Mulligan, and she has plenty more work out there. DiCaprio is another whose range and, now, length of performance history makes him a good candidate. My personal choices would be Peter O'Toole and Katharine Hepburn, and not only because they played opposite each other in *The Lion in Winter*. Of course, there's nothing to say you can't watch multiple films by someone still starting out. Think of Dev Patel in *Slumdog Millionaire* and *The Best Exotic Marigold Hotel*; that would be worth it if only to watch him play off all those British screen veterans, especially Dame Maggie Smith. The only thing that matters is that the actor interest you enough to watch him or her for extended periods.

And So On

You can do this, naturally, with more than actors. You probably already have favorite directors, so you've done this with Tarantino, maybe, or the Coen brothers or Judd Apatow without even thinking about it. What happens if you do the same with someone with a little more riding time? Woody Allen has fifty years of movies out in the world, as did Hitchcock before him. And they're not all the same, whatever people may say about "an Allen film" or "a Hitchcock film." You could even do second unit directors, those folks who handle the action sequences and wrangle stunt performers for a living.

This approach also works for composers, although it takes

a special effort of will for those of us who are not innately musical to focus on the score to the exclusion of all that visual information. Just pick a composer you like and follow the bouncing ball. Doesn't matter if it's John Williams or Thomas Newman or Erich Korngold or Bernard Herrmann. You can also do the same thing with cinematographers or even editors, although it will take a lot of concentration. I'm not sure you can extend the approach out to set painters, but you could certainly seek out art designers and costume designers.

Genre Studies

If you're like a lot of people, when we start talking "film history," your attention starts to wander and your eyes glaze over. So how about looking at the movies over time by means of a single genre? That sounds like more fun, especially since you get to pick the genre. Most people have a favorite or two. What are yours? Sci-fi? Rom-com? Mystery? Thriller? Horror? I'm not big on horror, but if I were undertaking a personal course there, I'd choose something early—the original *Frankenstein* or *The Cabinet of Dr. Caligari*—then jump to *Psycho* and maybe *Carrie* or *The Shining*, throw in *The Exorcist* just to make sure the devil gets in there somewhere, and on to more recent entries such as *The Blair Witch Project* and some examples of the zombie phenomenon. You'll probably think of something better if you know the genre reasonably well already.

Or maybe I'd just do Dracula and related vampire movies from *Nosferatu* forward. That way, differences between subgenres would be a nonissue. If we changed genres and went for Westerns, I could put together a dozen lists with no repeats—and not one of them would have the Johnny Depp vehicle *The Lone Ranger*. Here's the thing: you don't need my help. There are plenty of sources to find somebody's idea of the all-time Rom-Com list, or top political thrillers, or feminist noir films, or pretty much any category you care to name—and maybe a couple that haven't been named. From there, you can read descriptions and see what appeals.

Whatever path you choose, what you want to notice are how both understanding of the genre in question and technical considerations change the look and feel of movies over time. What passed for horror acting in the 1930s, for instance, would be dismissed as mugging for the camera now. And what passes for acceptable violence now would have been unthinkable—both in terms of volume and vehemence—even fifty years ago.

Technical Features

Pick some topic we've discussed—lighting, framing, mise-en-scène, whatever—and make that an object of special study. For, say, the next five movies you watch, you're going to concentrate on that technical element. You'll probably want to watch the movie twice, once just to enjoy and take in the storyline basics and a second time with special focus on that component. What you'll find is that after a handful of movies where you single out an element for special study, you'll soon start noticing how it functions without any particular effort on your part. It's kind of like listening for the woodwinds in a symphony (okay, the harmony singers in a pop song): you get good at something by consciously paying attention. Pretty soon, you can't *not* notice the thing you once had to work to notice.

So What About a List?

For those of you who want a list, here are the films discussed in the book, along with a few that were almost discussed, were discussed in an earlier draft but didn't make the final cut, or that should have been there all along but didn't occur to me at the time.

The Artist

All Is Lost

American Sniper, Unforgiven, Gran Torino, Pale Rider (and
plenty more Eastwood)

Annie Hall, Manhattan, Midnight in Paris, To Rome with Love

Batman Begins (but feel free to watch the entire *Dark Knight*
trilogy)

Beasts of the Southern Wild

The Best Exotic Marigold Hotel

The Big Chill

The Bishop's Wife / The Preacher's Wife

Birdman

Blazing Saddles

Blow-Up

Blue Jasmine

Body Heat

The Bourne Identity

Breaking Away

Bullitt

Butch Cassidy and the Sundance Kid

Casablanca

Citizen Kane

City Lights, The Gold Rush, Modern Times, The Kid (and all
things Chaplin—there's a whole film education right
there)

A Clockwork Orange

Dr. Strangelove

Fantasia

Far from the Madding Crowd

*A Fistful of Dollars, For a Few Dollars More, The Good, the Bad
and the Ugly, Once Upon a Time in the West, Once Upon a
Time in America* (is that enough Leone for you?)

The French Connection

The French Lieutenant's Woman

From Here to Eternity
Girl with a Pearl Earring
The Godfather Trilogy
The Grand Budapest Hotel
Great Expectations, A Passage to India, Lawrence of Arabia
  (among several David Lean wonders)
The Great Gatsby
Hamlet (the Zeffirelli/Mel Gibson one, but also the
  Kenneth Branagh and Laurence Olivier versions)
Her
The Hundred-Foot Journey
Jeremiah Johnson
The King's Speech
Life of Pi
The Lion in Winter
Little Caesar
Lord of the Rings
Mad Max: Fury Road (which will lead into the earlier
  installments)
The Magnificent Seven
The Maltese Falcon
*M*A*S*H*
The Matrix
The Mission
Mr. Turner
North by Northwest, Notorious, (*Psycho, The Birds, Rebecca,*
  Vertigo, and anything else by Hitchcock)
On Golden Pond
Raiders of the Lost Ark
The Red Balloon
The Road to Perdition
Safety Last!
Saturday Night Fever
Schindler's List

Shane
The Shootist
Singin' in the Rain
Slumdog Millionaire
Some Like It Hot
Stagecoach
Steamboat Bill, Jr. (*The General*, *The Navigator*, *Sherlock, Jr.*, to
   give Buster Keaton his due)
The Sting
A Streetcar Named Desire
Superman (1978, with Christopher Reeve, but feel free to
   compare any others)
Swing Time
The Third Man
The Thomas Crown Affair (both)
Titanic
To Kill a Mockingbird
Tom Jones
Top Gun
True Grit (1969 and 2012)
UP
Wait Until Dark
West Side Story
Who Framed Roger Rabbit
Wings
The Wizard of Oz
Woman in Gold

About the Author

THOMAS C. FOSTER is the *New York Times*–bestselling author of *How to Read Literature Like a Professor, How to Read Novels Like a Professor,* and *Twenty-five Books That Shaped America*. He is Emeritus Professor of English at the University of Michigan–Flint, where he taught classes in modern and contemporary literature as well as creative writing and composition. He has written several books on twentieth-century British and Irish fiction and poetry, and lives in East Lansing, Michigan.

BOOKS BY THOMAS C. FOSTER

HOW TO READ LITERATURE LIKE A PROFESSOR, Revised Edition
A Lively and Entertaining Guide to Reading Between the Lines
Available in Paperback and Ebook

"A smart, accessible, and thoroughly satisfying examination of what it means to read a work of literature. Guess what? It isn't all that hard, not when you have a knowledgeable guide to show the way. Dante had his Virgil; for everyone else, there is Thomas Foster."
—Nicholas A. Basbanes, author of *A Gentle Madness*

TWENTY-FIVE BOOKS THAT SHAPED AMERICA
How White Whales, Green Lights, and Restless Spirits Forged Our National Identity
Available in Paperback and Ebook

Thomas C. Foster applies his combination of know-how, inimitable wit, and analysis to look at the great masterworks of American literature and how each of them has shaped our very existence as readers, students, teachers, and Americans.

HOW TO READ NOVELS LIKE A PROFESSOR
A Jaunty Exploration of the World's Favorite Literary Form
Available in Paperback and Ebook

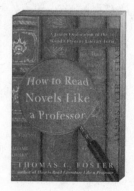

Out of all literary forms, the novel is arguably the most discussed—and the most fretted over. In *How to Read Novels Like a Professor*, Thomas C. Foster leads readers through the special "literary language" of the novel, helping them get more—more insight, more understanding, more pleasure—from their reading.

Available Wherever Books Are Sold